Praise for The Assassination of James Forrestal

David Martin's book *The Assassination of James Forrestal* focuses on the historic truths related to the systemic harassment and consequent death of James Forrestal in May, 1949, at the Bethesda Naval Hospital. It is a long-overdue, hugely important, work of "revisionist history." The timeworn myths intended to support his "suicide" – which had originally been planted by such muckraking columnists as Drew Pearson and Walter Winchell, then repeated by the authors of several biographies of Forrestal – have been systematically deconstructed by Martin (a.k.a. "DCDave).

This profoundly important book describes in detail one of the earliest plots of the "Deep State" as it was constituted post-WWII: The plot to remove all impediments to the creation and successful launch of the nation of Israel, through silencing the most influential and prescient voice cautioning his country, and the world, about the long and possibly endless tail of retaliations, recriminations and retributions that lay ahead. The history of that land, still resonating with the repercussions he predicted, proves James V. Forrestal's legendary wisdom.

--**Phillip F. Nelson**, author of *LBJ, the Mastermind of the JFK Assassination; LBJ, from Mastermind to "The Colossus;" Remember the Liberty;* and *Who Really Killed Martin Luther King, Jr.?*

The Assassination of James Forrestal

David Martin

McCabe Publishing
Hyattsville, Maryland

Acknowledgments

Grateful acknowledgment is made to the John Birch Society for permission to quote extensively from *The Death of James Forrestal* by Cornell Simpson, to Simon & Schuster, Inc., to quote from *Truman*, by David McCullough, and to Penguin Random House for the use of quotations from a number of publications. The cover photograph is used with permission of the U.S. Navy, Courtesy of Harry S. Truman Library and Museum.

David Martin/McCabe Publishing
www.DCDave.com

The Assassination of James Forrestal/ David Martin. —1st ed.
ISBN 978-0-9673521-2-1

Contents

To Alfred M. Lilienthal, the brave and principled man whose positive reaction to the first installment of "Who Killed James Forrestal?" in 2002 encouraged me to continue my quest for truth in the case and to P.A. Leonard, Deputy Director, (Claims, Investigations and Tort Litigation), of the U.S. Navy's Judge Advocate General's office who sent me the Navy's official inquiry into Forrestal's death in 2004. That inquiry, which I dubbed the Willcutts Report after Admiral Morton D. Willcutts, the head of the National Naval Medical Center who appointed the review panel, had been kept secret for 55 years.

Inconvenient Lives

To our south they're "disappeared;"
Up here they're "suicided."
To achieve a similar end,
A similar means is provided.

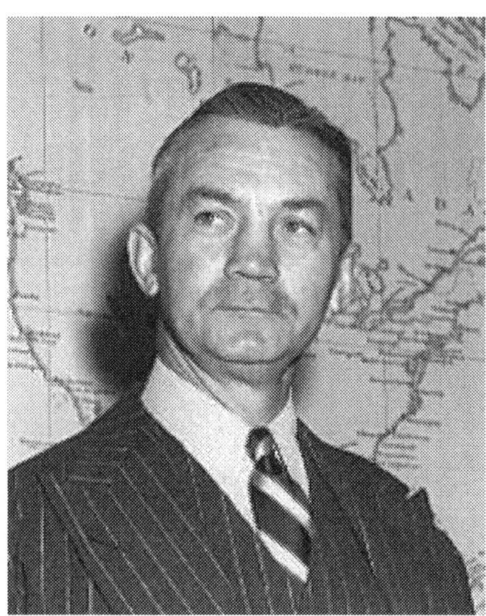

James Vincent Forrestal, February 15, 1892, - May 22, 1949

Main tower of Bethesda Naval Hospital, view from the back

Main tower front view. Note bay window upper left, matched on the back but obscured by trees.

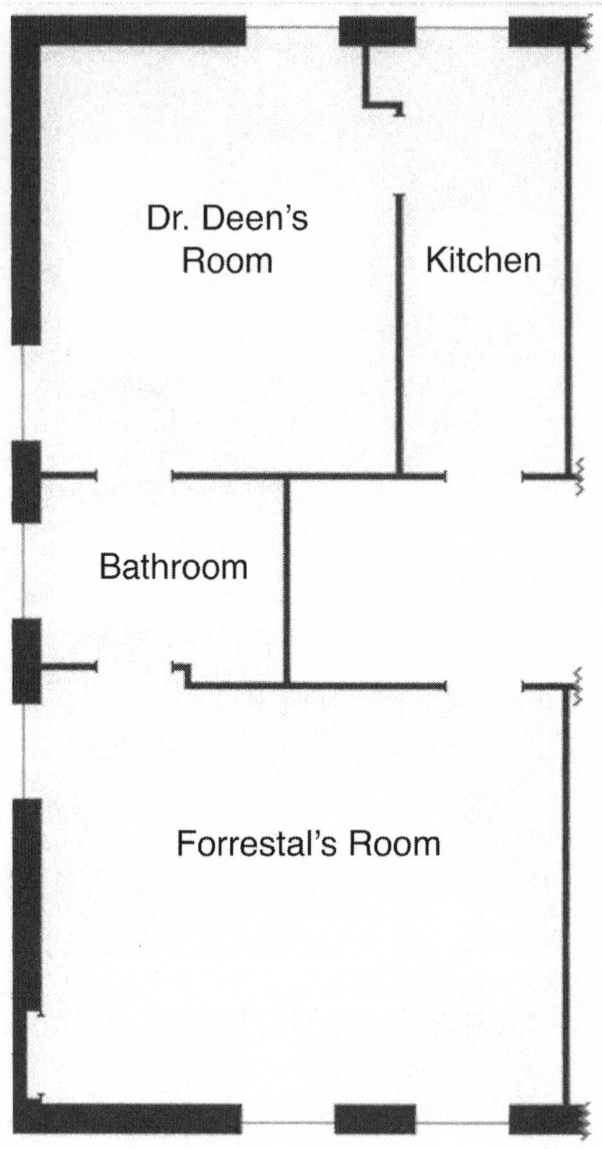

Right wing of 16th floor of the hospital. Wall with two windows of Forrestal's room is at the front of the building

Forrestal's vacated hospital room sometime May 22, 1949

Forrestal's hospital room, another angle

Kitchen with open window from which Forrestal fell, sometime May 22, 1949

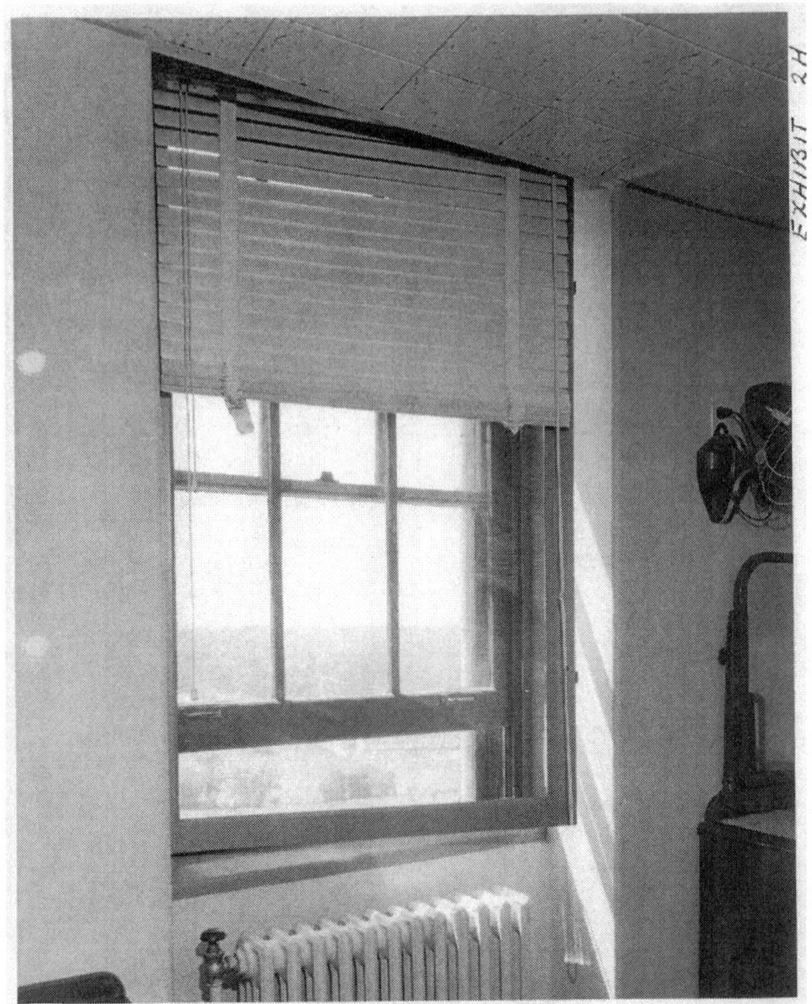

Window in Forrestal's room showing security screen

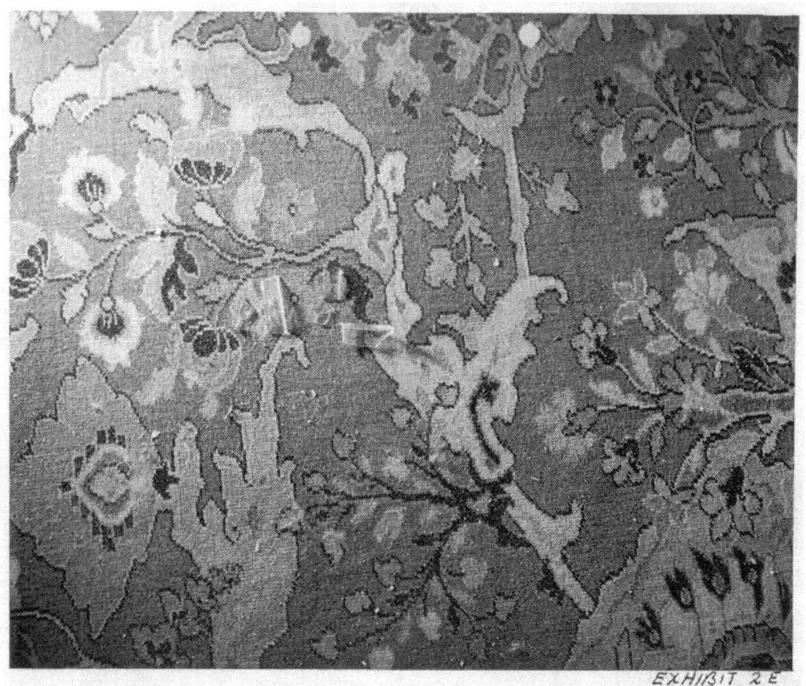

Carpet in Forrestal's room showing broken glass

X

THE SECRETARY OF DEFENSE
WASHINGTON

My dear Mr President:

As a result of your letter, the Dupont people have consented to let Don Carpenter stay for six months.

I am working on Arthur Drefs of St. Louis, or Dwight Palmer, to come in as his successor when his time is up.

Thanks for the help.

Respectfully,

James Forrestal

Actual Forrestal handwriting sample

CLASS OF SERVICE

This is a full-rate Telegram or Cablegram unless its deferred character is indicated by a suitable symbol above or preceding the address.

WESTERN UNION

A. N. WILLIAMS
PRESIDENT

SYMBOLS
DL=Day Letter
NL=Night Letter
LC=Deferred Cable
NLT=Cable Night Letter
Ship Radiogram

(05) 847 OCT 2

The filing time shown in the date line on telegrams and day letters is STANDARD TIME at point of origin. Time of receipt is STANDARD TIME at point of destination

WAWP47 PD=TDBRD QUOGUE NY 2

HON JAMES FORRESTAL=
PENTAGON BLDG=

THAT WAS A GOOD SPEECH=
:OHARA:

To John O'Hara, Esq
Quogue, L.I.

John:
I was somewhat confused by this but I doped it out. Thanks for the OK.
JF

:OHARA:

THE COMPANY WILL APPRECIATE SUGGESTIONS FROM ITS PATRONS CONCERNING ITS SERVICE

Actual Forrestal handwriting sample

THE SECRETARY OF THE NAVY.
WASHINGTON.

My dear Mr. President:

You know by now, better than I, that your address of yesterday clicked with all hands — Congress, the press and the people. They liked your humility and earnestness and lack of dramatics.

You start with a great reservoir of good will. It is up to those of us who are working directly for you to maintain that bank account. I shall do my best to perform my part, as long as you want me.

Respectfully,
James Forrestal

P.S. Don't bother to acknowledge. F

Actual Forrestal handwriting sample

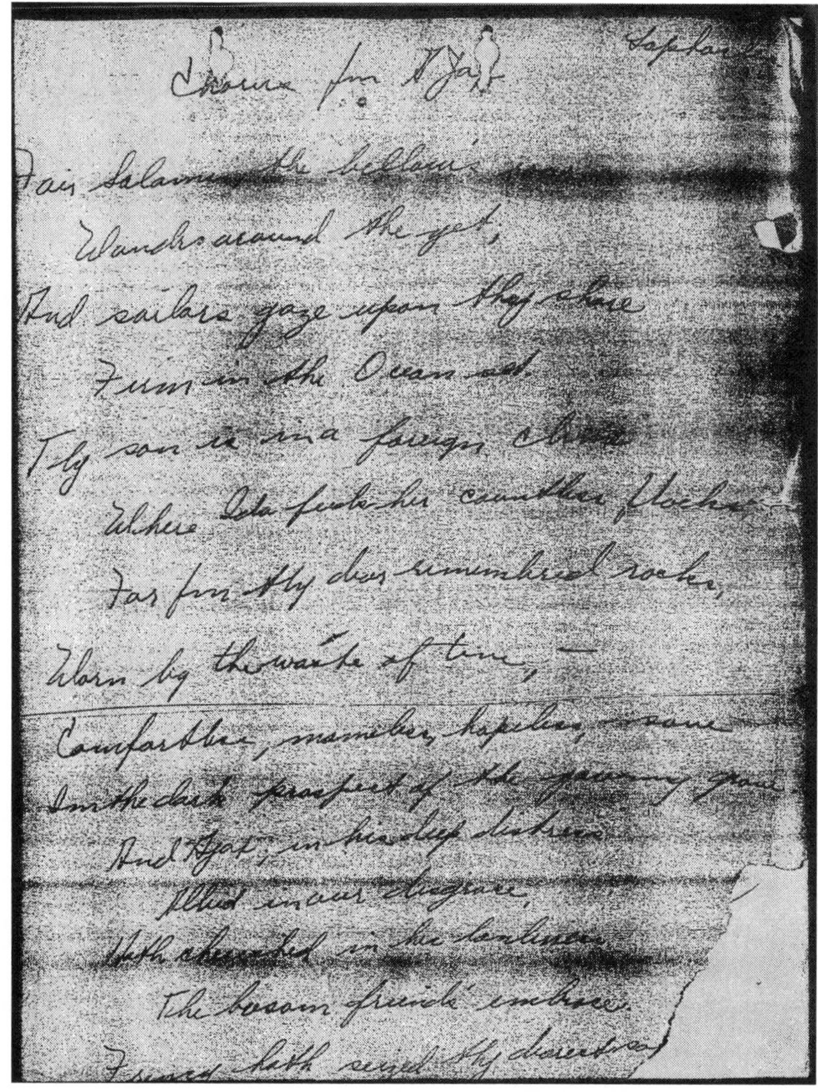

Sophocles

Chorus from Ajax

Fair Salamis, the billows' roar,
Wanders around thee yet,
And sailors gaze upon thy shore
Firm in the Ocean set.
Thy son is in a foreign clime
Where Ida feeds her countless flocks,
Far from thy dear remembered rocks,
Worn by the waste of time, —
Comfortless, nameless, hopeless save
In the dark prospect of the yawning grave.
And Ajax, in his deep distress
Allied in our disgrace,
Hath cherished in his loneliness
The bosom friend's embrace.
Frenzy hath seized thy dearest

Poem transciption purportedly found in Forrestal's vacated room

President John F. Kennedy visiting Forrestal's grave, Memorial Day, 1963

Foreword

Historic Assassination

While exploring the national attic,
I discovered something quite chilling:
It seems that James V. Forrestal
Was a victim of targeted killing.

How did it happen that I came to be interested in the death of America's first Secretary of Defense, James Forrestal, I am often asked? It all began with another mysterious death of a high government official, one that occurred in 1993, a little more than 44 years after Forrestal's plunge from a 16th floor window of the main tower of the Bethesda Naval Hospital. I am speaking of President Bill Clinton's deputy White House counsel, Vincent W. Foster, Jr. What follows is a summary of the political odyssey that led me to become the lone figure to look seriously and honestly into Forrestal's death since his fall from that window in the early hours of Sunday morning, May 22, 1949.

I've heard it said that the politics of most men is set by the time they are twelve years old, and it is the politics of their father. That was very much true in my own case for the first fifty years or so of my life. My father, a small-town North Carolina school principal, was a liberal Democrat from a large, fairly prominent liberal-Democratic Party family. His oldest brother was the longtime editor of the left-leaning *Winston-Salem Journal* and another older brother, the chief lobbyist for Wachovia Bank in Raleigh, was the chairman of the state Democratic Party for most of the 1940s. His next older brother, also a school principal, served one term in the state legislature after his retirement, having been elected as a liberal Democrat in one of the few North Carolina counties that had voted Republican since the end of the Civil War.

The dictum concerning one's politics is certainly more likely to hold true, I believe, if one is college educated and one's father happens to be of a liberal political persuasion, because, at the typical American college, one is likely to have such politics reinforced. I took only one course in American history in college, and that was on the country's history in the 20th century. A man who was at least as big an admirer of President Franklin D. Roosevelt as was my father taught it. That says a lot, considering the fact that my father had named my younger brother "Franklin D." after the man.

In 1964, I exercised my first opportunity to vote for president of the United States by casting my ballot for Lyndon Johnson, naturally. To vote for the archconservative Barry Goldwater would have been completely out of the question. I might note that, up to that point, the only president I had ever seen in the flesh was Harry Truman, who, as an ex-president by that time, addressed the attendees of the annual Nash County Harvest Festival in 1960, stumping for John F. Kennedy in the election of that year. I felt completely in the spirit of the moment as people shouted, "Give 'em hell, Harry, " from the open-air audience.

From 1968 through 1992, when I voted for Bill Clinton, I dutifully voted for whomever the Democratic Party nominated for the presidency. Everything began to change for me, though, in 1993. I was working in Washington, D.C., and on July 20 Foster's body was found lying in the back of a Civil War relic known as Fort Marcy Park, off the George Washington Parkway, which runs overlooking the Potomac River for a ways on the Virginia side of the river. I had lived in Fairfax County where the park is located since 1982 and had driven along that scenic stretch of road a number of times and had never even noticed it. The turnoff comes just when the drive becomes markedly less scenic, after two parking overlooks of the river and Washington, D.C., on the other side, and you lose the view of the river and beyond. At that point your mind tends to turn to whatever your next destination might be.

How was it, I wondered, that Foster, a relative newcomer to Washington, would even know about Fort Marcy Park? If he were in such a bad state of mind as to take the extreme step of killing himself, why would he have even gone to work that day? In the first few days, everyone seemed puzzled as to what his motivation might have been, and yet, all the news organizations called it an "apparent suicide," when, to me, there was hardly anything "apparent" about it. Another thing was noticeable in the news coverage. That is that nobody made any mention of the nearest federal facility to Fort Marcy Park, that is, the headquarters complex of the Central Intelligence Agency, which is hardly more than a mile away as the crow flies.

Although I had not known Foster, he was just two years behind me at Davidson College and, at about the same height, we had matched up against one another in intramural basketball competition. That fact increased my interest in his death. In due time, I became something of a scholar on Foster's death, which, in turn, made me a major critic of America's news media.

Repeatedly, I noticed, press reports referred to Foster as "the highest ranking federal official to commit suicide since Secretary of Defense James Forrestal." Since it had become apparent to me that Foster had not actually committed suicide, in spite of the virtually unanimous efforts of the nation's molders of public opinion to convince us that he had, my curiosity about what had actually happened to Forrestal was piqued.

Then, while browsing at the local used bookstore, I happened to run across the biography of the noted conservative journalist, Walter Winchell.[1] I discovered there that Winchell, who shared Forrestal's strong anti-Communist philosophy, had turned into a virulent Forrestal opponent in the last year of Forrestal's life. The author, Neal Gabler,

---

[1] Neal Gabler, *Winchell: Gossip, Power and the Culture of Celebrity*, Vintage Books, 1994.

surmised that that was because of Forrestal's opposition to U.S. support for the creation of the state of Israel. Winchell, who was Jewish, was an ardent Zionist. I also learned from Gabler that probably the most prominent liberal journalist of the day, Drew Pearson, like Winchell, had also written a series of articles scurrilously attacking Forrestal in the weeks leading up to Forrestal's forced resignation from the Harry Truman administration in March of 1949. The one big thing that Pearson, who was not Jewish, had in common with Winchell was that he was also a big Israel supporter.

The good-liberal-versus-bad-conservative view of things that I had learned from my father didn't work in this case. An important part of my early political education had been listening to the Sunday night radio programs by these two national newspaper columnists. We loved Pearson, and we hated Winchell. Something more powerful that we aren't supposed to see was apparently at work here.

At this point, my suspicion of foul play in Forrestal's death rose to a new level. I was already aware that Jewish terrorists had freely used assassination as a weapon in pushing the Zionist agenda, although I did not yet know the degree to which they had done so. Two notable examples were the assassination of Britain's Secretary of State for the Colonies, Lord Moyne, in 1944 and Swedish Count Folke Bernadotte, the United Nations Mediator in Palestine, in 1948.

The only thing I knew about Forrestal at that point was what Gabler had written about his Israel opposition and what I had read in David McCullough's celebrated 1992 biography of President Harry Truman in which he gives a matter-of-fact account of how Forrestal more or less went out of his mind and jumped out of the window of a hospital where he was being treated for depression. It was time to take a closer look.

Introduction

Fear Factor

The truth may be there to see
But it won't, like magic, appear.
You must seek it diligently,
And not be restrained by fear.

James Vincent Forrestal was born on February 15, 1892, in the town of Matteawan, New York, on the Hudson River in Dutchess County between West Point and Poughkeepsie. In 1913, the town merged with adjacent Fishkill Landing and adopted the name, "Beacon," after Beacon Mountain, the most notable landmark in the small urban area. His father, also named James, had emigrated from County Cork in Ireland to the town in 1857 at the age of nine, where he joined his mother, who had emigrated after her husband had died, and she had remarried. The new husband was named Patrick Kennedy, but the stepson kept his birth name of Forrestal.

Forrestal was the youngest of three children, all sons. Until he left college and went off to work on Wall Street, he went by the name of Vince, to distinguish him from his father. His father had apprenticed in carpentry and was accomplished and enterprising enough to form his small construction company. His mother, born Mary Anne Toohey, was the daughter of Irish immigrants, was a schoolteacher, a devout Roman Catholic, and a strict disciplinarian at home. She may be given a good deal of the credit for young James's notable self-discipline and his strong work ethic.

Young James was an excellent student and an enthusiastic participant in athletics, playing baseball, basketball, and tennis in high school, probably gaining the greatest proficiency in tennis. Boxing was also very popular in the area at the time, but his mother forbade him to participate. Only later did he violate the prohibition while at college, sustaining the somewhat flattened nose that he wore proudly for the rest of his life.

His mother fancied him to be ideal material for the priesthood, but his breadth of interests attracted him to a different sort of education than the seminary. While in high school he set his sights on Princeton University, but it took him a few years to reach that goal.

After graduating at age 16, in 1908, he spent three years working for three area newspapers, the *Matteawan Evening Journal*, the *Mount Vernon Argus*, and the *Poughkeepsie News Press*. Journalism was in his blood, and he had expressed a desire to return to it upon leaving government, but it was never to be.

He entered Dartmouth College in 1911 and then transferred to Princeton after his freshman year. He was a better than average student, but he distinguished himself more in his various extracurricular activities, particularly student journalism. Working first as a reporter for *The Daily Princetonian*, he ascended to its editorship at the end of his junior year. Like the reporting work he continued to do during summer vacations for the *Matteawan Evening Journal*, the editor's job also helped his always-precarious financial situation because it was a paying job.

In his senior year, his classmates voted him "Most Likely to Succeed." With all he had going for him, it's a bit of a mystery that he never graduated, leaving Princeton on credit short of the required number. There is speculation that it might have involved confusion over the credits that were transferred from Dartmouth.

Upon leaving Princeton, he took a couple of odd jobs in the New York City area before landing in a position more suitable to his background and taste, as financial reporter for the New York *World* newspaper. It wasn't long, though, before that job opened his eyes to the much greater career possibilities that he would have actually doing the sort of Wall Street work that he was reporting on. Recalling a contact he had made at Princeton, he interviewed with William A. Read and Company in 1916 and was promptly offered a job as bond salesman, which he accepted.

Given the heavy responsibility of sales for upper New York State, he pitched in with the sort of total commitment that would mark his entire career, both in the private sector and in public service. He was known to stay on the job frequently until at least nine o'clock at night. He also traded heavily on the many contacts he had made during his Princeton years. His diligence, his enthusiasm, and his contacts paid off when he was made a partner in the firm in 1923, vice-president in 1926, and president of the company in 1937.

The same year that Forrestal was made a partner, 1923, the firm's name changed to Dillon, Read and Company after the new controlling owner, Clarence Dillon. Dillon had been born Clarence Lapowski in San Antonio, Texas, the son of a prosperous Jewish clothing merchant. His father, Samuel Lapowski, had sent him to Worcester Academy in Massachusetts and then to Harvard, changing the family name to Dillon after his wife's family name when Clarence was in college. Exhibiting exceptional financial skill after joining William A. Read, Dillon had become a partner in 1916, the same year in which William A. Read died of a sudden illness.

Dillon had recognized Forrestal's talent and later took him under his wing as something of a protégé, but the younger man's rapid ascent in the investment banking firm was interrupted in 1917 when President Woodrow Wilson took the country into the great war in Europe.

At this point Forrestal made another career move of the sort that would typify his life. Out of a sense of patriotic duty he signed up for military service. Discovering that with his first choice, the Marines, his road to becoming an officer might not be as short as he would like it to be, he joined the Navy and trained to be an aviator. Successfully completing training with the Royal Flying Corps of Canada, he achieved the rank of lieutenant, but was never sent overseas. He spent most of his tour of duty at the office of Naval Operations in Washington, DC.

Just as World War I had done, World War II would pull Forrestal away from his highly successful and lucrative investment banking career. In mid-1940, the war in Europe was already a full-scale conflagration, and U.S. participation in it was beginning to take on the appearance of inevitability. Forrestal, a Democrat by family background, had already worked behind the scenes with Securities and Exchange Commissioner William O. Douglas in implementing Franklin Roosevelt's Wall Street reforms. Roosevelt had subsequently made Douglas a Supreme Court Justice. With war on the horizon, FDR saw the need for recruitment of some to the best talent from the private sector to help in the mobilization effort. One of the people Douglas recommended was his friend Forrestal.

The position to which he was initially appointed was in the White House as administrative assistant to the president. He was a part of a group of close advisers that varied in number through the years from four to six. The most famous person to hold the position is probably the influence-peddling lawyer Thomas "Tommy the Cork" Corcoran and, as things stand now, the most infamous is the Soviet agent Lauchlin Currie. Should the revelations in this book ever gain wide currency, a man who joined the team in 1942 and stayed on through the early years of the Truman administration, David Niles, might well supplant Currie at the top of the infamy totem pole.

Forrestal spent slightly less than two months in that job in the summer of 1940. Frank Knox, the Secretary of the Navy chose him for the new position of Under Secretary after New York lawyer and World War I war hero, William J. Donovan, later the head of the Office of Strategic Service (OSS) and Knox's Chicago banker friend Ralph Bard turned him down. Forrestal began his seven years with the Department of the Navy on August 22. In the capacity of Under Secretary he was the person most responsible for the Navy's mobilization for the war on the horizon.

Forrestal would remain in that vital position until May of 1944, when victory in World War II was in sight. America's naval success in the war owed largely to sheer numbers of ships and planes, as well as their rapidly improving effectiveness. To the extent that any one man could claim credit for that part of the battle, it was James Forrestal.

When Secretary Knox died unexpectedly on April 28, 1944, Forrestal was the consensus choice in Washington to succeed him. Nominated as expected by President Roosevelt, he was unanimously approved by the Senate, becoming Secretary on May 19. The press was just as approving as was official Washington. In the run-up to the nomination, *Business Week* had put him on its May 6 cover.

Secretary of the Navy was a much more important position at that time than it has been since the consolidation of the armed services under the Department of Defense, created by the National Security Act of 1947. Forrestal took the reins firmly and remained widely popular. Continuing in office when Vice-President Harry S. Truman succeeded Roosevelt on May 19, 1945, upon the latter's death, his popularity was reflected by his appearance on the cover of *Time* magazine on October 29, 1945.

The public remained unaware of the foreign policy breach that was slowly opening up between Forrestal and much of the rest of the team, even before Truman had inherited them from Roosevelt. As the end of the Pacific War neared, the firmly anti-Communist Forrestal was most concerned with preventing the Soviet Union from grabbing any of the spoils of victory over the Japanese, with whom they had had a non-aggression agreement throughout the war. Through information he received through Naval Intelligence, he knew better than anyone how desperate the Japanese military situation was and worked behind the scenes to achieve a negotiated surrender, but he was not backed up by the Roosevelt administration.[2]

Forrestal was not part of the official delegation to the Potsdam Conference that met in that suburb of Berlin with the war allies shortly after the German surrender to formulate terms for the end of the Pacific War.

---

[2] David Martin, "Forrestal Ignored: China Lost to Reds, Korean War Fought," March 5, 2012, http://www.dcdave.com/article5/110530.htm.

However, he flew privately to Germany hoping to have some input, taking with him the young Navy veteran son of his friend, former Ambassador to the Great Britain, Joseph P. Kennedy, the future President John F. Kennedy, but arrived after the conference had completed its work.[3]

The Potsdam Declaration emanating from that conference, signed by the United States, Great Britain, and China, as Forrestal feared, remained silent about the future of the Emperor of Japan and did not waver from the call for Japanese "unconditional surrender." Though the surrender terms actually reflected, to a degree, Forrestal's moderate approach, the Japanese rejected it, and only 11 days later, on August 6, 1945, the atomic bomb was dropped on Hiroshima. Even after another atomic bomb was dropped on Nagasaki three days later and devastating conventional bombing was continued on other Japanese cities, the Japanese still appeared to be holding out. However, on August 10 they sent out a radio message in which they said they would agree to the terms of the Potsdam Declaration, "with the understanding that said declaration does not comprise any demand which prejudices the prerogatives of His Majesty as a sovereign ruler."

Since that hardly constituted the unconditional surrender that the American public had been led to expect, Truman, urged on by his Secretary of State, James Byrnes, was leaning toward rejecting it. At that point, Forrestal suggested to the President that we accept the Japanese offer upon the condition that the Emperor would be subject to orders of the American military governor, while still calling it, for public consumption, "unconditional surrender." That formulation was accepted by Truman and subsequently by the Japanese and the war came to an end.[4] Forrestal's intervention at that moment saved a countless number of lives and who knows how much further gain by the Soviet Union in the region. Joseph Stalin had finally declared war on Japan immediately after the dropping of the second A-bomb.

---

[3] David Martin, "James Forrestal and John Kennedy," August 6, 2014, http://dcdave.com/article5/140806.htm.

[4] David Martin, "Oliver Stone on the Japanese Surrender," January 22, 2013, http://dcdave.com/article5/130122.htm.

In the immediate post-war period Forrestal became most closely identified with the transformation of U.S. policy towards the Soviet Union from general accommodation to what has been characterized as "containment." He circulated the now famous 1946 "long telegram" of Soviet specialist, George F. Kennan, stationed in the U.S. Embassy in Moscow to key members of the government and was responsible for its publication in *Foreign Affairs* in 1947. That document described the implacable, almost messianic attitude of Soviet Communism toward capitalism and the West. The containment policy manifested itself in active U.S. support for the anti-Communist forces in Greece and Turkey and became known as the Truman Doctrine after President Truman laid it out in a speech to Congress in July of 1947. Forrestal's identification with the Truman Doctrine has made him a target of leftist history writers to the present day.

As Secretary of the Navy, Forrestal also got caught up in the bitter internal skirmishing that went on over the military consolidation bill that eventually became the National Security Act of 1947. That legislation created the Department of Defense with the various military branches under it, separated fixed-wing aircraft from the Army under the newly created Air Force, and also created the Central Intelligence Agency. Forrestal, representing the sentiments of the officers that he supervised, had been a strong advocate for the continued independence of the Navy. In spite of his opposition to the legislation that created the post, when the holder of the eliminated position of Secretary of War, Robert Patterson, declined Truman's offer of the job, Truman nominated Forrestal for the job and he became America's first Secretary of Defense on September 17, 1947.

The year and a half of Forrestal's tenure in the newly created position was a period of considerable turbulence. Forrestal continued to resist what he considered to be dangerously rapid demobilization of the armed forces, and the consolidation of those forces hardly ran smoothly. A particular thorn in his side was the newly named Secretary of the Air Force,

Stuart Symington, of Missouri. Symington aggressively sought the aggrandizement of the new branch in an abrasive and arrogant manner that seriously undermined Forrestal's authority. His Missouri connections in Truman's White House, however, made it virtually impossible for Forrestal to replace him.

The largest source of disquiet for Forrestal in his new position, however, was the controversy over Palestine. Great Britain had been in control of the territory, formerly part of the Ottoman Empire, under a mandate of the League of Nations, established in 1923. By 1947, Zionist terrorism against the British authorities caused them finally to throw up their hands and to dump the matter into the hands of the United Nations.

Forrestal, with his responsibility for supplying our armed forces during World War II, was keenly aware of the nation's growing dependence on oil from the Middle East, and that Zionist aspirations were putting the nation on a collision course with the nation's that supplied the oil. He feared, furthermore, that the relatively tiny nation of Israel, which the Zionists intended to create, could not be sustained without the assistance of U.S. military force, endangering our access to oil and pushing the Muslim countries in the region into the lap of our primary geopolitical adversary, the Soviet Union.

Secretary of State George C. Marshall, the former Army general who had been Chief of Staff throughout World War II, shared Forrestal's view as did most of the foreign policy establishment within the government. Forrestal, however, was blunter and more outspoken on the question, and with his private-sector background, was more easily painted as simply a tool of the big oil companies who were worried about the threat to their profits.

Over Forrestal's objections, the Truman government not only supported the United Nations vote on November 29, 1947, to partition Palestine but actively worked to pressure enough countries into supporting the measure for it to succeed. Britain announced that its Mandate would terminate on May 15, 1948. The Zionists proclaimed the creation of the new state of Israel in the part of Palestine that the UN had allotted to the Jews, and the United States immediately granted it recognition as a state.

In the meantime, Forrestal saw his treatment by the American media take a complete turn. From being one of the heroes in the victory over the Axis Powers, he was turned into a money-grubbing villain. The two leading voices in his vilification were the left-leaning "muckraker," Drew Pearson, and the putative conservative, but FDR-admiring, primarily gossip columnist, Jewish arch-Zionist, Walter Winchell. Their objective seemed to go beyond getting him out of the government. Rather, it seemed that their purpose was to destroy his reputation for all time.

When Truman was surprisingly re-elected in November 1948, the die was cast for Forrestal to leave the government. He got along very poorly with Truman's Missouri cronies and he had even met privately with the Republican nominee, New York Governor Thomas E. Dewey, expecting like almost everyone else did that Dewey would be the new president.

Forrestal thought he had a private agreement from Truman that he would leave the government on May 1, 1949, but on March 4 Truman made the abrupt announcement that Forrestal was going to be replaced by West Virginia lawyer Louis Johnson, the man who had been Truman's main fund-raiser during the campaign and also a person for whom Forrestal had very little respect. Johnson's swearing-in ceremony took place on March 28, and things went quickly downhill for Forrestal from that point.

The unexpected acceleration of the timetable for Forrestal to step down has been attributed to Truman's realization that he was in the throes of some sort of emotional breakdown and therefore had to be replaced quickly. That argument, as we shall see, falls under the overall category of what we might call Forrestal-destruction propaganda. By the best evidence available, up until the day Johnson's swearing in, Forrestal seemed to be perfectly normal. He also seemed to be quite normal only minutes before he went out the 16th floor window of the Bethesda Naval Hospital, some seven weeks later.

The latest manifestation of Forrestal-destruction propaganda has the psychological strain on him resulting not from the vicious press vilification campaign that he suffered on account of his stand on Palestine but because of the stress of the internal battle over unification of the military services. That line of argument, as far as we can tell, made its debut, Soviet style, in an article in *The Washington Post* on the occasion of the 50th anniversary of Forrestal's death, which we discuss in Chapter 5. By 2008 that revisionist explanation for Forrestal's supposed psychological decline had been incorporated into the first mainstream history book to use evidence surrounding Forrestal's death uncovered by this writer, which we discuss in Chapter 12.

Again, the best evidence indicates that the late anti-Zionist writer, Alfred M. Lilienthal, was dead accurate in including Forrestal among an illustrious group of victims of Zionism:

> The roster of renegade libertarians, liberals and conservatives alike, who over the past thirty years have tried to buck the tide of Jewish-Zionist nationalism and then found themselves victims of a smear campaign, reads like an international Who's Who. Included in this illustrious list drawn from top educational, clerical, literary, political and journalistic circles are: Yale's Millar Burrows, Harvard's William Ernest Hocking, Dean Virginia Gildersleeve, Dr. William Sloane Coffin, Henry Van Dusen, Dean Francis Sayre, Rabbi Elmer Berger, Dr. A. C. Forrest, Dr. John Nicholls Booth, Father Daniel Berrigan, Morris Ernst, Arthur Garfield Hays, Vincent Sheean, Dr. Arnold Toynbee, Norman Thomas, Howard K. Smith, J. William Fulbright, James Abourezk, Ralph Flanders, General George Brown, James Forrestal, Henry A. Byroade, Moshe Menuhin, Dr. Israel Shahak, Dorothy Thompson, Willie Snow Ethridge, Margaret McKay, Hannah Arendt, Sir George Brown, Folke Bernadotte, Dag Hammarskjold, Bruno Kreisky, Georges Pompidou, and Charles de Gaulle.[5]

Looking carefully at the list we see a name near the end whose fate bears the closest resemblance to that of James Forrestal, that is the Swedish Count Folke Bernadotte, the U.N. mediator of the Arab-Israeli conflict. Bernadotte was assassinated by Zionist terrorists in Jerusalem on September 17, 1948. The death of another prominent Swede on the list, U.N. Secretary General Dag Hammarskjold from an airplane crash in Af-

[5] Alfred M. Lilienthal, *The Zionist Connection II: What Price Peace*, North American, 1978, p. 422.

rica on September 18, 1961, remains shrouded in mystery and controversy.

CHAPTER 1

The Case for Assassination

Not for Human Consumption?

The water from the well of truth
Is to most folks undrinkable.
That is because of their distaste
For things they find unthinkable

World War II had ended less than three years before. It was becoming increasingly apparent that, for all its losses, the big winner of that war had been the Soviet Union and world Communism. On March 10, 1948, the body of one of the leading holdouts against the Communist advance was found in the courtyard beneath the window of his office. National authorities called the death a suicide, but reports in opposition countries concluded that it had been a murder, a political assassination by the secret police. I am speaking of Foreign Minister Jan Masaryk, the last non-Communist government minister of Czechoslovakia, which was the last Eastern European country not yet taken over completely by the Communists.

On May 22, 1949, the body of the man generally regarded as the leading government official warning of the Communist menace abroad and within the United States government, the nation's first Secretary of Defense, James V. Forrestal, was found on a third-floor roof 13 floors below a 16th-floor window of the Bethesda Naval Hospital. He had been admitted to the hospital, apparently against his will, diagnosed as suffering from "operational fatigue" and kept in confinement in a room with security-screened windows on the 16th floor since April 2, some seven weeks before. The body had been discovered at 1:50 a.m., and the last edition of the May 22 *New York Times* reported the death as a suicide, although the belt, or sash, of his dressing gown was tied tightly around his neck, a more suspicious happenstance than anything associated with Masaryk's death.

Books on Forrestal

A suicide it has remained in the newspapers and magazines of the United States to the present day. Three notable books have also been written about Forrestal, each of which discusses his death in considerable length. The first was *James Forrestal, A Study of Personality, Politics, and Policy* by California political science professor, Arnold A. Rogow.[6] If the *Book Review Digest* is any indicator, it was the most heavily publicized, if not the best received, of the books in question. Nineteen reviews are listed, and a few are summarized. Most take the author to task for the general shallowness of his effort and his attempt at post-mortem psychoanalysis, what some have called a psychological autopsy. None of them, however, challenge Rogow's conclusion—which is really almost his starting place—that Forrestal's death was an obvious suicide caused by his "mental illness," something that Rogow dwells upon almost *ad nauseam*.

The second book was *The Death of James Forrestal* by Cornell Simpson, published by Western Islands Publishers in 1966. *Book Review Digest* does not mention it, but, in fact, it did have one reviewer in the

[6] The MacMillan Company, 1963.

American media, that was a little-known publication called *American Opinion* in its April 1967 edition. We shall have more to say about that review in Chapter 3. As it happens, *American Opinion* was the house organ of the right-wing John Birch Society and Western Islands Publishers was the in-house Birch Society publishing company. Your local municipal or university library probably does not have a copy.[7] Obscure though it might be, as vouched for by contemporary news reports, it is far more accurate and better documented in matters concerning the details of Forrestal's last weeks, days, and hours, than even the celebrated third, and most recent, of the books written. [8]

Driven Patriot

The book we are speaking of is the 587-page biography, *Driven Patriot, the Life and Times of James Forrestal,* by Townsend Hoopes and Douglas Brinkley. [9] In their two chapters on Forrestal's decline and death, Hoopes

---

[7] From our home in Fairfax County, Virginia, outside Washington, DC, we find searching worldcat.org that only five libraries within 100 miles have the book. The National Defense University and Howard are the only college libraries in the nation's capital that have it, and the former is not exactly a regular college library. It's in only one library in Virginia, the Jerry Falwell Library of Liberty University. Only one library in Maryland has it, the Lewis J. Ort Library of Frostburg State University.

[8] We were able to obtain a used copy through the Internet at a reasonable price in 2002, something less than $20. Now, thanks in large measure to our reawakening of interest in the case of Forrestal's death at http://www.dcdave.com, no copy of this book, which has long been out of print, can be obtained for less than $100 when shipping and handling costs are figured in.

[9] Alfred A. Knopf, 2003. From their Wikipedia pages we learn that Hoopes, a former Under Secretary of the Air Force, among many government positions he held, was a member of the Skull and Bones secret society at Yale University and that Brinkley, who is a commentator on CNN, is a member of the Council on Foreign Relations. He was also the protégé of popular historian, Stephen E. Ambrose. As establishment historians, Hoopes and Brinkley's credentials are impeccable.

and Brinkley reference Simpson's book only once, and they do that very dismissively at the conclusion of their chapter on Forrestal, versus 23 references to Rogow. We shall have a good deal more to say about the Rogow and Simpson books later in this chapter, but first, let us examine the work that has long been considered to be the last word on the subject of Forrestal's life in general and his death in particular. This biography, by a former Under Secretary of the Air Force and a young man who has gone on to become perhaps the best-known academic historian in the country, was named a Notable Book of the Year (1992) by *The New York Times*, although the *Book Review Digest* records only seven reviews in periodicals. In their concluding paragraph to Chapter 32, which is entitled "Breakdown," they make their lone reference to the Simpson book, in order to shoot it down. They admit that there have been doubters of the suicide story, led by Forrestal's own older brother, Henry, who suggest that either "the Communists" or "the Jews" did him in, with the help of the Truman government, but they dismiss the notion with a wave of the hand, based upon what they say are "the facts of the case."[10]

It is interesting, indeed, to learn that in this case a man as close to Forrestal as his older brother Henry did not believe that the death was a suicide, so what were the "facts of the case" on the night of the death, as recounted by Hoopes and Brinkley?

Those supposed "facts" are in the preceding pages of the chapter, and they are very cleverly laid out with lots of details as though the authors were flies on the wall observing everything. Forrestal had seemed calm and even in high spirits on the two preceding days, a Friday and a Saturday, they tell us, but now it looked like the usual Sunday-night radio pounding from Drew Pearson had gotten the better of him. The Navy corpsman assigned to keep watch on him up until midnight had observed him pacing the floor and had grown worried. Forrestal had told the corpsman that he did not want to take the usual prescribed sedative because he planned to stay up and read. The corpsman had tried to alert the doctor on duty, sleeping in the room next to Forrestal that something

---

[10] Hoopes and Brinkley, p. 468.

was wrong with Forrestal's emotional state, but the doctor brushed him off and went on to bed.

Another corpsman came on at midnight. He was new to the job, a stand-in for the regular guy who, according to the authors, had gone absent without leave on a drunken bender. The new man, they say, looked into the room at about 1:45 and saw Forrestal copying a morbid poem from Mark Van Doren's *Anthology of World Poetry*, "The Chorus from Ajax," in which Ajax, they say, in a forlorn state of mind contemplates suicide. The book, they tell us, was bound in red leather in decorated in gold. Then they furnish the lines that Forrestal supposedly actually had copied:

> Fair Salamis, the billows' roar
> Wander around thee yet,
> And sailors gaze upon thy shore
> Firm in the Ocean set.
> Thy son is in a foreign clime
> Where Ida feeds her countless flocks,
> Far from thy dear, remembered rocks,
> Worn by the waste of time–
> Comfortless, nameless, hopeless save
> In the dark prospect of the yawning grave....
>
> Woe to the mother in her close of day,
> Woe to her desolate heart and temples gray,
> When she shall hear
> Her loved one's story whispered in her ear!
> "Woe, woe!' will be the cry–
> No quiet murmur like the tremulous wail
> Of the lone bird, the querulous nightingale–[11]

---

[11] Ibid., pp. 464-465. The authors have no explanation for the ellipsis after the word, "grave," suggesting that something is missing. Examining the original poem we see that, in fact, lines 11-20 are not there. We are not told whether those lines were skipped in the original transcription. In all likelihood, neither Hoopes nor Brinkley, nor even Rogow, whose section they were practically copying verbatim, knew the answer to that question. Editor Walter Millis (with the collaboration of E.S. Duffield) had it that way in *The Forrestal Diaries*, The Viking Press, 1951, p. 555, and Rogow, no doubt, was just copying Millis. The contem-

The copying supposedly ended right at the word, "nightingale." This fact sends the authors off onto a flight of fancy, based upon the speculation of John Loftus, that Forrestal must have been overwhelmed with feelings of guilt at that point for having authorized a CIA operation with the code name of "Nightingale" that infiltrated expatriate Ukrainian spies into the Soviet Union, many of whom were former Nazi collaborators guilty of horrible atrocities against Jews.[12]

Then the authors tell us precisely where Forrestal inserted the sheet of paper into the book and then, as if they were there observing it, that he walked out of the room to the kitchen across the hall, tied the sash from his dressing gown to the radiator beneath the window, and tried to hang himself outside the window, but the sash "gave way" and he fell 13 floors to the 3rd floor roof of a hallway below, dying instantly from the fall. The corpsman wasn't there to prevent it, they tell us, because Forrestal had ordered him off on an errand to get him out of the way.

Meanwhile, the corpsman who had been on duty earlier, we are told, had returned to his barracks but he had been unable to sleep. He returned to get a cup of coffee at the hospital at a "canteen," which was presumably still open, when he encountered a great commotion. Somehow, he knew without being told what had happened, and, sure enough, he encountered the young doctor on duty whom he had tried to warn and was given the tragic news. [13]

The Hoopes and Brinkley account might sound persuasive to the uncritical reader, but there is a great deal of missing information. They tell us nothing from the people in the position to know, the Navy corpsman and the doctor who were on duty there on the 16th floor at the time of the death. Interestingly, Hoopes and Brinkley even withhold their names, as though they are afraid that someone might track them down and find out what they saw and heard that fateful night. We also hear nothing

---

porary press, as we shall discuss in Chapter Four, was inconsistent as to which lines of the poem were transcribed.

[12] John Loftus, *The Belarus Secret,* Alfred A. Knopf, 1982.

[13] Hoopes and Brinkley, pp. 463-466.

from the nurse who was supposed to be in charge of the floor that night. Their central character, instead, is the one person whom they do name, one Edward Prise, but he had left for the night almost two hours before Forrestal's death.

We might note, as well, that the name of this Edward Prise appears in none of the contemporaneous accounts of the death in the major newspapers, and his story contradicts some of the basic facts in those stories. For instance, news accounts place the time of the declining of the sleeping pill at 1:45 a.m., not much earlier in the evening as Prise tells us through Hoopes and Brinkley. The news accounts also note nothing irregular or unusual about the corpsman who was on guard at the time of the death. He is named as Apprentice Robert Wayne Harrison, Jr., and he is nowhere described as a substitute for the regular person on duty. By those early accounts, it was not a case of an inexperienced corpsman not recognizing danger signals who allowed himself to be wheedled into leaving his post. Rather, the guard, according to the hospital, had simply been relaxed from 100% of the time to checks on Forrestal every five minutes. So great had been Forrestal's improvement, so little did anyone fear that he would commit suicide, that not only was he routinely being permitted unobserved, ready access to an easily-opened 16th-floor window, but he was also "being allowed to shave himself and... belts were permissible on his dressing gown and pajamas." And Harrison's guard shift did not begin at midnight as told in the Prise account, but at 9:00 p.m. as related by *The Washington Post* on May 23, 1949.

So where, we must wonder, did Hoopes and Brinkley get their Edward Prise story? Their three references are as follows:

> [John] Osborne, "Forrestal," unpublished manuscript outline; Rogow, James Forrestal, pp. 16-17; and Lyle Stuart, *Why: the Magazine of Popular Psychiatry* I, no. 1 (November 1950), pp. 3-9, 20-27.

Let's take them in reverse order.

Why? The Magazine of Popular Psychiatry is truly obscure. According to a search at the Library of Congress, only two libraries in the country have back issues of this long-defunct periodical, and when we tried to get a copy we found that their collections did not go back to the cited premier issue. At any rate, that would appear to be a rather poor secondary source.

The second reference, for its part, flatly contradicts the Prise account. According to Arnold Rogow, the Navy corpsman to whom Forrestal declined the offer of a sedative for sleeping was the same one who later looked in on Forrestal to see him copying the poem. Like the newspapers, Rogow makes no mention of this man being a substitute for the regular man on duty. Furthermore, according to Rogow, the corpsman's absence from the scene was innocent, not because he had been ordered away by Forrestal to give him the opportunity to take his plunge. He was merely off on an "errand," apparently of his own volition. And Rogow goes Hoopes and Brinkley one better when it comes to not naming people. Not only does Edward Prise play no role in his account, but Rogow doesn't name anyone, not even Harrison, who had already been named in the newspapers of the day.

We might also note that the Rogow account is also in conflict with contemporaneous news stories with respect to the rejection of the sedative. Rogow says that that happened late on Saturday night, but the newspapers say that it took place when Harrison looked in on Forrestal at 1:45, which would be Sunday morning, and found him awake, after he had appeared to be sleeping at 1:30. Forrestal's declining of the pill, by news accounts, even prompted Harrison to go wake up the staff psychiatrist on duty on the 16th floor, Dr. Robert R. Deen, and ask him what they should do about it.

On page 16, Rogow reveals that Hoopes and Brinkley are apparently wrong about a steak dinner that Admiral Morton Willcutts, the head of the National Naval Center of which the Bethesda Naval Hospital is a part, watched Forrestal eat. He is in agreement with Simpson that that took place on Friday, not Saturday as Hoopes and Brinkley say.

That brings us to the unpublished manuscript of journalist John Osborne, who died in 1981 after working as a journalist for the Associated Press and as an editor for *Time* and *The New Republic*. We were eventually able to locate it among his papers bequeathed to the Library of Congress. Sure enough, there we find the elusive and clairvoyant Edward Prise, playing the central role of the drama. Curiously, though, Osborne writes that he was able to interview all the key people surrounding Forrestal's death, but the only one whose account he gives us is from a person who was not actually there when Forrestal went out of the window.

Daughter of Key Forrestal Witness Surfaces

We received the following email message on September 26, 2017:

> I started reading your article on the Forrestal death. I got to the part about Edward Prise's story being irrelevant. He was my father and I can tell you he lived in fear of something happening because of information he knew about the case. We grew up hearing whispers between our parents in reference to this matter but were not allowed to ask for details. Even up until a year prior to my father's death in 1991 he had called me and was in fear that he was going to be questioned again about the issue. It might have been irrelevant to you but it was not irrelevant to my family, it was always a shadow in our lives.

The article to which she refers is the one that this first chapter is built upon, first published in 2002.[14] It is clear that Prise's daughter had only just discovered the article, almost 15 years after its first posting on the Internet, because, as we can see, she reacted strongly and negatively to what seemed to be the minimization of the importance of her father in the article. Had she waited until she had finished Part 2, posted in 2004, her reaction would have been very different, because we restore Prise to

[14] "Who Killed James Forrestal, Part 1," November 10, 2002, http://dcdave.com/article4/021110.html.

a place of great importance in that installment, as we shall see in Chapter Four.[15]

We can also see that in that one brief paragraph Edward Prise's daughter completely reverses the role for which her father had been cast, first by Osborne in his unpublished work and then by Hoopes and Brinkley. The words that those writers put in his mouth would never have made him afraid to talk about what he knew of the Forrestal death, as we see was the case, even to his own children. From the daughter we get the distinct impression that there was something very dark and menacing surrounding Forrestal's death, something quite different from the routine suicide that the world has been given to believe, and Prise's account reinforces according to Hoopes and Brinkley. Their book would have been in progress in 1991, and it is likely that one of them had questioned Prise in that year, prompting his agitated call to his daughter.

Secret Investigation Report

So why did Hoopes and Brinkley have to reach so far for this source, especially when he is apparently a very poor witness who wasn't even around when Forrestal took his tragic plunge? What about the findings of the review board that was appointed by the same Admiral Willcutts who observed Forrestal dining on steak on Friday? Here's how *The New York Times* described the board's upcoming work on May 24:

> The board will consider all the circumstances of Mr. Forrestal's illness and of what happened in the few minutes when he was left unattended, walked out of his room into a diet kitchen and jumped. Today the board outlined the procedures it would follow and visited the scene of the death. Tomorrow it will hear witnesses, including Capt. [George] Raines, the psychiatrist attending Mr. Forrestal.

---

15 "Who Killed James Forrestal, Part 2," September 19, 2004, http://dcdave.com/article4/040922.html.

Why, you might ask, didn't Hoopes and Brinkley simply go to the transcript of those hearings and tell us what the most immediate witnesses had to say? At this point, the best expression that comes to mind is one frequently used by the former *Miami Herald's* humorous columnist, Dave Barry, "I'm not making this up." The hearings were secret and the transcript was still secret when Hoopes and Brinkley wrote their book.

It is true that Admiral Willcutts, Admiral Leslie Stone, the Bethesda Hospital commandant, Dr. George N. Raines, the Navy psychiatrist in charge of the case, and Dr. Frank J. Broschart, Montgomery County (Maryland) coroner, all publicly called the death a suicide virtually immediately after it happened (in violation of the basic investigative rule of police that all violent deaths should be treated as murder until sufficient evidence is gathered to prove otherwise). But, on what basis, one might ask, did the duly appointed investigative body, Admiral Willcutts' review board, conclude that it was, indeed, a suicide?

Dave Barry's favorite expression is appropriate once again. I'm not making this up. The answer is that it didn't. Here is what the investigation concluded, as reported on page 15 of the October 12, 1949, *New York Times*. The full article, including the headlines, is given here:

> Navy Absolves All in Forrestal Leap Investigating Board Report on Death Submitted May 30, Revealed by Matthews
>
> Special to the New York Times
>
> Washington, Oct. 11. Francis P. Matthews, Secretary of the Navy, made public today the report of an investigating board absolving all individuals of blame in the death of James Forrestal last May 22. The former Secretary of Defense leaped to his death from an upper story of the Naval Medical Center at Bethesda, Maryland.
>
> The text of the report declared:
>
> 1. That the body found on the ledge outside of Building 1 of the National Medical Center at 1:50 A.M. and pronounced dead at 1:55 A.M. Sunday, May 22, 1949, was identified as that of the late James V. For-

> restal, a patient in the neuropsychiatric service of the United States Naval Hospital National Medical Center.
>
> 2. That the late James V. Forrestal died about 1:50 A.M. on Sunday, May 22, 1949, at the National Naval Medical Center, Bethesda, Maryland, as a result of injuries, multiple extreme, received incident to a fall from a high point in the tower, Building 1.
>
> 3. That the behavior of the deceased during the period of the stay in the hospital preceding his death was indicative of a mental depression.
>
> 4. That the treatment and precautions in the conduct of the case were in agreement with accepted psychiatric practice and commensurate with the evident status of the patient at all times.
>
> 5. That the death was not caused in any manner by the intent, fault, negligence or inefficiency of any person or persons in the naval service or connected therewith.
>
> The board, appointed by Rear Admiral Morton D. Willcutts, then head of the Naval Medical Center, submitted its report on May 30. The Navy announcement today gave no explanation of the delay in making the findings public.
>
> Shortly after Mr. Forrestal's death, Navy psychiatrists explained that their patient had reached a stage in his recovery where a necessary "calculated risk" had to be assumed in permitting him more liberty of movement and less supervision. He climbed through the window of a kitchen during the temporary absence from his floor of an orderly, who otherwise would have seen him and who could have prevented the jump.

At least *The New York Times* is consistent. Its very first report in the last edition of its May 22 newspaper begins, "James Forrestal, former Secretary of Defense jumped thirteen stories to his death early this morning from the sixteenth floor of the Naval Medical Center." Notice, though, that it only took the Willcutts review board a week to wrap up its inquiry, but the Navy took over four months to release this inadequate little summary of the findings, which was buried away on an inside page of *The New York Times.*

And look at the Navy's conclusions. They tell us only that Forrestal died from the injuries caused by the fall and that no one associated with the hospital or the Navy was responsible in any way for the fall. What they don't say is what caused the fall. They don't even venture to remind us that the sash of a hospital gown, presumably Forrestal's, was tied tightly around the neck of the corpse, which they thoroughly establish was that of Forrestal. By not mentioning it, they are relieved of any requirement to explain, or even to speculate upon, its purpose and who might have done the tying of the sash.

Hoopes and Brinkley say quite confidently that Forrestal had tied one end of the sash to a radiator below the window and that it "gave way," whatever that means. All *The New York Times* had to say about the sash in its front-page May 23 article was as follows:

> There were indications that Mr. Forrestal might also have tried to hang himself. The sash of his dressing-gown was still knotted and wrapped tightly around his neck when he was found, but hospital officials would not speculate as to its possible purpose.

And to this day no one in authority has told us what that sash was doing there. Might that be because the attempted hanging scenario is not just nonsensical, but it is impossible? If Forrestal was bent on killing himself, wouldn't he have simply dived out the window, particularly when the attendant was likely to return at any minute? After the sash had been wrapped and tied tightly around his neck, was there enough of it left over for it also to have been tied at one time around the radiator beneath the window? Were there any indications from the creases in the sash that an attempt had been made to tie it around something at one end? How likely is it, anyway, that Navy veteran Forrestal would have been so incompetent at tying a knot that it would have come undone? Most importantly, how do we know that skilled assassins, working for people with ample motives to silence this astute and outspoken patriot (more about those people later) did not use the sash to throttle and subdue Forrestal before pitching him out the window?

The willingness of the authorities to withstand the thoroughly justified charge of cover-up by not releasing the results of their investigation, including the transcripts of witness testimony, speaks volumes, as does the extraordinarily deceptive description of the case by the likes of such establishment figures as Townsend Hoopes and Douglas Brinkley. Their account is replete with deceptions, but there is none greater than this withholding of the information that all the key witness testimony has been kept secret, along with the results of the investigation itself, and that the investigation did not conclude that Forrestal committed suicide. Even Arnold Rogow states in a very matter-of-fact manner in a footnote on page 19, that the Surgeon General and the Navy both conducted inquiries and that the results of neither had been released.[16] Actually, as we have seen, the *results* of the Navy inquiry were released. The problem is that the transcript of the inquiry itself was kept secret. That is to say, *prima facie*, there has been a cover-up and no one in the media or in the history community has had one word to say about it. Hoopes and Brinkley make their cover-up contribution by neglecting to mention that there ever *was* any such Navy inquiry.[17]

"Evidence" without Sources, and Sins of Omission

By leaving out the vital information that the official record of the case has been suppressed, Hoopes and Brinkley, cobbling together an account based on a hodgepodge of dubious sources, leave the reader with the impression that we know more about what happened than we really do. Take, for instance, the matter of Forrestal's copying of a poem, interpreted as an advocacy of suicide, in the wee hours of the night. How do we know that the copying was done by Forrestal, himself, and not by someone who saw it as a clever substitute for a more difficult to compose fake suicide note? Well, they say that the substitute corpsman saw him copying away when he looked in on him at 1:45. And how do they know that? Their sole reference for that observation is Arnold Rogow, and, sure

---

[16] This is the only mention that we have seen of any Surgeon General's report. That office knew nothing of any such report upon our inquiry in 2002.

[17] Simpson writes on page 185, "...the entire report issued on this brief, token inquiry was illegally classified as secret and is withheld from the public to this day." Readers can hear the author call in to C-SPAN and question Douglas Brinkley about his book's crucial omission by scrolling to just past the 2:47 mark of this televised interview on December 7, 2003:
https://www.c-span.org/video/?179432-1/depth-douglas-brinkley.

enough, that's what Rogow says, although Rogow's observer is apparently the regular guard, *uh attendant,* and not a substitute.

So how does Rogow know? We have no way of knowing, because he has no reference. One may surmise at this point that the Rogow account upon which Hoopes and Brinkley rely is not true. All *The New York Times* and *The Washington Post* have to say about the 1:45 encounter is that the corpsman found Forrestal awake, and he declined a sedative or sleeping pill. If the corpsman had actually witnessed him writing, with the poetry book open in front of him, the newspapers would surely have taken that opportunity to tell us, because they certainly do want us to believe that he was the transcriber. Here's *The New York Times* account of May 23:

> Mr. Forrestal had copied most of the Sophocles poem from the book on hospital memo paper, but he had apparently been interrupted in his efforts. His copying stopped after he had written "night" of the word "nightingale" in the twenty-sixth line of the poem.

Clearly, this is conjecture, and not based on what the corpsman had to say. This presumably copied poem by Forrestal was played up big by all the newspapers from the very beginning, because it was from that, as much or more than anything else, that the suicide conclusion that all of them immediately reached was made to seem plausible. It is highly unlikely that the newspapers would have passed up actual eyewitness evidence that Forrestal was transcribing the tragic lines just minutes before he had his fatal fall. We shall see later that our early deduction that Rogow had made up the story that Forrestal was witnessed transcribing the poem was accurate, because we were later able to get the words of the witness himself.

By now it should be clear to the reader that authors of well-publicized and distributed books in the United States on James Forrestal have taken no oath to tell the truth, the whole truth, and nothing but the truth. Take, as well, the treatment of Forrestal's older brother, Henry, a solid and successful businessman who lived in the family home in Beacon, New York, where they and an older brother had grown up. We have seen that Hoopes and Brinkley note Henry's doubts about the official verdict on Forrestal's death, but they brush him aside and make him appear a tad outrageous with his suggestion that "the Communists" or "the Jews" might have been behind it, with the connivance of the highest officials in the U.S. government. As with the missing testimony of the witnesses, how much better would it have been to hear what Henry had to say himself about this matter! The authors had access to Cornell Simpson's 1966 book, *The Death of James Forrestal*, and they could have given us at least something of the flavor of what one finds there.

The author Simpson tells us that he visited the brother Henry at his home in Beacon, New York, and Henry could not have been more certain that Forrestal did not kill himself. In fact, he was "the last person in the world" who would have committed suicide and he had absolutely no reason for doing so. Henry was bitter about how his brother had been kept confined within the hospital for such a long time in "virtual imprisonment" and how he had not been permitted the visitors that he wanted to see.

He was outraged at how the authorities had called the death a suicide immediately with no investigation at all, when he had seemed perfectly normal in conversation with his attendant just minutes before he went out the window with that belt tied around his neck. Furthermore, his appearance and demeanor had also seemed to be completely normal when he had had recent visits by President Truman, his own successor as Defense Secretary, Louis Johnson, and by Henry himself. The timing of the death Henry found particularly suspicious because he was coming to take his brother out of the hospital a few hours later that very same day.

He was especially bitter about how the hospital authorities had prevented any visit by Forrestal's close confidante, Monsignor Maurice Sheehy. Sheehy, according to Henry, was another person who did not believe the suicide story, although, as we shall see, he seems to have sung a different tune later for public consumption.

> Monsignor Sheehy said that when he hurried to the hospital several hours after Forrestal hurtled to his death to try to learn what he could of the circumstances of the tragedy, a stranger approached him in the

> crowded hospital corridor. The man was a hospital corpsman, not young Harrison, but a warrant officer wearing stripes attesting to twenty years of service in the navy. He said to Monsignor Sheehy in a low, tense voice: "Father...you know Mr. Forrestal didn't kill himself, don't you."
>
> But before Monsignor Sheehy could reply or ask the man's name, he said, others in the crowded corridor pressed about him closely, and the veteran warrant officer, as if fearful of being overheard, quickly disappeared.
>
> What did this man know about Forrestal's death? What was it he did not dare tell even a priest?
>
> What really happened in the hospital that fatal night?[18]

Hoopes and Brinkley also say in a matter-of-fact manner that Henry had visited his brother at the hospital four times, but they don't tell us what we learn in the obscure 1966 Simpson book. According to Simpson, Henry had been rebuffed several times by the lead psychiatrist Dr. George Raines and the acting hospital commandant, Captain B.W. Hogan when he tried to visit his brother. James Forrestal had been admitted to the hospital on April 2, and, according to Simpson, the hospital authorities relented only after Henry told Captain Hogan that he was going to the press and threatened legal action. Once he did get to visit his brother briefly, he found him "acting and talking as sanely and intelligently as any man I've ever known," in Henry's words to Simpson.[19]

There is no hint from Hoopes and Brinkley that Henry was ever kept away from his brother by the hospital. They *do* tell us of Henry's futile efforts to persuade Dr. Raines to allow Forrestal's friend and Catholic priest, Monsignor Maurice Sheehy, to visit, although they don't tell us that, in fact, Raines turned Sheehy away on six separate occasions.

Otherwise, the accounts of Hoopes and Brinkley and Simpson are very similar on this prevention of Sheehy's visit to Forrestal over the entire nearly seven-week period. The principal difference is that the

---

[18] Simpson, pp. 29-30.

[19] Ibid., p. 9.

former make the preposterous excuse for the authorities that they possibly feared that Forrestal might divulge sensitive classified information to a priest during a confessional, a supposed fear that would rule out giving any practicing Roman Catholic a security clearance. Hoopes and Brinkley tell us that on May 18 Henry Forrestal and Sheehy together took their complaint about Sheehy being denied permission to visit to Navy Secretary John L. Sullivan and he had overruled the Bethesda authorities, but before the meeting took place, Forrestal was dead. What they don't tell us, as Simpson does, is that Henry had plans to take James out of the hospital the very day of James's fatal plunge, according to Simpson.[20]

Simpson made no excuses for the inexcusable policy of Dr. Raines with respect to Father Sheehy. Rather, he says, "The priest later commented that he received the distinct impression that Dr. Raines was acting under orders. One might ask, under whose orders?"[21]

When Father Sheehy contacted Secretary of the Navy Sullivan, the Secretary seemed surprised to learn of the ban on his visiting. Simpson reaches the conclusion that the orders that Dr. Raines was following came from the White House, the same as the orders that had caused him to be committed to the hospital in the first place and kept there in near isolation on the top floor for seven long weeks.

Simpson goes on to reveal that Father Paul McNally, S.J. of Georgetown University had also tried and had been prevented from seeing Forrestal by Dr. Raines, as had at least one other important friend, unnamed, who "urgently wanted to talk with him."[22]

Yet, *The Washington Post* reported on May 23, "During the past few weeks, Forrestal was allowed to have any visitors he wanted to see, a medical officer on duty said, adding that no log was kept of such visitors." We shall see later that both assertions attributed to that anonymous medical officer are untrue. Maybe that's why he wanted to remain anonymous, or perhaps *The Washington Post* simply made the story up. A log of visitors was kept, but it was apparently not a completely honest

---

[20] Hoopes and Brinkley, pp. 462-463; Simpson, pp. 8-9.

[21] Simpson, p. 10.

[22] Ibid., p. 11.

one. We know from other sources that there were people who visited Forrestal whose names do not appear on the log.

Odd Choice of Permitted Visitors

At the same time that Forrestal was being prevented visits by those he most wanted and needed to see, unwanted guests were being allowed in. These included his successor as Secretary of Defense, Louis Johnson, a man whom, according to Hoopes and Brinkley, Forrestal held in very low regard. As Assistant Secretary of War in the Roosevelt administration in the late 1930s, Johnson had been fired by FDR for undermining the authority of the Secretary, Harry Woodring, Forrestal aide John Kenney had described him as an overly ambitious troublemaker and Forrestal had told Kenney that Johnson was incompetent and felt degraded at the very idea of being replaced by such a man.[23] Apparently the main thing that commended Johnson for the position was that he badly wanted it and that he had been Truman's chief fund-raiser in the 1948 presidential campaign.

Interestingly, *The New York Times* of May 23, 1949, alongside its articles about Forrestal's death is the headline, "Johnson Took Post on Forrestal Plea." That article reported that on May 17 Louis Johnson had addressed a group called the Post Mortem Club and had told them at that time that he was reluctant to accept the post, but Forrestal had pleaded with him to take over the job from him. One might wonder if Johnson knew at that time that Forrestal would never be able to contradict him, although what is more likely is that Johnson knew that Forrestal was too big a man to do such a petty thing as to contradict him publicly over such an ultimately small matter.

Another guest who was probably unwanted, two weeks before Forrestal's death, was the man who had actually made the decision to re-

---

23 Hoopes and Brinkley, p. 431.

place Forrestal with this crony and far lesser man, none other than President Truman, himself. Townsend Hoopes also learned in a January 1989 interview of top Forrestal aide, Marx Leva, that even young Congressman Lyndon Baines Johnson "managed to gain entrance to the suite 'against Forrestal's wishes'."[24]

This is a very strange revelation. LBJ, at that time, was a man of much less stature than Forrestal. It would have been extraordinarily presumptuous of him to bull his way into Forrestal's hospital room when his visit was frankly not wanted. A likely reason why Forrestal would have considered Johnson a member of the enemy camp, albeit a low-level one, was Johnson's great partisanship toward the fledgling state of Israel. As a Congressman, Johnson was considerably ahead of his time in that respect, at least for a Congressman outside the state of New York. We might imagine something of Forrestal's attitude toward LBJ by noting a May 23, 1949, *Washington Post* article headlined, "Delusions of Persecution, Acute Anxiety, Depression Marked Forrestal's Illness." That article concludes as follows:

> His fear of reprisals from pro-Zionists was said to stem from attacks by some columnists on what they said was his opposition to partition of Palestine under a UN mandate. In his last year as Defense Secretary, he received great numbers of abusive and threatening letters.

One must truly wonder why Lyndon Johnson would have wanted to visit Forrestal in his hospital room and what on earth the two adversaries might have had to say to one another. Could LBJ have been playing something of a foot-soldier role for the orchestrators of Forrestal's demise? Might he have been there to size up the overall situation, and at the same time contribute to "making his bones," as it were, by participating in such an important operation?

We must wonder as well why none of Forrestal's closest professional associates are known to have visited or attempted to visit him. One would think that men like Ferdinand Eberstadt, Robert Lovett, and Marx Leva, who, as we shall see, were at his side during his days of decline,

---

[24] Ibid., p. 462.

would have exhibited continuing personal concern for his well-being by periodic visits to the hospital. Did they all realize at that point that it would not be good for their future in the government to be suspected of being too close to Forrestal, who they could see from an insider's reading of the political tea leaves was a doomed man? That speculation seems particularly apt in the case of Eberstadt, whom author Jeffery M. Dorwart characterizes as Forrestal's closest friend and who was at his side during the days before Forrestal's commitment to the hospital. Eberstadt's son, Frederick, in fact, "found it unimaginable" that his father failed to pay even one visit to his friend in the hospital.[25] It might well have had something to do with an observation that Eberstadt had made some weeks before, that is, "My friend has apparently gotten himself in very wrong with the Zionists."[26]

Something we need not wonder about is whether Dr. Raines and the Naval Medical Center made decisions based upon what was best for the patient in this case. Clearly, they did not. Their visitor policy would appear to be more closely akin to torture than to therapy, or closer to the state-serving psychiatric profession of the old Soviet Union. Here's what the aide, Leva, had to say about it in an interview for the Truman Library:

> By the way, psychiatry, he was never permitted to see the people he should have seen. I'm not sure he should have seen me, I would have reminded him of too much, but friends of his, people who loved him; Senator Leverett Saltonstall, just to mention one name, not really a political ally but just someone who really loved him; Kate Foley his secretary.
>
> The great vice of military medicine is that you see who they want you to see. Louis Johnson came out to see him and he saw him and that was the last person that he should have seen you know. Captain Raines couldn't say no to Louis Johnson, but that's the last thing that should have been done...

---

[25] Jeffery M. Dorwart, *Eberstadt and Forrestal: A National Security Partnership*, Texas A & M University Press, 1991, p. 169.

[26] Ibid., p. 159.

> And only a Navy doctor could put a VIP patient on the seventeenth floor [sic] you know. I mean nobody else would put anybody above the second floor with that particular illness. Who is to know whether that had gone so far? I mean he apparently was beyond being neurotic, I mean it was apparently paranoid (sic) but I didn't see it at all. It's a long way to tell you that I did not see it at all until the day after he left office.[27]

Forrestal's Condition

However much he might have improved, whether because of or in spite of his treatment at the Naval Hospital, one must wonder if Forrestal wasn't a bit off in the head and therefore possibly prone to suicide, as even Leva grudgingly seems to have accepted. A number of statements made in the wake of the death could leave one with hardly any other impression. This is from the May 24 *New York Times:*

> Captain George M. Raines, the Navy psychiatrist who had been treating Mr. Forrestal, said that the former Secretary ended his life in a sudden fit of despondency. He said this was "extremely common" to the patient's severe type of mental illness.

And in the May 24 *Washington Post,* although Dr. Raines "categorically denied that Forrestal attempted suicide previously during his stay at the hospital" (which had been charged by columnist, Drew Pearson, who also said he had tried to hang himself, slashed his wrists, and had taken an overdose of sleeping pills while at Hobe Sound, Florida, where he had gone for relaxation), Raines did say:

> There was a history of an alleged suicide attempt obtained by Dr. Menninger which is said to have occurred on the night before the patient was seen by him (at Hobe Sound). At no time during his residence with the Naval Hospital had Mr. Forrestal made a suicidal gesture or a suicidal attempt. His feelings of hopelessness and possible suicide had been a matter of frank discussion between the two of us throughout the course of the therapy.

Please notice the firmness of the denials of actual suicide attempts versus the extreme vagueness of the apparent affirmation of suicidal

[27] Harry S. Truman Presidential Library and Museum, Interview of Marx Leva by Jerry N. Hess, https://trumanlibrary.org/oralhist/leva.htm.

tendencies and of the "alleged suicide attempt." Arnold Rogow also got in on the act. Speaking of Forrestal's stay at Hobe Sound, he said that Forrestal "made at least one suicide attempt," and then he goes on to describe the various possibly dangerous things his friends kept away from him like belts, knives, and razor blades and how they kept a close watch on him when he was in the water. He's full of details about the various suicide-prevention measures taken, but he is very vague about that supposed suicide attempt.[28]

Hoopes and Brinkley muddy the water still further with respect the "suicide attempt," saying only that he talked of suicide, according to Captain Raines who had flown down from Bethesda to observe him, but he had done nothing to act upon it. Then they quickly turn around and contradict Dr. Raines with a third account. The business journalist, Eliot Janeway, they say, was told by Ferdinand Eberstadt privately that Forrestal had "made one suicide attempt" while there at the private retreat of Under Secretary of State Robert Lovett.[29] Once again, the actual details of that supposed attempt by Forrestal to take his own life are still quite noticeably lacking.

Hoopes and Brinkley also say that before the decision was made that Forrestal should go to Florida to rest, he told his friend and fellow Wall Street magnate turned high government consultant on national security matters, Ferdinand Eberstadt, that "his life was a wreck, his career a total failure, and he was considering suicide."[30] And what is their reference for that? Like their account of the witness to the transcription of the poem, it is only Arnold Rogow. Rogow says that Forrestal told Eberstadt that he was a complete failure and considering suicide, but, once again, Rogow has no reference, neither an interview of Eberstadt nor any writing by him. Rogow also has no reference for his rather detailed description of

---

[28] Rogow, p. 6.

[29] Hoopes and Brinkley, p. 456.

[30] Ibid, p. 450.

Forrestal's apparently forcible transfer from the relaxing beach resort in Florida to the Bethesda Naval Hospital.

He tells us that even though Forrestal had been sedated, he was highly agitated during the flight from Florida. He talked, said Rogow, of all the people who were out to get him and mentioned possible suicide again. He lamented his falling away from the Catholic Church, even the fact that he had married a divorcee and that it was possible that he was being punished for it. In spite of the reassurances of those with him that no one wished him ill, he even made several attempts to get out of the moving car on its way from the airport to the hospital and said that he did not expect to leave the hospital alive.[31]

On page 454, Hoopes and Brinkley repeat Rogow's passage almost verbatim, leaving out the part about his talking of suicide again and supplying the information that Eberstadt, aide John Gingrich, and the noted psychiatrist, Dr. William Menninger, who had been summoned to Florida to examine Forrestal, accompanied him on the trip. They cite only the sourceless Rogow, however, as their source. Maybe the more recent authors omitted the suicide talk, knowing that it would hardly ring true in such close juxtaposition to Forrestal's manifestation of his serious Roman Catholicism. Catholics regard suicide as a grave sin, but one must wonder how they learned who was with Forrestal on that fateful last trip to the hospital.

Of particular interest are the supposed words of reassurance, repeated by both the Rogow and Hoopes and Brinkley books, given by Forrestal's traveling associates that no one was out to get him. At this point one must ask who was off his rocker here. The unprecedented campaign of defamation to which he had been subjected, led by columnists and radio commentators Drew Pearson and Walter Winchell, ever since his position against recognition of the state of Israel had become public, and the "great numbers of abusive and threatening letters" about the matter that the *Washington Post* said he had received demonstrated beyond a doubt that large numbers of people wished James Forrestal ill. It is also

---

[31] Rogow, pp. 8-9.

abundantly obvious that there were a number of people who wanted to destroy him as a man of influence. The only question was how much power they might have had and how far they thought it necessary to go.

The Hoopes and Brinkley account of what transpired upon Forrestal's arrival at the Bethesda Naval Hospital, which directly follows the account of his troubled trip, is most intriguing. Admitted to the Bethesda Naval Hospital, as we have noted, on April 2, Forrestal was talked to by Dr. Menninger on April 3 and again on April 6, but then Menninger bowed out of the picture. Dr. Raines took over completely from that point, or, at least, appeared to take over. Hoopes and Brinkley strongly suggest, however, that he was not really the person in charge of Forrestal's "care." Dr. Robert P. Nenno, who had been an assistant to Dr. Raines from 1952 to 1959 said in 1984 that Dr. Raines had told him that it was not his decision to place Forrestal in the 16th floor VIP suite. Had it been left to him, any depressed or potentially suicidal patient would have been housed in one of the two single-story facilities next to the main tower that were set up specifically for emotionally disturbed patients. As for who made that call, their direct quote from Nenno is, "I have always guessed that the order came from the White House."[32]

If the White House made the decision on where Forrestal should be locked up, there is a good chance that Monsignor Sheehy's suspicion as related by Simpson that they were also specifying the visitors he should receive was also correct.

Who Was Calling the Shots?

Concerning the extent of White House involvement in Forrestal's treatment, the following 1968 excerpt of an interview by the Truman Library's Jerry Hess of Harry Truman's appointments secretary for his full time as President, Matthew J. Connelly, is of considerable interest. Connelly had previously been Truman's executive assistant when Truman

[32] Hoopes and Brinkley, p. 454.

was Vice President and when he was Senator, and before that he was the chief investigator on the Senate committee through which Truman rose to prominence as chairman, the Committee to Investigate the National Defense Program. The first and last parts of the excerpt are included to support other suggestions in this paper that there was a big drop-off in leadership quality in the fledgling Department of Defense when Louis Johnson replaced James Forrestal:

> HESS: The next man who served for just a short period of time until the unification was Kenneth C. Royall. He appears again as Secretary of the Army so we'll discuss him as Secretary of the Army, if that's all right.
>
> The next category is Secretary of Defense. Of course, the first Secretary of Defense under the unification act was James Forrestal. Why was he chosen as the first Secretary of Defense?
>
> CONNELLY: Forrestal was Secretary of the Navy prior to the merger of the branches of the Army, Navy and Air Force. Mr. Forrestal had been in Washington under the Roosevelt administration, was a highly intellectual fellow, and was a good administrative officer. When the merger was completed to create the Defense Department, Mr. Truman looked on him as the superior of the other members of the military establishment and appointed him as Secretary of Defense, which office he held very successfully until an illness overtook him.
>
> HESS: Do you recall any instances, any evidences on the job of the mental deterioration that overtook Mr. Forrestal, unfortunately?
>
> CONNELLY: Yes, I recall Mr. Forrestal called me and told me that his telephones were being bugged, his house was being watched, and he would like me to do something about it. So I had the chief of the Secret Service detail at the White House make an investigation of Mr. Forrestal's home; I had him observe it, I had him check his phones, and found out that he was just misinformed, that it wasn't being watched, and there was no indication that there was any wiretapping in Mr. Forrestal's home. That really upset me, because I realized that the Secret Service would do a thorough job, and I told the President that I was worried that Mr. Forrestal might be a little bit wrong.
>
> HESS: What did the President say at that time? Do you recall?
>
> CONNELLY: He asked me what I thought and I said, "I think Mr. Forrestal is cracking up."
>
> So he said, "Why don't we arrange to have him go down to Key West and take a little vacation?"

So, Mr. Forrestal did go to Key West. There was a repetition down there. Mr. Forrestal had hallucinations about things that were going wrong at Key West and he called me from Key West and told me that something was wrong down there. So I checked very carefully with the Navy, who supervises Key West, and Mr. Forrestal later was transferred from Key West to the naval hospital in Bethesda.

HESS: Do you recall what he thought was going wrong at Key West at this time?

CONNELLY: He thought that the same things were happening, that people were annoying him, and he felt he was under surveillance down there, he felt that he was being watched, and in other words, he was being personally persecuted. So as a result of that, we had him very quietly removed to Bethesda hospital in Washington. And history will disclose that is where he jumped out a window.

HESS: The next man to hold the position was Louis Johnson. Why was he chosen for that position?

CONNELLY: Louis Johnson was chosen for two reasons. Number one, Louis Johnson had been Commander of the American Legion. He was a perennial candidate for President. He was a very effective political organizer, and during the campaign of 1948 when things were not very good for Mr. Truman, Louis Johnson accepted the position as treasurer of the Democratic National Committee. He gave up his law practice. He devoted all of his time to raising money for the campaign in '48. He was a highly successful lawyer in Washington, and Mr. Truman turned to him after the death of Mr. Forrestal to take over the Pentagon operation.

HESS: During this time, two important events took place, the cutting back of the Armed Forces and the invasion of Korea. Some people had blamed Louis Johnson for the reduction in the Armed Forces. Is that valid?

CONNELLY: That is valid. He had promised that he would cut to the bone the expenditures of the Defense Department and set out to do so, with the result that when the Korean war developed we found ourselves very unable to meet our commitments for our appearance in Korea.

HESS: Was this done strictly for reasons of economy? Wasn't it seen that this was a dangerous thing to do in the world situation at that time, or not?

CONNELLY: Well, World War II was over and Mr. Johnson thought that the appropriation for the Defense Department could be cut to reduce the overhead we had in maintaining the equipment over here and overseas, and he put on an economy program and without the Korean war at that time being imminent, he succeeded in his objectives. However, when the Korean thing developed we were too thin on supplies and materiel.

HESS: In the Korean War the North Koreans invaded South Korea, we'll get to that a little bit later, on June the 24th, on a Saturday, of 1950. Just when was the decision made to replace Louis Johnson. What can you tell me about the resignation of Louis Johnson?

CONNELLY: I don't recall.

HESS: Was that offered willingly, do you recall?

CONNELLY: I don't believe so. I think that the President by this time became dissatisfied with Johnson because of his inability to get along with other members of the Armed Forces.

HESS: How did he get along with the other members of the Cabinet?

CONNELLY: Louis Johnson was somewhat of an individualist, and Louis Johnson was not what you would call a cooperative member of the Cabinet. He was running his own show, and he didn't want any interference from anybody else, and I don't think he asked very often for opinions from anybody else.[33]

The first thing to notice here is that Connelly's statement apparently contradicts both the Hoopes and Brinkley and the Rogow accounts as to who was behind the decision to send Forrestal down to Florida, and later to have him placed in the Bethesda Naval Hospital. Both books have Forrestal's friend, Ferdinand Eberstadt, as the prime mover in the decision to go down to the estate of State Department official and friend, Robert Lovett, where Forrestal's wife, Josephine Ogden, "Jo," Forrestal was already vacationing. As we shall see, the most immediate witness to Forrestal's apparent nervous breakdown, Forrestal aide, Marx Leva, supports their version. One curiosity is that, although Eberstadt did not die until 1969, six years after Rogow's book was published and 20 years

---

[33] Truman Library Oral History Interviews with Matthew Connelly, https://www.trumanlibrary.org/oralhist/connly.htm.

after Forrestal's death, no one seems to have any sort of formal statement from Eberstadt directly about these matters, including Forrestal's supposed suicide attempt at Hobe Sound or his talk of suicide. As for the decision to move Forrestal to Bethesda, Hoopes and Brinkley have it as a "tacit agreement" among several people at Hobe Sound, including Dr. Menninger, whom Eberstadt had apparently called in, Dr. Raines, who they say had been sent down at the behest of the White House (though not as the "agent" of the White House) and Forrestal's wife. The wife, they say, had been influenced toward the Bethesda decision by a telephone conversation with Truman. Rogow says simply that Bethesda "was deemed" preferable to Menninger's psychiatric clinic but doesn't say by whom.

Considering the fact that Forrestal, having been officially replaced as Defense Secretary by Johnson on March 28, was a private citizen at this point, it is certainly reasonable to assume that Forrestal's extra-legal transportation to Florida on a military airplane and confinement and treatment in the Naval Hospital at Bethesda was not done without approval at the highest level. Therefore, the Connelly account is probably essentially correct, although some area of dispute may remain as to who was the prime mover behind the decisions that were made. What appears not to be factually correct in the Connelly account is his placing of the Florida vacation site as Key West instead of Hobe Sound. Hobe Sound is on the southeast coast of Florida, north of Jupiter and West Palm Beach and more than 100 miles from Key West. One would like to think that he just slipped up on the name, but he is so definite about the Navy's role in everything, and the U.S. Navy does have facilities at Key West. Perhaps it was the active role of Navy doctor, Captain Raines, that caused his confusion.

As we have seen, although they don't go quite so far as Connelly, Hoopes and Brinkley do hint at a heavy behind-the-scenes presence by the White House in Forrestal's treatment. Not only do they suggest that the White House was responsible for Forrestal being confined to the

16th floor, but one can easily see political pressure as opposed to sound medical considerations behind the curious choice of visitors that they tell us Forrestal was permitted. Arnold Rogow doesn't take that chance. He did, as we have seen, mention in passing, though without comment in a footnote, that the report of the official investigation was kept secret, but generally he is far guiltier than Hoopes and Brinkley of withholding vital information from the reader.

Rogow's Psychological Autopsy

Rogow keeps the hand of the White House completely hidden in his account. Rather, the voice we hear over and over is that of Dr. Raines and of the psychiatric community. One is greatly reminded of Kenneth Starr's heavy reliance upon "suicidologist" Dr. Allan Berman and his "100% degree of medical certainty" that Deputy White House Counsel Vincent Foster committed suicide.

Rogow tells us that Dr. Raines diagnosed Forrestal as suffering from something called "involutional melancholia," which was, indeed, a depressive condition specific to people of late middle age in the eyes of certain elements of the psychiatric community at the time. Rogow also quotes from a psychiatric textbook that mentions paranoia as one of the symptoms and that there is a risk of suicide from sufferers of the disorder. Not leaving anything to chance, he reminds us at that point that Forrestal had expressed concerns that there were "plots" and "conspiracies" against him. Rogow carefully leads the reader to the conclusion that Dr. Raines had made the proper diagnosis.[34]

---

[34] Rogow, pp. 9-10. Wikipedia brings us down to earth with these words: "Involutional melancholia is not recognized as a psychiatric disorder by the DSM-5 (Diagnostic and Statistical Manual of Mental Disorders), the American Psychiatric Association's (APA) classification and diagnostic tool." https://en.wikipedia.org/wiki/Involutional_melancholia. See also the commonsense rejoinder to Rogow by Oklahoma State University sociologists, Mary Akashah and Donald Tennant, "Madness and Politics: The Case of James Forrestal," (Proceedings of the Oklahoma Academy of Science, Vol. 60, 1980) available online at http://digital.library.okstate.edu/oas/oas_pdf/v60/p89_92.pdf. The following paragraph provides a good summation of their conclusions: "We do not deny that Forrestal was under great stress at the end of his career. How-

Rogow does mention, again almost in passing, that Forrestal's brother, Henry, was not happy with the treatment at the Bethesda Naval Hospital, and he quotes from the December 1950 article by William Bradford Huie in the December 1950 *New American Mercury* to that effect. He also tells us that Father Sheehy had tried six times "during the week before [Forrestal's] death" to see him at the hospital but "he told reporters, he was turned away by Raines because Raines did not believe that such a visit 'would be in the patient's best interest.'"[35]

No reference is given for the Sheehy talk to reporters, but the Huie article is clear that the six attempts by Sheehy to visit took place before Henry's last visit with Raines on May 12, ten days before Forrestal's death, and probably over a period of time much longer than one week. Huie tells us that on April 12, "Henry Forrestal also told the doctors (Raines and Hogan) that his brother wished to talk with Father Sheehy. Captain Hogan replied, according to Mr. Forrestal: 'Yes, he has asked to see the Father several times. And, of course, he will.'"

The prevention of any meeting between Sheehy and James Forrestal was obviously not the last minute sort of thing that Rogow would apparently want us to believe that it was.

Sheehy, in a very short article in the January 1951 *Catholic Digest* entitled "The Death of James Forrestal" responding to Huie's *American Mercury* article, offers the opinion that "the psychiatrist in charge was acting according to his principles." Father Sheehy, who also reveals in the article that his efforts to see Forrestal took place virtually over the whole period of the confinement, writes here in such a politically circumspect

---

ever, we have found no convincing evidence that he was dangerously psychotic or incapable of discharging his duties while in office. There is no justification for saying that his policies and positions were somehow the products of a diseased mind, unless we are willing to make the same assumptions about literally millions of people who have entertained similar beliefs. Nevertheless, they have been interpreted as such in Forrestal's case."

[35] Rogow, p. 45.

manner that one wonders what anyone could possibly have had to fear in letting him talk to Forrestal.

Rogow, for his part, even manages to come half clean with respect to doubts that Forrestal's death was actually a suicide. In a passage that is not referenced by Hoopes and Brinkley, he informs us that the widow in June of 1949 filed a $10,000 insurance claim on the basis that the death was an accident. In a footnote he tells us that he was unable to find out if the insurance company paid up.[36]

We hear nothing from Rogow, though, of brother Henry's vigorous denial that Forrestal had committed suicide as we saw in the passage from the Simpson book. To be sure, Rogow did not have the Simpson book to quote from since his book predated Simpson's by three years, but he had something even better. He had Henry Forrestal himself. In his acknowledgments on page 375 he thanks Henry for his great cooperation on the work and on page 58 he has the little detail furnished by Henry that his younger brother was almost always strapped for money at college even though the family had provided him with about $6,000 while he was at Princeton.

Clearly, Henry made himself available to Rogow and told the man everything he wanted to know. No doubt, in desperate hope of finally getting his own considered opinion that his brother was murdered out to the public, he also told Rogow everything that he wanted Rogow to know. One can only imagine the sense of betrayal he must have felt upon reading what Arnold Rogow ended up writing. The experience probably left him more "damned bitter" than ever, and ever more at a loss as to what he could do.

The Gospel According to Rogow

In the absence of an official "Warren Report" or "Fiske Report" or "Starr Report" on Forrestal's death, Rogow's flawed account has become the surrogate "official" version of what happened. We have seen how Hoopes and Brinkley lean on it for important evidence that is not elsewhere sup-

[36] Ibid., p. 46.

ported, like the naval corpsman witnessing Forrestal transcribing the Sophocles poem and Forrestal's supposed talk of contemplated suicide to Ferdinand Eberstadt. It has also become the standard reference for accounts of Forrestal's death in popular books like *The Puzzle Palace*, by James Bamford, *The Agency*, by John Ranelagh, and *The Secret War against the Jews*, by John Loftus and Mark Aarons. Otto Freidrich, in his book, *Going Crazy*, uses Rogow as his source and refers to Forrestal as "mad as King Lear."[37]

We have noted that Rogow, like Hoopes and Brinkley, leaves out the name of vital witnesses such as the naval corpsman and the doctor on duty on the 16th floor on the night of May 21-22, 1949. He even goes Hoopes and Brinkley one better and omits the name of Special Assistant and General Counsel to the Secretary of Defense, Marx Leva, the man who first witnessed Forrestal's breakdown on March 29, the day after his replacement as Defense Secretary by Louis Johnson and shortly after he was honored at a ceremony of the Committee on Armed Services of the House of Representatives. In the course of two paragraphs Rogow refers to an anonymous "aide" or "assistant" no less than five times. In each case he is talking of Leva.

Forrestal Protégé, Marx Leva

Since it is evident that Rogow didn't want readers to seek out Leva and hear or read for themselves what he had to say, I shall provide his account here from the previously cited Truman Library interview by Jerry Hess:

> HESS: What do you recall about the unfortunate mental breakdown that overtook Mr. Forrestal?
>
> LEVA: Well, I may have been in the position of not being able to see the forest for the trees because I was seeing him six, eight, ten, twelve times a day and both in and out of the office. A lot of his friends have said since his death, "Oh, we saw it coming," and, "We knew this and we

[37] Quoted by Akashah and Tennant.

knew that." The only thing that I knew was that he was terribly tired, terribly overworked, spending frequently literally sixteen hours and eighteen hours a day trying to administer an impossible mechanism, worrying about the fact that a lot of it was of his own creation. I knew that he was tired, I begged him to take time off. I'm sure that others begged him to take time off.

I tried to arrange, and on one occasion did arrange, a fishing trip for him with his friend Ferdinand Eberstadt, which he canceled, he didn't take it. I tried to tell him he ought to go south, go somewhere, and rest. I did realize that. But I did not—I had no background with mental illness, I had no knowledge of how it manifested itself and I did not equate exhaustion and mental illness. I just thought he was terribly tired and he ought to take time off.

I even came up with what I thought was a very ingenious device because he told me he didn't have any under secretary; he didn't have any assistant secretaries, he couldn't leave. And I even gave him a legal opinion (I hope not written because it was not very valid), in which I said that, I think I told him this: That because the 1947 unification act didn't create an under secretary or any assistant secretaries, but did have a number of presidential appointees in the Pentagon, it would be quite all right for him to designate any one of the three secretaries as the acting Secretary of Defense in his absence because they were the next level of presidential appointees. And I said, "If you feel that Secretary Symington cannot be objective on a Navy matter and Secretary Sullivan cannot be objective on an Air Force matter, then you have Royall as a possible man, since the Army is less partisan, or if you feel that it would be an insult to one of the secretaries to have one of the others and what you want is a caretaker for a couple of weeks, you can appoint a fellow like Gordon Gray, who was my specific recommendation, who is the Assistant Secretary of the Army, or perhaps then Under Secretary" And I said, "Nobody could be insulted, everybody respects him and he is a presidential appointee. I'm sure Mr. Truman would approve, and you could just let him run the department administratively, and we can always get you on the phone when we need to," which I thought was a rather ingenious solution, but nothing came of it.

That is a long answer to your question, or a long non-answer, I did not know what was happening. Now my observation of what did happen is as follows: Louis Johnson, who I had not met before he was sworn in, was to have been sworn in on March the 31st of 1949. Forrestal apparently just thought he couldn't hold on any longer, I didn't realize that until later, and asked that this ceremony be moved up to March the 28th. It was moved up to March 28th and while Forrestal was terribly tired, it was—he spoke briefly but well. The ceremony went off fine.

I believe that either Forrestal went to an office that had been set aside for him afterwards, or he went home. In any event, we had an appointment on the Hill the next day, March 29th before the House Armed Services Committee because Chairman Vinson had said to me, "Be sure to have Mr. Forrestal there." They wanted to take note of his outstanding service, etc. So I arranged that Mr. Forrestal would be there. He came to the Pentagon.

I rode up to the Hill with him. That was the day after Johnson was sworn in, and we appeared before the House Armed Services Committee and Forrestal was sort of overwhelmed by the compliments of Carl Vinson and the ranking Republican member, Dewey Short, from the great state of Missouri. And he was a little teary eyed, I think, but he responded very beautifully and said that anything that he had been able to accomplish was because the Secretaries of Army and Navy and Air Force had been working so closely with him, etc. He made a, you know, good routine response. My further recollection at that time is that Stuart Symington said to me, "Marx, old fellow, would you mind if I rode back to the Pentagon with Jim; there's something I want to talk to him about." I don't know what it was.

I said, "Sure."

So, I rode back with Royall because Forrestal and I had driven over together. When I got back to the Pentagon I went back to my office. Forrestal had been given an office down from the Secretary of Defense a little, next door to mine. So I stuck my head in—it was next door to my office—and he was sitting there just like this with his hat on his head, just gazing. And I went in and I said, "Mr. Secretary, is there anything I can do for you?"

He was almost in a coma really. That was when I first knew and that was when I first got scared. So I said, "Do you feel faint?" I don't remember what I said.

He said, "No, no, I want to go home."

So, he got up and headed for the door and I said, "Where are you going?"

He said, "I'm going for my car." Well, he didn't have a car.

So, I ran like hell. I remember whose car I got; I got Dr. Vannevar Bush's driver, who was then head of the Research and Development Board, and I said, "Take Mr. Forrestal home and phone me when you get him there." I knew Mrs. Forrestal wasn't in town, and I told the driver to make sure that the butler knows that he's there, etc. And then I phoned, as it happened, Mr. Eberstadt who was testifying on the 1949 amendments to the unification act before the Senate Armed Services Committee. And I said, "I don't like what I see. Can I meet you?"

He said, "Yes, I'll meet you at the house."

So, I met him at the house and the butler said he had gone upstairs. I don't know, anyway—I'm sort of short-circuiting this. That wasn't exactly what happened. We first phoned the house, Eber and I got together, the butler said, "He won't speak to anybody."

Eber said to the butler, "You tell James (Eber and others of the Princeton group called him James), you tell James he can get away with that with a lot of people but not with me." And so he came to the phone and apparently babbled a lot of stuff about the Russians—apparently it was just like that. I don't know. The only further thing I knew is that I did drive to the house, I waited while Eber had the butler pack his clothes. Eber came out once and said, "Can you get a plane to take him to Florida?"

And I said, "Certainly."

And I phoned and we got a Marine plane, I think, I don't know. And so Forrestal came down and Eber sat in the back seat of my old, old Chevrolet and Forrestal sat in front with me and then the butler came running back, came running after us. He brought the Secretary's golf clubs. So I opened the trunk, we put in the golf clubs and I drove out to the private plane end (we didn't go to the military planes), private plane end of National Airport. And on the way out Forrestal said three times, the only thing he said, Eber tried to speak to him and he would say, "You're a loyal fellow, Marx." "You're a loyal fellow, Marx," three times. I remember that, I think I remember that. And we put him in the plane and I had also phoned to be sure to have a military aide there to look after him and then I said to Eber, "I hate for him to be going down there by himself but I know Bob Lovett is down there," who was a close friend.

And I said, "I'm going to phone Bob to be sure to meet the plane." So I phoned Bob and Bob did meet the plane. I never saw him after that.

By the way, psychiatry—(omit two paragraphs previously quoted)

Actually, as I understood later from Mr. Eberstadt—Mr. Eberstadt sent a plane down, chartered a plane, and sent Dr. Menninger from Topeka and wanted the Secretary to fly up to the Menninger Clinic, but Mrs. Forrestal and Mr. Truman agreed that it would be—neither of whom knew anything about psychiatry either—that there would be less stigma at being at the naval hospital.

And only a Navy doctor could put a VIP patient—(Previously-cited paragraph omitted.)

HESS: What would be your evaluation of his general effectiveness and his administrative ability and Mr. Forrestal's overall value to the United States?

LEVA: Oh, I think he was one of the ablest public servants I have ever known. I think that he was simply tremendous in everything that he went into. I think that most people's memories have been clouded by the end of the story without any attention to the early chapters or the middle chapters.

I think in particular of a column that Arthur Krock wrote that impressed me very deeply. The day after Forrestal was sworn in, which now has us to September '47, in which Arthur wrote, in substance, "He entered on his new duties as Secretary of Defense with a measure of public respect and esteem unequaled in the memory of this correspondent." It's easy to lose sight of that. He apparently did a simply fantastic job at the Navy during World War II both as Under Secretary and as Secretary. I only got there when it was over but those who were there say that that multibillion procurement program that he put together, hiring for the purpose the best and the most outstanding lawyers anywhere in the country to make sure that the country got its money's worth, and what he did on a crash basis, and I'm sure what [Robert] Patterson did in a similar context in the Army, was simply a fabulous administrative achievement. I think within the limit of what one could do in the very difficult framework of starting unification, he did magnificently.

The first thing to note is that Leva's candid, non-medical view that prior to the breakdown on March 29 the only thing noticeable about Forrestal's condition was that he was badly exhausted and overworked. Leva was not alone in not seeing any evidence that Forrestal was actually "cracking up." Hoopes and Brinkley say virtually the same thing with respect to everyone who worked closely with him. Those co-workers attribute their failure to notice any change in him, like Leva, to the continuous nature of their contact with him as well as to his very self-contained, businesslike manner. [38]

---

[38] Hoopes and Brinkley, p. 426.

Given the extent and pace of his decline, it is astonishing that colleagues at the Pentagon, including members of his inner staff, failed to recognize it. In retrospect they attribute their failure to Forrestal's formidable self-control, his brusque, impersonal method of dealing with staff, and the simple fact that they saw him too frequently to note much change in his condition or demeanor.

These observations are in curious contrast to what Monsignor Sheehy wrote in his *Catholic Digest* article:

> The day he was admitted to the hospital, Forrestal told Dr. Raines he wished to see me. The word reached me through the executive officer of the hospital. I dismissed a class, because I had seen his collapse coming on for some weeks, and knew his condition was serious. The psychiatrist told me that he wished my help, but that Jim was so confused I should wait some days before seeing him.

Sheehy does not elaborate. Perhaps he is talking about the growing exhaustion. Setting aside what some have seen as "paranoid" previous claims by Forrestal that some people were out to get him, because there is every reason to believe that they were, his truly strange behavior began very abruptly after that automobile ride with Secretary of the Air Force (and later Senator and Presidential aspirant) Stuart Symington. It should be noted that in their index under "Symington, Stuart, double-dealing tactics of," they list pages 368-70, 380-83, 446, and 447. It is a relatively safe assumption that whatever it was Symington had to say to Forrestal affected the latter very, very greatly and in a very negative way. It would not have been out of character for Symington, if one accepts the Hoopes and Brinkley portrait of the man, for that to have been his intention. That impression of Symington's motives is reinforced by the fact that Symington later said that no such trip had taken place or that he and Forrestal were ever alone together, but Leva and Forrestal aide John Ohly was in strong agreement with Leva on the matter.[39]

---

[39] Ibid., p. 447.

The Symington Revelations

The reader may excuse us if we engage in a bit of speculation at this point as to what the subject matter of that conversation might have been. One must agree, we believe, that this speculation is at least as valid as the suggestion that the word "nightingale" in that poem by Sophocles, because that was the name of an American intelligence program to infiltrate anti-communist former Nazi sympathizers into the Ukraine, touched off such feelings of guilt in an apparently fully-recovered Forrestal that he rushed quickly across the hall, tied one end of his gown's sash tightly around his neck, attempted unsuccessfully to secure the other end to a radiator, and then flung himself out the window, dying from the fall instead of from the intended hanging.

The key to the subject matter of the Symington conversation is to be found in the five words that Forrestal kept repeating to Leva, "You are a loyal fellow. You are a loyal fellow." And why wouldn't he be, one might ask, and in contrast to whom? Now I think we can see why Arnold Rogow didn't want us to know Marx Leva's name. Marx Leva, if you had not guessed by this time, was quite thoroughly Jewish. The best guess as to the subject matter of Symington's conversation, I believe, is that it related to some enormity, some devastating power play by Jewish Americans that advanced the cause of Israel at the expense of what Forrestal perceived to be the interests of the United States. Forrestal was apparently overwhelmed by the contrast between the personal and the patriotic loyalty of Leva, a man he had elevated to his current position because of his dedicated service to the American government, and the large number of prominent and less-prominent Jews who had made Forrestal's life a hell over the past couple of years.

On the Beach

Expanding upon the reasons for the anti-suicide precautions, Hoopes and Brinkley make Forrestal sound absolutely nutty by his suggestion that he and Lovett not talk in the proximity of the permanent sockets for beach umbrellas for fear that listening devices might be planted there. What he wanted to talk about was how the Communists who had infiltrated the Roosevelt-Truman administration had singled him out as public enemy number one, but he was not the only one that they planned to assassinate. They actually were planning the assassination of the entire leadership of the government and the invasion of the country, and might even be already underway.[40]

Their lone reference for all this is Rogow and Rogow, as is typical with him, has no reference at all. Their passage is so close to a verbatim rendering of Rogow, in fact, that one could almost call it plagiarism, except that Hoopes and Brinkley have made it sound even more outlandish by adding the bit about the Kremlin's plan to assassinate the whole leadership in Washington.

The story about the supposedly bugged beach umbrella sockets is quoted in its entirety in *The Secret War against the Jews* and it is also recounted in *The Agency*. It certainly does make it sound like Forrestal was pretty far around the bend while at Hobe Sound, but there is simply no evidence that it is true.

Robert Lovett is long dead, but fortunately he gave an interview to Alfred Goldberg and Harry B. Yoshpe of the Office of the Secretary of Defense Oral History Project on May 13, 1974 (Lovett was Secretary of Defense under Truman from September 1951 to the end of Truman's term in January of 1953.). We quote the relevant portions:

> YOSHPE: It has often been said that the problems of trying to run the Defense establishment in the face of these difficulties undermined Forrestal's health. Is there any truth in that?
>
> LOVETT: I wouldn't say that those problems were the ones. Jim Forrestal was a very intense man anyway, but he had himself under strict control. He was never one to show emotion–containing that all the time was what I think put such extra tension on him. I remember that he was flown down to Hobe Sound after his breakdown. They phoned me and asked me if I would meet him, which I did—as I say, he was a very dear, close friend of mine. And when he got out of the plane over at the air

[40] Ibid., p. 451.

> base, we stood under the shadow of the tail plane because it was hot as the hinges at that time of day. When he came down and he offloaded his golf clubs, bag, and that sort of thing, I said to Jim, "I'm glad you brought your golf clubs because I'm going to take every dollar you've got here." Not a crack of a smile, and he finally turned to me and said, "You know, they're really after me."
>
> I'd been warned, of course, by Eberstadt over the phone that Forrestal was in bad shape. But to shorten the story, he was at that time a completely different person from the one I knew. We finally got him back to Washington. Ed Shea, his roommate at Princeton, came up from Texas and stayed there with him, and slept in the room with him the whole time. But he obviously was in very bad shape.
>
> Now part of that tension was not the result of the problems of running the Department but the fact that he had been dabbling a little bit in politics. In other words, he had been dealing with the Republican side while a Democratic appointee. Not in any sly way but simply maintaining his position–I think he wanted to continue in the job in case of the change. I believe that had something to do with it. But that, I would say, would not be for publication.
>
> YOSHPE; Some of the material, including the Forrestal diaries, seemed to indicate that he had expected to stay on at least until May.
>
> LOVETT: He had hoped, I think, to stay on. He was obsessed with the idea that his phone calls were being bugged and that "they" (it was hard to identify they) were some anti-Forrestal group in the Administration. They, the enemy, who was it? He was not of sound mind, in my view.

That's it. No examples are given to illustrate Forrestal's unsoundness of mind but the ones you see here. There is no talk of suicide and no mention of any suicide attempt. There is also no mention of suspicion of bugged beach umbrella sockets (although if one were to try to record conversations on a beach, putting bugs in pre-installed umbrella sockets would seem to be the best way to do it), nor is there any talk of Forrestal running out of his room in the middle of night claiming the Russians were attacking when a police siren awakened him. This latter tale is a story reported by Drew Pearson in his nationally syndicated column, but dismissed as untrue by Hoopes and Brinkley.

But Pulitzer Prize winner, Thomas Powers, reported in *The Man Who Kept the Secrets*, citing Daniel Yergin that not only did Forrestal say that "they" were after him, but that he had actually run through the streets yelling,"The Russians are coming. The Russians are coming. They're right around. I've seen Russian soldiers." Then he goes on to say that he died trying to hang himself "from his hospital window, but slipped and fell sixteen stories to his death."[41]

Yergin's reference for this story, and for Forrestal's "at least one suicide attempt" at Hobe Sound, turns out to be none other than Arnold Rogow. The idea that Forrestal slipped and fell while trying to hang himself is apparently original with Powers. In the Ranelagh and Loftus and Aarons versions, the reason Forrestal ends up falling instead of hanging is that the sash broke, another fanciful account that these authors seem to have invented independently, that is, unless there is some propaganda-central supplying these authors. (Here we are reminded of the supposedly independent reports of authors Ronald Kessler [*Inside the White House*] and Judith Warner [*Hillary Clinton, The Inside Story*] that Vincent Foster's pocket was where a hand-written list of psychiatrists turned up in that mysterious death case. That bit of evidence is inconsistent with the official story, which is that a search of Foster's clothing turned up nothing—except two sets of keys after a second search of the body at the morgue.)[42]

But we have not yet covered everything in the Lovett interview that bears upon the demise of James Forrestal:

> GOLDBERG: Another issue from this same period was raised with us by a number of people. It falls right into your State Department period. That was the Palestine problem. The Defense Department had very strong views on this, and the State Department did also.

---

[41] Thomas Powers, *The Man Who Kept the Secrets: Richard Helms and the CIA*, Alfred A. Knopf, 1979, p. 361; the Yergin referenceis to *Shattered Peace: The Origins of the Cold War and the National Security State*, Houghton Mifflin, 1977, p. 208.

[42] Concerning the various locations where that list of psychiatrists was said to have been found, see David Martin, "Vince Foster's Valuable Murder," November 26, 2000, http://www.dcdave.com/article3/001126.html.

LOVETT: I was the agent in State who had to take the rap in this thing and do most of the ground work so I've a lively recollection. Pick some particular question –

GOLDBERG; I really wanted to ask how State looked at the National Security aspects of the issue at that time. I know how the Defense Department was looking at it, and I've seen a lot of the State documents for the period, too, but we're interested in hearing about it from your level and General Marshall's.

LOVETT: Well, you remember the American position set forth by Senator Austin at the United Nations meeting. It was, in effect, that this small country of a million and one half people, surrounded by 40 million Arabs, was non-viable unless it could be assured of an umbrella of some sort. It was on that basis that the theory of the trusteeship was developed which would give them an independent country, but place them in the hands of a group of trustees until such time as they either matured into a viable nation or until some method of living could be worked out with the Arabs.

We were ultimately defeated on that. I say we, this country's point of view did not prevail, and it didn't prevail because it was fought vigorously by the Israelis. Now the atmosphere was embittered, and that was the thing which caused most of the attacks on Forrestal. In my view, it was one of the principal causes for his mental condition. The constant unrelenting attacks on Forrestal. I was less visible as a government official. They were bad enough, God knows, on me. I received telephone calls at 11 o'clock at night, with threats: "we'll get you, you so and so." And I got telegrams from every conceivable agency—Haganah, Hadassah, Rabbi Abba Hillel Silver—everybody pressuring me to do this, that, and the other thing. Give these people independence. You give them independence and they get overrun—what do you do then? So it was a sense of conscience in this country, being willing to help them and not leading them down the garden path to utter destruction. It was a very serious problem.

Compared to Forrestal, Lovett, by his own account, was relatively out of the line of fire over the Israel issue, but that did not prevent him from receiving late night threatening telephone calls and tons of pressure from all quarters. Lovett was subjected to none of the public vilification that Forrestal faced, so one can only imagine what Forrestal had to put up with privately.

Forrestal *Was* Bugged

Actually, we don't have to depend completely upon imagination. We can take it from pro-Zionist authors John Loftus and Mark Aarons in their book, *The Secret War against the Jews.* They confide to us from their Zionist sources that they had attempted to blackmail Forrestal, as Loftus and Aarons say they had blackmailed Nelson Rockefeller to get his Latin American friends to line up in favor of the partition of Palestine by the United Nations. The method was to use recordings they had of his dealings with the Nazis when he had been president of the Wall Street investment-banking firm, Dillon, Read, and Company. They didn't have enough on him to rein him in, they say, but it sent him around the bend in paranoia, convincing him that "his every word was bugged."[43]

Whether or not Forrestal's "every word" was bugged would appear from this revelation to be little more than a quibble over the degree to which his avowed enemies clandestinely monitored his dealings. After all, how would the Zionists have come into possession of tapes of Forrestal's most private business dealings except through the use of bugs and/or wiretaps? And if this account is to be believed, the fact of the monitoring had already been revealed to Forrestal by this dastardly attempted blackmail, an attempt to get Forrestal to go against what he thought was best for the nation by playing upon a hoped-for fear of revelations possibly detrimental to his own personal interests.

If the Zionists thought such rotten tactics, of which Loftus and Aarons seem almost to approve, would work on Forrestal, they had seriously misjudged their man. Hoopes and Brinkley have chosen the title of their Forrestal biography well, "Driven Patriot." Not in this writer's lifetime have we seen an American leader who has so determinedly and courageously put the interests of the American people first as did James Forrestal. At least twice that we know of, as Secretary of the Navy, he flirted with insubordination in the Truman administration in the waning days of the Pacific War. Through the Office of Naval Intelligence, he made un-

[43] John Loftus and Mark Aarons, *The Secret War against the Jews: How Western Espionage Betrayed the Jewish People,* St. Martin's Griffin, pp. 212-213.

authorized peace feelers toward the Japanese, ignoring our rigid public "unconditional surrender" terms that prolonged the war and resulted in the perhaps unnecessary bloody battles of Iwo Jima and Okinawa and the continued decimation of Japanese cities, culminating in the nuclear attacks on the defenseless and strategically unimportant cities of Hiroshima and Nagasaki.[44] Later, though pointedly not a part of Truman's official delegation, he would attend the Potsdam Conference outside the destroyed Berlin, taking with him on his flight the 28-year-old Navy veteran by the name of John F. Kennedy, the son of Forrestal's powerful friend, Joseph P. Kennedy.[45]

With regard to the Palestine question, Forrestal knew that he had all the leaders in the State Department and the military on his side. They knew that American interests would be compromised by the sponsorship of a new state made up primarily of recent European immigrants, smack in the heart of Arab territory, territory that was rich in oil upon which the West and our military apparatus had grown more dependent. He also feared greatly that we would be drawn in militarily in defense of the new and beleaguered little country against those with whom we should have a harmony of interests. Negotiations over Palestine were the direct responsibility of the State Department and the White House, so Forrestal was not really a player in the decisions that were made, but he was braver and more outspoken than was Secretary of State George C. Marshall, and he reckoned without the political weakness of Harry Truman, who personally had his own serious misgivings about the partition of Palestine and the creation of the Jewish state of Israel, but, as we have seen, he needed every last vote he could scare up to retain the presiden-

---

[44] David Martin, "Forrestal Ignored: China Lost to Reds, Korean War Fought," http://www.dcdave.com/article5/110530.htm.

[45] David Martin, "James Forrestal and John Kennedy," http://dcdave.com/article5/140806.htm.

cy in 1948.[46] In the final analysis, recognition of Israel proved to be a political winner for Truman because the Arabs still needed to sell their oil and we were their best market and the Israelis proved to be militarily a lot stronger than most people anticipated, and we did not need to send our own troops to defend them. In the longer run, however, Forrestal's misgivings over America's support for Israel have proved to be prescient, while, in the short run Forrestal managed to make of himself an object of "an outpouring of slander and calumny that must surely be judged one of the most shameful intervals in American journalism."[47]

More Zionist Weapons

We learn some more about the extent of their clandestine weaponry from Walter Winchell biographer, Neal Gabler. Gabler tells us that after the outbreak of the war in Europe, Winchell might well have been the strongest public voice in the country urging American involvement on the side opponents of the detested Nazis. To Winchell, the members of the very influential America First Committee, led by famous aviator Charles Lindbergh, were no better than traitors. He began to regale his readers and listeners to his weekly radio broadcast with "inside information" on the connections between various conservative anti-war leaders and the Nazis. Most people assumed, says Gabler, that he must be getting most of that information from the FBI, but the fact was that Winchell was more of a source for the FBI than they were from him. His primary provider of inside information was Arnold Forster, the New York counsel for the Jewish Anti-Defamation League (ADL).

Forster, Gabler tells us, had a whole stable of spies who used all manner of clandestine methods to gather intelligence. It practically drove

---

[46] Concerning Truman's reservations about the entire Zionist project, see David Martin, "'Jews' Tried to Kill Truman in 1947," http://dcdave.com/article5/120510.htm.

[47] Hoopes and Brinkley, pp. 402-404. They have taken the concluding quote from Robert A. Lovett, "Reflections on Jim Forrestal," unpublished book preface, March 12, 1985.

Mississippi Senator Theodore Bilbo crazy, says Gabler, "to see in the column or hear on the broadcast everything he said privately."[48]

The Winchell biographer, Gabler, by the way, is another one of those authors who draws very heavily upon Arnold Rogow in his account of Forrestal's death. Publishing his Winchell biography in 1994, two years after the Hoopes and Brinkley biography of Forrestal, he makes explicit use of their account as well.

> The ADL has continued its clandestine activity in the United States:
>
> ADL Found Guilty of Spying by California Court
>
> By Barbara Ferguson, Arab News Correspondent
>
> WASHINGTON: The San Francisco Superior Court has awarded former Congressman Pete McCloskey, R-California, a $150,000 court judgment against the Anti-Defamation League (ADL).
>
> McCloskey, the attorney in the case, represented one of three civil lawsuits filed in San Francisco against the ADL in 1993. The lawsuit came after raids were made by the San Francisco Police Department and the FBI on offices of the ADL in both San Francisco and Los Angeles, which found that the ADL was engaged in extensive domestic spying operations on a vast number of individuals and institutions around the country.
>
> During the course of the inquiry in San Francisco, the SFPD and FBI determined the ADL had computerized files on nearly 10,000 people across the country, and that more than 75 percent of the information had been illegally obtained from police, FBI files and state drivers license data banks.
>
> Much of the stolen information had been provided by Tom Gerard of the San Francisco Police Department, who sold, or gave, the information to Ray Bullock, ADL's top undercover operative.
>
> The investigation also determined that the ADL conduit, Gerard, was also working with the CIA.

---

[48] Gabler, pp. 294-295.

Two other similar suits against ADL were settled some years ago, and the ADL was found guilty in both cases, but the McCloskey suit continued to drag through the courts until last month.

In the McCloskey case, the ADL agreed to pay (from its annual multimillion budget) $50,000 to each of the three plaintiffs Jeffrey Blankfort, Steve Zeltzer and Anne Poirier who continued to press charges against the ADL, despite a continuing series of judicial roadblocks that forced 14 of the original defendants to withdraw. Another two died during the proceedings.

The ADL, which calls itself a civil rights group, continued to claim it did nothing wrong in monitoring their activities. Although the ADL presents itself as a group that defends the interests of Jews, two of three ADL victims are Jewish.

Blankfort and Zeltzer were targeted by the ADL because they were critical of Israel's policies toward the Palestinians.

The third ADL victim in the McCloskey case, Poirier, was not involved in any activities related to Israel or the Middle East. Poirier ran a scholarship program for South African exiles who were fighting the apartheid system in South Africa.

At the time, the ADL worked closely with the then anti-apartheid government of South Africa, and ADL's operative Bullock provided ADL with illegally obtained data on Poirier and her associates to the South African government.

But the conclusion of McCloskey's case does not mean the end to the ADL's legal problems.

On March 31, 2001, US District Judge Edward Nottingham of Denver, Colorado, upheld most of a $10.5 million defamation judgment that a federal jury in Denver had levied against the ADL in April of 2000.

The jury hit the ADL with the massive judgment after finding it had falsely labeled Evergreen, Colorado residents 'William and Dorothy Quigley; as "anti-Semites." The ADL is appealing the judgment.[49]

Post-Mortem Smear Artists

A couple of more things from Loftus and Aarons need comment upon. "At the end," they say, "Forrestal allegedly could be heard 'screaming that the Jews and the communists were crawling on the floor of his room

[49] http://www.fpp.co.uk/docs/ADL/ADLitems/McCloskey270402.html.

seeking to destroy him.'" That is obviously a false statement, ranking right up there with this one from Jack Anderson:

> While at Hobe Sound, Forrestal made three suicide attempts, by drug overdose, by hanging, and by slashing his wrists. On the night of April 1, the sound of a fire engine siren prompted him to rush out of the house in his pajamas screaming, "The Russians are attacking!"[50]

Actually, the Loftus and Aarons observation is even worse, because it gives the impression that Forrestal's mental state had continued to deteriorate while he was in the hospital, but we have seen from the observations of Henry Forrestal, Harry Truman, and Louis Johnson, and the statement to Dr. Raines to brother Henry that Forrestal was "essentially okay" and the general relaxation of his observation, that that was certainly not the case. Loftus and Aarons give Charles Higham as their reference.[51] Higham, though, attributes his wild claims about Forrestal's supposed behavior in his latter days in the hospital simply to unnamed newspaper reports. The author in his research has not encountered anything resembling such newspaper reports. Higham also writes that Forrestal was suffering from "advanced paranoid schizophrenia," a claim that goes farther even than the unsupported claims of Rogow, and a charge that we should bear in mind as we learn more in the course of this book.

So the end of the trail turns out to be anonymous "newspapers," who if they ever reported such a thing were likely making it up themselves or had had it fed to them by someone who was. We might note, as well, how greatly this report of Forrestal's condition in his final days contrasts with the observations of the man in charge of the hospital. Rear Admiral Willcutts told reporters right after Forrestal's death that he was shocked and

---

[50] *Confessions of a Muckraker: The Inside Story of Life in Washington during the Truman, Eisenhower, Kennedy and Johnson Years* (with James Boyd), Random House, 1979. p. 158. And yes, Anderson quotes Rogow extensively as well.

[51] Charles Higham, *Trading with the Enemy: An Exposé of the Nazi-American Money Plot 1933-1949*, Barnes and Noble, 1983, pp. 210-211.

that after visiting with him on Friday he thought that he was "getting along splendidly."[52]

The Book on the Death

Now let us have a closer look at Cornell Simpson's virtually unknown work, mentioned by Hoopes and Brinkley only in an endnote disparagingly as a "murder-conspiracy" book.

Simpson tells us in his foreword that he completed the manuscript in its entirety in the mid-1950s but then put it aside after a previous would-be publisher decided that it was too controversial, too "dangerous" to publish. He also says that he purposely chose not to update it to maintain the "close perspective" of the era. That is a great shame, for in following this course he gave Arnold Rogow, who published his book three years before, a free pass. Simpson could have easily made it clear what a poorly documented and poorly argued case for the suicide theory of Forrestal's death Rogow had written.

Quite early in Simpson we get some clarification of the oft-repeated, but vague assertion that Forrestal had made "at least one suicide attempt" at Hobe Sound. Forrestal's friend Eberstadt, with Forrestal's agreement, according to Simpson, summoned the renowned psychiatrist, Dr. William Menninger, who at the time was president of both the American Psychiatric Association and the American Psychoanalytic Association.

> Dr. Menninger questioned Forrestal about a reported suicide attempt supposedly made by Forrestal after Dr. Raines's arrival at Hobe Sound, and Menninger subsequently told *The Washington Post* he had satisfied himself that there was nothing whatsoever to this tale:
>
> "Mr. Forrestal told me that the night before I arrived he had put a belt around his neck with the intention of hanging himself, but the belt broke. Since there were no marks on his throat or body, I consider this [only] a nightmare. Also, we never found a broken belt of any kind."

---

[52] Simpson, p. 16.

> In spite of Dr. Menninger's statement, the suicide story was later exploited by unscrupulous newspaper columnists and by a man who was present and knew its falsity.[53]

One does wish that Simpson had given the date of *The Post* edition in which the Menninger quote appeared. The man who was present at Hobe Sound, yet later exploited the attempted suicide story, from later observations by Simpson, appears to have been Dr. Raines. The Menninger statement is almost too bizarre not to be true. It also explains the vagueness of the various authors about the nature of Forrestal's attempt (except for the specific, but false, claims of the outrageously irresponsible and vicious Drew Pearson). Were they to get specific about the means of suicide they would have to come to grips with the Menninger interpretation of the matter. Still, they can satisfy themselves that they are not lying because, against Menninger's interpretation of what Forrestal told him and the lack of physical evidence, they have Forrestal's own words.

One would appreciate greater candor from all the authors who have written on the subject of Forrestal's mental state. Even noted historian, David McCullough, in his widely praised 1992 biography, *Truman*, repeated the mantra that Forrestal "made at least one attempt at suicide" while at Hobe Sound.[54] There is no doubt that at least for a few days the man was in a very bad way. If he could mistake a nightmare for an actual event he was clearly in need of help of some sort, but, in retrospect, forcible hospitalization hardly seems to have been called for. It very closely resembled, in fact, the notorious confinement of political dissidents to mental hospitals by the Soviet Union.

We also can't help but notice a strong resemblance between Soviet journalism and that practiced by the American press and book writers with respect to Forrestal's demise. There is ample reason to question whether Forrestal was ever truly suicidal, and there is even stronger reason to question whether he was anywhere near his Hobe Sound emo-

---

[53] Ibid., p. 6.

[54] David McCullough, *Truman,* Simon and Schuster, 1992, p. 739.

tional state some seven weeks later. When authors so regularly go beyond known and verifiable facts to create a desired impression, readers have a very good reason to be suspicious.

By contrast, Cornell Simpson portrays Forrestal, after his rest and recovery, as not only quite normal in manner in the judgment of everyone who saw him, but also as a man with a good deal more to live for than the average person. He was very well fixed financially and he was in basically good health. The newspapers would have us believe, as with Vince Foster, that he was depressed over how the press had treated him, but, according to Simpson, it was all to the contrary. Forrestal had always been a fighter and the press smears merely "got his Irish up." He had every intention, in fact, of setting the record straight by writing a book and plunging into the newspaper business himself. As for possible depression over losing his job, he had already realized that he didn't fit with Truman and his Missouri cronies and was already prepared to move on. He just didn't like the abrupt manner of his dismissal.[55]

Hoopes and Brinkley provide corroboration that Forrestal was seriously interested in taking a big plunge into the news, that is, the opinion-molding business. He had told powerful Wall Street friends like Clarence Dillon, Eberstadt, and Paul Shields that he was interested in starting a newspaper or a magazine modeled after *The Economist* of Great Britain, and they had demonstrated a willingness to help him raise the start-up funds.[56]

That was a couple of years before the press campaign against Forrestal, but he was still very well off financially and well connected on Wall Street. A James Forrestal in the publishing business would have been a serious force to be reckoned with in American public life, perhaps a greater force than he had been as a cabinet member.

Forrestal's writing and publishing plans provide the answer to the question, "Why would anyone bother to murder him when he had already been driven from office and disgraced by the taint of mental ill-

---

[55] Simpson, p. 15.

[56] Hoopes and Brinkley, p. 238.

ness?" Had Forrestal lived and gone on with his writing plans, Drew Pearson's lurid and irresponsible charges would have probably been all that anyone would have heard about Forrestal being "mentally ill." There would have been no Arnold Rogow book psychoanalyzing the man. James V. Forrestal was a formidable man who knew a great deal about the inner workings of the government under Roosevelt and Truman, and he didn't like the direction that the country was going.

The compelling reasons for Forrestal to want to continue living were also compelling reasons for his powerful enemies to see to it that he did not. Forrestal had left his top job at Dillon, Read, and Company in June of 1940 to become an administrative assistant to President Franklin D. Roosevelt. For most of World War II he served as Under Secretary of the Navy. He became the Secretary of the Navy in April of 1944, and he was appointed the first Secretary of Defense after reorganization of the armed services in September of 1947.

All during his period of high government service, Forrestal had kept a detailed diary. It would have been a gold mine for the book he planned to write. Who knows what he might have revealed, because Forrestal was thought of as a very forceful and independent-minded person, as nobody's yes-man? Some areas where his diaries might have been revealing were the disastrous war strategy that needlessly prolonged the conflict and invited massive communist expansion in both Europe and Asia, the wholesale infiltration of the Roosevelt and Truman administrations by Soviet agents, Communists, and Communist sympathizers, and the tactics employed by the Zionists to gain recognition of the state of Israel. Perhaps the underhanded means that, according to Loftus and Aarons, had worked on Nelson Rockefeller but failed on Forrestal, had also worked on some other high-level government officials.

Simpson Versus McCullough

The treatment of the question of the handling of Forrestal's diary by the prominent historian McCullough and the little-known writer, Simpson, makes a very interesting contrast. McCullough writes of "rumors" that the White House had ordered that "pages" of Forrestal's diary be "secretly removed" and that questions about the tragic death had persisted, like why had a person with suicidal tendencies been housed on the sixteenth floor? Had this strongest anti-Communist in the administration been "driven to his death" by "secret Communists on Truman's staff."[57]

If this approach reminds you of number three in my "Seventeen Techniques for Truth Suppression," it is with good reason.

> Characterize the charges as "rumors" or, better yet, "wild rumors." If, in spite of the news blackout, the public is still able to learn about the suspicious facts, it can only be through "rumors." (If they tend to believe the "rumors," it must be because they are simply "paranoid" or "hysterical.")[58]

We may contrast the McCullough virtual brush-off of suspicions with regard to Forrestal's diary with Simpson's long, serious treatment of the diary question.

In Simpson's view, the handling of the diaries holds the key to what was behind Forrestal's assassination. He tells us that altogether they amounted to some three thousand pages in fifteen loose-leaf binders. The White House would later claim that while he was at Hobe Sound Forrestal had sent word that he wanted President Truman to take custody of the diaries, something that Simpson regards as utterly preposterous. What is most likely is that as men like David Niles went over what was in those diaries during the seven weeks of his confinement at Bethesda, Forrestal's fate was sealed.[59]

The version of the diaries edited by FDR apologist and *New York Herald Tribune* journalist, the Yale graduate Walter Millis, was a severely edited version of the original. By the time Millis had done his chopping the diaries had been gone over by both the White House and the Pentagon and there can be little doubt that they took out the most damaging

---

[57] McCullough, pp. 740-741.

[58] David Martin, "Seventeen Techniques for Truth Suppression," http://dcdave.com/article3/991228.html.

[59] Simpson, p. 7.

and revealing things about the administration, the most important of which, according to Simpson, would have been how their policies were consciously aiding the Communist cause.[60]

The original diaries would very likely have named names like Harry Dexter White and Lauchlin Currie, people within the Roosevelt and Truman administrations who were doing the bidding of the Communists. Not only did Millis take a lot out, but he also put into the published version as much of his own analysis as that which came from Forrestal, often taking issue with Forrestal when he went against the approved "leftist line."

In addition to the sellout to Communism, another topic of great interest to Forrestal that was off limits in the published version of the diaries was anything having to do with the attack on Pearl Harbor. The closest that Millis gets to it is in his April 18, 1945 diary entry on Millis's page 46, when Forrestal presents a list of recommendations to Truman. Simpson calls our attention to the ellipses in Item 5:

> 5. PEARL HARBOR. I told him that I had got Admiral [H. Kent] Hewitt back to pursue the investigation into the Pearl Harbor disaster.... I felt I had an obligation to Congress to continue the investigation because I was not completely satisfied with the report my own Court had made....

What was in that recommendation that Millis leaves out, Simpson wonders. Might he not have been pointing the finger of responsibility at the Roosevelt administration, itself?[61]

The thing about the Millis version of the diaries, as Simpson sees it, rings particularly false is the generally favorable tone that is found there toward the man whom Simpson characterizes as Forrestal's "perpetual antagonist," General George Catlett Marshall. Every anti-Communist measure that Forrestal proposed, says Simpson, Marshall opposed. Forrestal's true feelings toward Marshall and his policies, though, would have been devastating for the Truman administration and therefore,

---

[60] Ibid., pp. 81-82.

[61] Ibid., pp. 83-84.

speculates Simpson, could simply not be permitted to see the light of day.[62]

Unfortunately, the version of the truth with respect to the Forrestal diaries that even the most serious history students are ever likely to see is that of McCullough, or maybe that of Hoopes and Brinkley, and not that of Simpson. Hoopes and Brinkley say nothing in their text about the confiscation of diaries by the White House. They do, at the beginning of their notes on sources, credit Millis as a valuable source, while noting that government censors had deleted portions of it "on the grounds of national security." They then reassure us that "all of these unpublished entries" have been made available for scholars at several research libraries.[63]

One wonders how these authors can be so confident, in the absence of the diaries' author, that everything that Forrestal put into the original version is now available in complete, unedited form. It only seems reasonable that the White House would have permanently removed anything that might be seen as wrongdoing on the part of the Roosevelt and Truman administrations. The contrast between Simpson's claim that Millis left out 80 percent of the original to "a number of diary entries" were deleted for national security purposes—like McCullough's rumors of "pages" being removed—is also striking.[64]

To be sure, not everything that Cornell Simpson has written should be taken at face value, either. Nowhere does he tell us how he knows with such precision that there were originally exactly 3,000 pages in 15 notebooks in the Forrestal diaries. Simpson, himself, is something of a mystery man. This book on Forrestal's death seems to be the only one he has written, and a search of the Internet for his name turns up only references to *The Death of James Forrestal*.[65] He is a polished and skillful writer, and his knowledge of the degree of infiltration of the Roosevelt

---

[62] Ibid., p. 85.

[63] Hoopes and Brinkley, p. 483.

[64] Simpson, p. 83.

[65] We shall see later that our early suspicion, hinted at here, that "Cornell Simpson" was a pen name was correct.

and Truman administrations seems almost like that of an insider. Many of the charges in his book, which echo those of Forrestal in his waning days in government, have been borne out by more recent discoveries. This is from the noted historian, Thomas Fleming:

> There was scarcely a branch of the American government, including the War, Navy, and Justice Departments, that did not have Soviet moles in high places, feeding Moscow information. Wild Bill Donovan's Office of Strategic Services, the forerunner of the CIA, had so many informers in its ranks, it was almost an arm of the NKVD. Donovan's personal assistant, Duncan Chaplin Lee, was a spy.[66]

> By count from the Venona decrypts (secret Soviet cable traffic from the 1940s that the United States intercepted and eventually decrypted, which became available to historians in 1995), there were 329 Soviet agents inside the U.S. government during World War II. The number of rolls of microfilm shipped to Moscow from the NKVD's New York headquarters leaped from 59 in 1942 to 211 in 1943, the same year during which the American press and publishing industry were gushing praise of the Soviet Union. In the single year 1942, the documents leaked by one member of England's Cambridge Five filled forty-five volumes in the NKVD archives. The Russian agent in charge of Whittaker Chambers's spy ring boasted to Moscow: "We have agents at the very center of the government, influencing policy." The OSS and the British SIS did not have a single agent in Moscow.[67]

David Niles, the Communist

One man in particular with some dubious connections was in a very strategic position to do harm to Forrestal. That is one of the few staff aides that Truman had inherited from Roosevelt, David Niles (Others were speechwriter, Samuel Rosenman, press secretary, Jonathan Daniels, press aide, Eben Ayers, and correspondence secretary, Bill Hassett.). In the foregoing, when we have said that "the White House" may have taken some action or other with respect to Forrestal, those actions might well

---

[66] Thomas Fleming, *The New Dealers' War: F.D.R. and the War within World War II*, Basic Books, 2001, p. 319.

[67] Ibid., p. 322. See also this writer's extensive documentation of Communist infiltration of the Roosevelt and Truman administration at this web site: http://ariwatch.com/Links/DCDave.htm#TheRedDecadeAndAfter.

have been the work of Niles, Harry Truman's famous aphorism about where the buck stops notwithstanding.

Hoopes and Brinkley tell us that White House aides Harry Vaughn and Matthew Connelly (remember him?) were pushing Truman to replace Forrestal as was Niles, who "disliked Forrestal intensely." There were a number of things they had against him. As Navy Secretary he had opposed the unification of the armed services under the new Department of Defense; his wariness of the Soviet menace had made him oppose Truman's new ceiling on military spending; he was trying to take personal control over the newly created National Security Counsel and its staff. What was likely most important, though, was his adamant opposition to the partition of Palestine. Hoopes and Brinkley characterize these internal Forrestal opponents as "small-minded loyalists."[68]

Tracking down Cornell Simpson's numerous references to Niles leads the reader to suspect that Niles was a bit more than a small-minded White House loyalist. (The sentence fragments are in the original.):

> Soviet spy Alger Hiss, fair-haired boy of the State Department, who went to Yalta as Roosevelt's advisor and who was a chief planner of the present United Nations.
>
> Harry Hopkins, Lauchlin Currie, David Niles, Michael Greenberg, Owen Lattimore, Philleo Nash and others identified in sworn testimony as pro-Communists or outright Russian spies operating through the White House, who for years secretly influenced United States presidents and shaped policy decisions to benefit the USSR.
>
> With characters such as the above and countless more like them dictating U.S. government policy, it is little wonder that Forrestal often felt he was the only pro-American in a nest of Communists. In December 1945 he made a brilliantly simple indictment of the wholesale treason in Washington when he told the newly elected U.S. Senator Joseph R. McCarthy (R., Wis.): "Consistency never has been a mark of stupidity. If the diplomats who have mishandled our relations with Russia were merely stupid, they would occasionally make a mistake in our favor."[69]
>
> ----------

[68] Hoopes and Brinkley, pp. 428-429.

[69] Simpson, p. 53.

Another was David Niles, alias Neihuss, a powerful advisor to Roosevelt and Truman. The mysterious Niles, who had an office in the White House, operated very secretively; however when various Fifth Amendment Communists were asked by congressional committees if they knew Niles, they refused to answer on the grounds that if they did so they might incriminate themselves.[70]

Congressman Martin Dies of Texas, first chairman of the House Committee on Un-American Activities, told this writer that a short time before [former U.S. Supreme Court Justice Frank] Murphy died, Mrs. Dies and he met Murphy at the home of the late celebrated Washington hostess, Mrs. Evelyn Walsh McLean.

"Justice Murphy was highly excited," Congressman Dies explained. "In fact, he was the most emotionally disturbed man I've ever seen. He paced back and forth, unable to sit down. He said he had recently 'gotten religion' and had returned to the Catholic church.

"And then he told us, very excitedly, 'We're doomed! The United States is doomed! The Communists have control completely. They've got complete control of Roosevelt and his wife as well. It's impossible for anyone to see him now unless the appointment is cleared by David Niles and his gang.[71]

The campaign against Forrestal had a threefold purpose: to discredit Forrestal in the eyes of the American people, thereby permanently eliminating him as a public official; to harass and persecute him personally and drive him to a nervous breakdown if possible, thus wrecking his capacity to fight the Communist conspiracy even as a private citizen; to intimidate all other anti-Communists by instilling in them a fear of the terrible reprisals awaiting those who dare oppose Communism at home and abroad.

Monsignor Sheehy and others have said they suspected that the long smear campaign against Forrestal may have been secretly directed by Communists and pro-Communists in the White House itself—perhaps by the powerful David Niles.[72]

---

[70] Ibid., p. 90.

[71] Ibid., p. 134.

[72] Ibid., p. 161.

Authors Herbert Romerstein and Eric Breindel provide other insights into the connections and the character of David Niles.

> Meanwhile, Josephine Adams remained active on the political scene. In October 1944 she wrote to Mrs. Roosevelt, "Last evening it was requested through [presidential assistant] D. [David K.] Niles that E. B. [Earl Browder] withdraw from the radio debate with [George] Sokolsky on the election." Filed with the letter in the Roosevelt Library was an unidentified newspaper clipping reporting that Browder had canceled the debate with Sokolsky. The letter was marked to be shown to the President. The election was a month away. The Communists actively supported Roosevelt's reelection, but public support from Earl Browder was not an asset in most of the country.
>
> Niles, a mysterious political operative for President Roosevelt, had other associations with the Communists. An NKVD Venona message from New York to Moscow reported on a plan to send a husband and wife team of NKVD "illegals" to Mexico. The message said, "Through Roosevelt's advisor David Niles—will take three-four days will cost $500.... [A]round Niles there is a group of his friends who arrange anything for a bribe. Through them Michael W. Burd ["Tenor"] obtains priority and has already paid them as much as $6,000. Whether Niles takes a bribe himself is not known for certain." Burd was a Soviet agent and an officer of the Midland Export Corporation in New York City.
>
> On August 2, 1944, the New York *Rezindentura* reported to Moscow that "Niles refused to intervene in the case explaining that he had only recently interceded for one refugee and recommended approaching Congressman [Arthur] Klein." When this did not work, Niles intervened. And although the project was held up because Niles was busy with the Democratic convention, the matter was finally taken care of—Burd handled the paperwork.
>
> Whittaker Chambers reported to the FBI an odd story about Niles that he had heard from a fellow Soviet agent named John Hermann in 1934 or 1935. A Soviet agent named Silverman (not George Silverman) was living in the next building from Alger Hiss. This Silverman apparently had an obviously homosexual affair with David Niles. Silverman had told Niles of the work of the underground apparatus in Washington, and Niles later threatened to expose the activities of the Communist group unless Silverman left his wife. To solve the problem, J. Peters, the head of the American Communist underground, ordered Hermann and Harold Ware to get Silverman to leave Washington, D. C. immediately. [73]

---

[73] Herbert Romerstein and Eric Breindel, *The Venona Secrets, Exposing Soviet Espionage and America's Traitors*, Regnery Publishing, 2000, pp. 180-181.

That James Forrestal was "disliked intensely" by the likes of a David Niles would seem to be something of which Forrestal could be justly proud.

There is something missing, however, in the portrait painted by Cornell Simpson of Forrestal as public enemy number one of the Communists. He neglects to mention that the fiercely anti-Communist columnist and radio commentator, Walter Winchell, enthusiastically joined his leftist counterpart, Drew Pearson, in the Forrestal smear campaign. The big thing they had in common, as previously observed, was that they were both strong Israel advocates. Neither Israel nor Zionism appears in Simpson's index. He vilifies Pearson as a virtual Communist spokesman, but mentions Winchell only once, and that is favorably for his exposure of Harry Truman's supposed lies about Truman's former membership in the Ku Klux Klan. His only allusion to possible Zionist enmity toward Forrestal he handles defensively as follows:

> Others chose to tar Forrestal with anti-Semitism when they spotted a chance to distort his stand on the Palestine partition issue. Forrestal was not anti-Semitic; he had simply urged that Truman not play domestic politics with the Palestine question and had explained his position as follows:
>
> "If we are to safeguard western civilization in this crisis, the British and American fleets must have free access to Near Eastern oil. That is a fact, however unpleasant it may be.... I am interested in justice in Palestine, but this interest must remain secondary to my primary interest, which is the protection of America and the West from the gravest threat we have ever faced [Soviet Russia]. No minority has the right to jeopardize this nation for its own selfish interest."[74]

David Niles, the Zionist

We'd never get it from Simpson, but there is very good evidence that David Niles used his power as a gatekeeper for Roosevelt and Truman at least as much for the Zionists as he did for the Communists. For evidence

[74] Simpson, p. 162.

of that, we turn to another source, Edwin Wright. Wright was Army general staff G-2 (intelligence) Middle East specialist in Washington, 1945-46; Bureau Near East-South Asian-African Affairs Department of State, since 1946, country specialist 1946-47, advisor U.N. affairs, 1947-50, and advisor on intelligence, 1950-55. The first passage is from his 1975 work, *The Great Zionist Cover-up*, originally prepared for and by request of The Harry Truman Library, Independence, Missouri.[75]

> Mr. Loy Henderson, Director of NEA (Near East-Africa Division of the State Department), on November 24, 1947, sent a Memorandum to Acting Secretary Robert Lovett to pass on to President Truman. In it is this passage, "It seems to me and all the members of my office acquainted with the Middle East, that the policy we are following in New York, (at the United Nations, where the U.S. Delegation was favoring the establishment of a Zionist Jewish State on territory overwhelmingly Arab) is contrary to the interests of the United States and will eventually involve us in international difficulties of so grave a nature that the reaction throughout the world, as well as in this country, will be very strong.-- We are incurring long-term Arab hostility -- the Arabs are losing confidence in the friendship and integrity of the USA.--(It will encourage) Soviet penetration into important areas as yet free from Soviet domination" and as vast quantities of petroleum were being discovered in Arab lands, it was essential that normal and mutually advantageous relations with the Arab world should be preserved.
>
> Before these memoranda could get to the Oval Office in the White House, they had to pass through the screening of Sam Rosenman, Political Advisor of the President, and David (Nyhus) Niles, Appointments Secretary, both crypto-Zionists. One of these memoranda was returned unopened with a notation, "President Truman already knows your views and doesn't need this." That President Truman's attitude toward the NEA had been poisoned is evident from his remarks in his Memoirs that he could not trust his advisors in the State Department because they were, "anti-Semitic." Being low on the totem pole in this group, I can testify that I have never worked with a more honest or conscientious group of men, who when they were asked their opinion gave it honestly - and were insulted for their loyalty.

---

[75] Edwin M. Wright, *The Great Zionist Cover-up*, The Northeast Ohio Committee on Middle East Understanding, Inc., 1975, pp. iv-v. Available online at https://www.scribd.com/document/105756948/Wright-Edwin-The-Great-Zionist-Coverup-en-1975-142-S-Text.

There are other telling references to Niles in the July 26, 1974, Truman Library interview of Wright by Richard D. McKinzie.[76]

> These many Israeli Government propaganda organizations did all they could to discredit those men in the State Department, whom they identified as "pro-Arab." For further details: Alan R. Taylor, *Prelude to Israel* (Philosophical Library, 1959), especially the Chapter VIII, "The Zionist Search for American Support," pp. 77-113.] They kept whispering in his ear, "Don't trust the State Department." The result was he did not trust the State Department, the people who knew what was going on.
>
> David Niles was another one. He was the protocol officer in the White House, and saw to it that the State Department influence was negated while the Zionist view was presented. You get this from Mr. Truman's book, but also there are many stories that are not known.
>
> ---------
>
> Foreign policy cannot be operated intelligently if it's to be the football of domestic lobbies, and this was Mr. Truman's great mistake. In this issue he gave way to a domestic lobby. What did (New York Congressman) Emmanuel Cellar know about the Middle East? The answer is nothing. What did these other men, David Niles or (former Truman business partner) Eddie Jacobson know about the Middle East? Zero. The result was he listened to a group of propagandists who gave him the wrong ideas and he came across with this fatal decision that we would support a Jewish state in the area.
>
> --------
>
> One day I was sitting next to Mr. Henderson , he had his notes out and was dictating to me some letters when the telephone rang. It was Mr. Niles of the White House, and Mr. Niles told him (I got the story later on) that the night before some member of the State Department had been at a dinner party and had criticized President Truman's statement on a Jewish state. Mr. Niles said, "We are not going to tolerate any criticism of the President on this issue, and you let your staff know that if this happens again they must be disciplined."
>
> Mr. Henderson called a meeting of the staff and told them of the message of Mr. Niles. He said, "None of you people are to speak in public about this issue, because if you do we'll have to send you off to some Si-

[76] Truman Library, Oral History Interview with Edwin M. Wright, https://www.trumanlibrary.org/oralhist/wright.htm.

beria if any of you publicly express your private opinions, even to private groups, and it gets to the White House, you will be purged."

What happened was that Clark Clifford went to Mr. Truman, evidently upon the request of [Zionist leader and first president of Israel, Chaim] Weizmann, who was also hanging around Washington. Washington was loaded with Zionists at that time, they were all hanging around there talking to their Congressmen, getting Eddie Jacobson on the job and others. They were pulling all the strings. It's very difficult for the person outside to know just what did go on, because this has not yet been published. We'll have to find, if David Niles ever publishes any documents, as to what part he played in it. I don't know that his book has come out yet.

Anyhow, through David Niles, they had a meeting of Clark Clifford, political adviser to the President; [Eliahu] Elath, at that time still called himself Epstein; and the President. On the morning of the 13th of May, Epstein argued, "Please recognize Israel immediately, because we need that recognition for legitimacy." They had quite a discussion, but Mr. [Secretary of State George C.] Marshall was never called in or asked about this at all. [F.R.U.S. 1948, Vol. V, pp. 974-77, Secretary of State's memo of May 12, 1948 describes the acrimonious debate between Clark Clifford and Secretary Marshall.]

We were committed to certain things and we didn't know what we were committed to. As these situations unfolded, and the Secretary of State made no decisions, I can assure you of this: They were all made in the White House. Mr. David Niles knew what was going on, Emmanuel Cellar knew what was going on, but the State Department often just had these announcements coming out and they'd find out afterwards what'd been decided.

MCKINZIE: At what point was it apparent to you that you weren't supposed to say anything?

WRIGHT: The day that Mr. Henderson told us what Mr. Niles' instructions were: "Discipline these fellows if they disagree with the President." From then on we knew that we played no part in what was going on.

A final excerpt from the Wright interview reveals completely the ascendancy of the Zionist power over America's foreign policy apparatus:

There were influences to get rid of anyone who was called "pro-Arab." They were not pro-Arab, I must insist upon this, they were acting in accordance with America's larger interests in the Middle East. The Zionists gave them the title "pro-Arab" and that was enough to destroy them. You had to be pro-Zionist or keep quiet in order to stay in the State Department, and the net result was a whole generation of officers who are simply "Uncle Toms." They don't dare to speak or publish things. They are afraid that they will be sent off to Africa, or who knows to some other part of the world, and will stay there the rest of their lives.

One of these men was Henry Byroade. Henry Byroade made a talk in Philadelphia in April 1954. Before he made this talk he had two men work with him on it. One was Parker T. "Pete" Hart, who was the head of the NE, the Near Eastern Section, and the other was myself. We went over to his house and worked out his talk. In it he made this statement: "I have some advice for both Arabs and for Jews. Israel should think of itself as a state living in the Middle East and that it must live with its Arab neighbors. The Arabs must cease to think of themselves as wanting to destroy Israel and should come to terms with Israel itself." [Fred J. Khouri The Arab-Israeli Dilemma, Syracuse Press, 1968, p. 300 adds that even the Israeli Government protested this statement]

The next morning Henry Byroade got a call from Nathan Goldman, who was in California. [Nathan Goldman was president of the World Jewish Congress and many years president of the World Zionist Organization. He acted as though he were president of a World Jewish State and had a bitter fight with Ben-Gurion after 1948.] He used his first name and said, "Hank, did you make that speech in Philadelphia that was reported in the papers today?"

Byroade said, "Yes, I made that speech."

He said, "We will see to it that you'll never hold another good position."

That was the control, from California, that Nathan Goldman held over the State Department. All they had to do was go to the President or to Congress, and the demand would come for this fellow to be sent off and put in some obscure area, where he no longer would influence the situation. This has been going on for 26 years in the Department of State as the result of Mr. Truman's first decision to purge Loy Henderson.

It destroyed the efficacy of the Department of State in that particular area. The Zionists consider that they have control of the Department of State, can dictate who is going to be in it and who is going to say what policy should be. It's sort of silent terrorism that they have applied and kept up ever since.

Zionist Enemy Number One

One must wonder if James Forrestal realized the power of the forces he was up against in opposing the push of the Zionists for a state of their own in Palestine. From the treatment he received in the press, it was apparent whom they regarded as their principal enemy in the United States. If there is any doubt left, it is erased by these excerpts from Chapter Seven of *The Secret War against the Jews*, entitled "A Jewish-Communist Conspiracy":

> In this chapter we discuss the following allegations by our sources in detail:
>
> - The United States' first secretary of defense, James V. Forrestal, was the leader of a cabal of senior State Department and intelligence officials within the Truman administration that worked behind the president's back to block the creation of the State of Israel.
>
> - Forrestal was, in fact, a corporate spy for Allen Dulles within the Truman administration, while Dulles was working to elect the president's opponent, Governor Thomas E. Dewey.
>
> - When the Zionists realized right before the UN vote on partition of Palestine that they might not have enough votes, they blackmailed Nelson Rockefeller, who delivered the largely hostile votes of the Latin American bloc.
>
> The secret history of the birth of Israel has never been told before. Let us begin with the principal villain, the man who nearly succeeded in preventing Israel's birth.
>
> -----
>
> Despite deep dissatisfaction with the president [Roosevelt] and his successor, Forrestal rose through the ranks to become undersecretary and then secretary of the navy, and finally the first secretary of defense in September 1947. Truman did not realize for another year that Forrestal was quietly going mad. Virtually the entire American defense policy, indeed much of its strategy toward the Zionists, was in the hands of an *extremely bigoted lunatic.*[77] (emphasis added)

[77] Loftus and Aarons, pp. 155-156.

It could hardly be clearer that the extreme animosity toward Forrestal that motivated the slander campaign in the press in 1948, and was behind the threatening letters and telephone calls in the last months of his life, is alive today in the writings of people like John Loftus, Mark Aarons, and Walter Winchell biographer, Neal Gabler.

The First Christopher Ruddy?

Curiously, though, the only suspects Cornell Simpson even considers in Forrestal's likely murder are the Communists. His book is divided into two sections. The first is named, "Suicide or Murder?", and he leaves little doubt in the reader's mind that it was the latter. Section Two is titled, "Who Could Have Murdered Forrestal–and Why? The section consists of four chapters. The titles of the first three are questions: "Who Gained Most by the Death?", "Who Gained Most by the Death (continued)", and "Who Murders in a Matching Pattern?" The answer in each case is "The Communists and the international Communist conspiracy." Yes, Simpson also shows that the Truman administration itself also benefitted from the death, but only because it helped conceal the degree of its penetration by Communists and the extent to which its policies, particularly those of Truman's predecessor, Franklin Roosevelt, aided the Communists.

The final chapter, in case you still don't get the picture, is titled, "What the Communists Did to Forrestal." These passages give one the flavor of Simpson's summing up:

> ...it was the Communist *Daily Worker* that openly launched the vicious barrage against our first secretary of defense. And the defamation was quickly snatched up and embellished by all those newspaper columnists and radio and TV commentators who march in closed ranks behind the Communist party line.[78]
>
> -----

[78] Simpson, p. 182.

> After Forrestal was killed, the *New York Sun* reported that [Drew] Pearson's stories depicting the former defense secretary as a mental case were picked up and published prominently in the Russian press. Here again Pearson's smears were valuable to the Kremlin, for it is standard Communist technique to question the sanity of all anti-Communists.[79]
>
> ----
>
> Two days after the former defense secretary was killed, Tris Coffin, another Washington columnist, came out with a story that used a classic smear technique–the anonymous source. Coffin claimed that an unnamed informant had visited Forrestal at the hospital and had found Forrestal disheveled, deranged and obviously suicidal. Other visitors and hospital officials agreed that Forrestal had been in excellent spirits and was immaculately groomed. Coffin also claimed that Forrestal's "wrists were bandaged," implying that Forrestal had tried to slash them. This lie was printed the day after Dr. Raines had stated in a press release that Forrestal had not made any suicidal gestures in the hospital.
>
> Two and a half years after the death, *Time* magazine reissued some of the original "suicide attempt" lies. It also implied that Forrestal's mind had slipped, as evidenced in a habit he had developed of scratching his head while thinking.
>
> Note that Forrestal's enemies, even long after his death, continued to print lies designed to establish not only that he had frequently tried to kill himself but had been hopelessly out of his mind, all of which served to discredit his entire anti-Communist stand.[80]

Indeed it did, but as we have seen, the Forrestal smears and misrepresentations keep coming, right up to the present day, and they are not coming from the Communists. They were neatly packaged by Arnold Rogow in a book that was published three years before Simpson's, which Simpson chose to ignore, perhaps because he was unable to paint Rogow as a Communist or Communist sympathizer.

One must wonder why Cornell Simpson is so intent on steering his readers away from the obvious prime suspects in Forrestal's death. It was not the Communists who were known to have threatened Forrestal, Robert Lovett, and other government officials in the last months of For-

---

[79] Ibid., p. 163.
[80] Ibid., p. 166.

restal's life.[81] And though they might have had some small influence with the American press that slandered him, distorted the facts about his last few weeks of life, and failed to raise a hue and cry about the ongoing secrecy of the investigation of his death, it was minor compared to that of the Zionists, and it is now non-existent.

Simpson actually gives himself away in the fourth paragraph of his book's foreword:

> ...on November 22, 1963, while riding in a motorcade in Dallas, president Kennedy was shot and killed by Lee Harvey Oswald, a mysterious young American Communist recently returned from a lengthy stay in Soviet Russia. While in Russia, Oswald, according to his own writings, had been paid large sums of money by the Soviet secret police, which is the terrorist "enforcement" arm of the Soviet government and which is notorious for political assassinations both inside and outside Russia. Why the Soviet secret police would have had the future assassin of a U.S. president on its payroll never has been disclosed.[82]

To be sure we have learned a great deal more about the Kennedy assassination than we knew in 1966, but it is very hard to believe that a man as perspicacious and as skeptical of the government and the press as Cornell Simpson has shown himself to be in the Forrestal death, could accept as face value the official line that Oswald killed Kennedy. Here he reminds us of no one so much as the reporter and now Newsmax editor and publisher and most recently President Donald Trump crony, Christopher Ruddy. Ruddy, with his reports in the *New York Post* and the *Pittsburgh Tribune Review*, and his book, *The Strange Death of Vincent Foster*, has been the only American journalist to challenge the official verdict of suicide in the death of Deputy White House Counsel, Vincent W. Foster, Jr., but he scoffs at skeptics of the Warren Report and other apparent cover-ups, calling them "conspiracy theorists." One can only conclude that Ruddy is an operative for someone, and the fiercely pro-Israel orientation of Newsmax strongly suggests who that someone

---

[81] And Communists did not send a letter bomb to Truman in the White House in 1947. See "'Jews' Tried to Kill Truman in 1947," op. cit.

[82] Ibid., p. vii.

might be.[83] May not the same suspicion be raised of Simpson, who gives voice to the skepticism over the Forrestal death felt by many of his contemporaries, but then directs that doubt and skepticism down a rabbit trail leading away from the most likely suspects?

Seasoned Assassins

The Communists are hardly the only ones noted for political assassinations. Just eight months before Forrestal's death, members of future Prime Minister Yitzhak Shamir's "Stern Gang" gunned down the United Nation's chief mediator in Palestine, the Swedish Count Folke Bernadotte. In November of 1944 that same organization was responsible for the murder of Lord Moyne, a high British official supervising that country's Mandate over Palestine. In July of 1946, agents of another Zionist terrorist organization, Irgun, led by another future Prime Minister, Menachem Begin, blew up the building where the British had their headquarters in Jerusalem, the King David Hotel, killing 35 people, including 17 Jews.

The most extreme of the Zionists in Israel have always had an inordinate amount of power and influence in the United States, right up to the present day. Criticism of their actions is much more prominently voiced in Israel, itself, than it is in this country.

Only a few months before James Forrestal's confinement to the Bethesda Naval Hospital (also famous, or infamous, we might remind readers, for the autopsy of John F. Kennedy and the rather suspicious death of Senator Joe McCarthy[84]) a group of the most illustrious Jewish intellectuals in the United States were moved to warn the country with the following message:

Letters to The Times

---

[83] For more on Ruddy, see David Martin, "Double Agent Ruddy Reaches for Media Pinnacle," http://dcdave.com/article5/140314.htm and "Christopher Ruddy on Brett Kavanaugh," http://dcdave.com/article5/180715.htm.

[84] David Martin, "James Forrestal and Joe McCarthy," http://www.dcdave.com/article5/110928.htm.

New York Times December 4, 1948

New Palestine Party Visit of Menachem Begin and Aims of Political Movement Discussed

Among the most disturbing political phenomena of our times is the emergence in the newly created state of Israel of the "Freedom Party" (Tnuat Haherut), a political party closely akin in its organization, methods, political philosophy and social appeal to the Nazi and Fascist parties. It was formed out of the membership and following of the former Irgun Zvai Leumi, a terrorist, right-wing, chauvinist organization in Palestine.

The current visit of Menachem Begin, leader of this party, to the United States is obviously calculated to give the impression of American support for his party in the coming Israeli elections, and to cement political ties with conservative Zionist elements in the United States. Several Americans of national repute have lent their names to welcome his visit. It is inconceivable that those who oppose fascism throughout the world, if correctly informed as to Mr. Begin's political record and perspectives, could add their names and support to the movement he represents.

Before irreparable damage is done by way of financial contributions, public manifestations in Begin's behalf, and the creation in Palestine of the impression that a large segment of America supports Fascist elements in Israel, the American public must be informed as to the record and objectives of Mr. Begin and his movement.

The public avowals of Begin's party are no guide whatever to its actual character. Today they speak of freedom, democracy and anti-imperialism, whereas until recently they openly preached the doctrine of the Fascist state. It is in its actions that the terrorist party betrays its real character; from its past actions we can judge what it may be expected to do in the future.

Attack on Arab Village

A shocking example was their behavior in the Arab village of Deir Yassin. This village, off the main roads and surrounded by Jewish lands, had taken no part in the war, and had even fought off Arab bands who wanted to use the village as their base. On April 9 (THE NEW YORK TIMES), terrorist bands attacked this peaceful village, which was not a military objective in the fighting, killed most of its inhabitants-240 men, women, and children-and kept a few of them alive to parade as captives through the streets of Jerusalem. Most of the Jewish community was horrified at the deed, and the Jewish Agency sent a telegram of apology to King Abdullah of Trans-Jordan. But the terrorists, far from being ashamed of their act, were proud of this massacre, publicized it widely, and invited all the foreign correspondents present in the country to view the heaped corpses and the general havoc at Deir Yassin.

The Deir Yassin incident exemplifies the character and actions of the Freedom Party.

Within the Jewish community they have preached an admixture of ultranationalism, religious mysticism, and racial superiority. Like other Fascist parties they have been used to break strikes, and have themselves pressed for the destruction of free trade unions. In their stead they have proposed corporate unions on the Italian Fascist model.

During the last years of sporadic anti-British violence, the IZL and Stern groups inaugurated a reign of terror in the Palestine Jewish community. Teachers were beaten up for speaking against them, adults were shot for not letting their children join them. By gangster methods, beatings, window-smashing, and wide-spread robberies, the terrorists intimidated the population and exacted a heavy tribute.

The people of the Freedom Party have had no part in the constructive achievements in Palestine. They have reclaimed no land, built no settlements, and only detracted from the Jewish defense activity. Their much-publicized immigration endeavors were minute, and devoted mainly to bringing in Fascist compatriots.

Discrepancies Seen

The discrepancies between the bold claims now being made by Begin and his party, and their record of past performance in Palestine bear the imprint of no ordinary political party. This is the unmistakable stamp of a Fascist party for whom terrorism (against Jews, Arabs, and British alike), and misrepresentation are means, and a "Leader State" is the goal.

In the light of the foregoing considerations, it is imperative that the truth about Mr. Begin and his movement be made known in this country. It is all the more tragic that the top leadership of American Zionism has refused to campaign against Begin's efforts, or even to expose to its own constituents the dangers to Israel from support to Begin.

The undersigned therefore take this means of publicly presenting a few salient facts concerning Begin and his party; and of urging all concerned not to support this latest manifestation of fascism.

ISIDORE ABRAMOWITZ, HANNAH ARENDT, ABRAHAM BRICK, RABBI JESSURUN CARDOZO, ALBERT EINSTEIN, HERMAN EISEN, M.D., HAYIM FINEMAN, M. GALLEN, M.D., H.H. HARRIS, ZELIG S. HARRIS, SIDNEY

HOOK, FRED KARUSH, BRURIA KAUFMAN, IRMA L. LINDHEIM, NACHMAN MAISEL, SEYMOUR MELMAN, MYER D. MENDELSON, M.D., HARRY M. OSLINSKY, SAMUEL PITLICK, FRITZ ROHRLICH, LOUIS P. ROCKER, RUTH SAGIS, ITZHAK SANKOWSKY, I.J. SHOENBERG, SAMUEL SHUMAN, M. SINGER, IRMA WOLFE, STEFAN WOLFE.[85]

Would men like Menachem Begin and his followers have hesitated at assassinating the most popular, outspoken, and powerful critic of the nascent state of Israel in the United States if given the opportunity? It certainly did not stop them when the perceived obstacles to Israeli ambitions were members of the British or the Swedish leadership and nobility. Would someone like David Niles have used his power and influence to assist the assassins, and did he have sufficient power and influence to see that the deed was accomplished? From the evidence we have presented, we believe the answer would have to be in the affirmative.

Would President Truman have countenanced such a thing? One likes to think that he would not, had it been in his power. But from his earliest days in politics as a member of the political machine, that is, the organized criminal conspiracy, of "Boss" Tom Pendergast of Kansas City, Truman had learned how to make the kinds of compromises that would leave him eventually, though President, powerless to prevent such an atrocity. (Do an Internet search of various combinations of "Truman" "corruption" "Pendergast" and "John Lazia" for evidence of the sort that you will not find heavily emphasized by Truman hagiographers like David McCullough.). We have seen the assertion, after all, by Zionist apologists John Loftus and Mark Aarons that David Ben-Gurion would freely use blackmail to advance Israel's interests.

Would America's press have participated in the cover-up of such a heinous crime? Considering what we have learned of the role they have played in the aftermath of the assassination of the Kennedy brothers,

---

[85] "New Palestine Party Visit of Menachem Begin and aims of Political Movement Discussed," https://www.marxists.org/reference/archive/einstein/1948/12/02.htm.

Martin Luther King, Vincent Foster, and Thomas Merton, the temptation to engage in sarcasm at this point is almost irresistible. Let us simply say that, considering who the most likely suspects would have to have been, one would sooner expect Pravda of the old days to question the official verdict in the Jan Masaryk "suicide."

CHAPTER 2

James Forrestal's "Anti-Semitism"

Terms of Opprobrium

"Anti-Semitic," "conspiracy theorist,"
Throw in "isolationist," too.
We don't need laws to limit out thoughts
When labeling language will do.

The year was around 2004, as I recall, and I was attending a house lunchtime lecture by a professor from Georgetown University at the Bureau of Labor Statistics in Washington on the subject of President Harry Truman's racial integration of the United States military. I beg the indulgence of the readers, but I have completely forgotten the professor's name. I do recall, though, that he was quite obviously Jewish.

During the question and answer period after his lecture I suggested that he might have fleshed his story out a bit more by noting that the real pioneer in the desegregation of the armed services was James Forrestal, who had ordered the integration of the Navy when he was Navy Secretary. The man's very emotional response really surprised me. "Forrestal was an anti-Semite," he said, in what was really a complete non sequitur, as he brushed away my observation. He seemed almost like Dracula with a cross being waved in his face at the favorable mention of the name of James Forrestal. The impression that this scholar imparted was that there is a continuing strong dislike—if not pure hatred—of Forrestal within an important element of the U.S. Jewish community.

Nowhere is the malicious belief about Forrestal's attitude toward Jews fostered more strongly than in the aforementioned *Secret War against the Jews.* The following sentence describing Forrestal's ultimate demise is most damning: "To his many critics, it seemed that James Forrestal's anti-Jewish obsession had finally conquered him."[86]

Did he have such an obsession? Loftus and Aarons certainly want us to think so. In their index we find under "Forrestal, James" the subcategory, "anti-Semitism of, 156-59, 177-80, 199, 208, 213-14, 327, 365." The primary evidence they give for the assertion are the business dealings of Forrestal's investment banking firm, Dillon, Read, and Co., with companies in Nazi Germany in the 1930s and Forrestal's opposition to the creation of the state of Israel, that is, his anti-Zionism.[87] Nowhere do Loftus and Aarons tell us that the controlling partner of Dillon, Read, Clarence Dillon, whom Forrestal replaced as president in 1938, was Jewish. He was born Clarence Lapowski in San Antonio, Texas, in 1882, the son of an affluent clothing merchant. Maybe this is the rock upon which the Zionists' blackmail attempt foundered.

They also have passages like this: "Forrestal himself admitted that he thought that Jews were 'different,' and he 'could never really understand how a non-Jew and a Jew could be friends.'"[88]

The passage finds an echo in Gabler's Winchell biography:

---

[86]Loftus and Aarons, p. 213.

[87] They don't even give us this passage from Forrestal's diaries: "*22 December 1945*: Played golf today with Joe Kennedy [Joseph P. Kennedy, who was Roosevelt's Ambassador to Great Britain in the years immediately before the war]. I asked him about his conversations with Roosevelt and Neville Chamberlain from 1938 on....Chamberlain, he says, stated that America and the world Jews had forced England into the war." Millis, pp. 121-122.

[88] Ibid., p. 157.

> Forrestal had never particularly liked Jews and, according to a friend, had never understood how Jews and non-Jews could be intimates. *Now he took his anti-Semitism into public policy*, arguing that a Jewish state in Palestine would needlessly antagonize Arabs and jeopardize oil supplies, that the Soviets would eventually be pulled into any Mideast crisis and that American troops would eventually have to defend the Jews there.[89] (emphasis added)

If the two books sound quite similar on this point it is because they have the same source, Arnold Rogow. Turning to Rogow, we see that his source is not only typically anonymous, but Loftus and Aarons and Gabler have used the passage very much out of context:

> Here, perhaps, his views were a direct reflection of his background. While Forrestal was not an anti-Semite, his attitude toward Jews was characterized by much ambivalence. Although he maintained good relations with his New York and Washington associates who were Jewish, notably Bernard Baruch (At this point Rogow has a long footnote mainly expounding upon Baruch's great admiration for Forrestal.), his Defense Department legal aide Marx Leva, and Navy Captain Ellis M. Zacharias, he had difficulty accepting Jews as social equals. One of his Wall Street colleagues recalls that Forrestal thought Jews were "different," and he could never really understand how a non-Jew and a Jew could be friends. I remember an occasion when I was involved in his presence in an argument with a Jewish friend. At one point I got overheated and I said something like "you son-of-a-bitch." Jim was shocked that I could talk that way to someone who was Jewish. He himself was always very reserved with people who were Jews. I think there was something about them he couldn't understand, or maybe didn't like. [90]

Or maybe not. Forrestal was also very reserved with people who were not Jews. What Rogow has given us here is clearly the very subjective impression of one man, on a very tricky subject.[91] Others have ex-

---

[89] Gabler, p. 385.

[90] Rogow, pp. 191-192. It should be noted that Zacharias, the Navy Captain mentioned here, was the head of the Office of Naval Intelligence through whom Forrestal operated in his attempt to bring about an earlier end to the Pacific War through unauthorized peace feelers to the Japanese. See Zacharias, "How We Bungled the Japanese Surrender," *Look* magazine, June 6, 1950, available online at http://ussslcca25.com/zach12.htm.

[91] On August 20, 2007, we were able to interview John Spalding, Forrestal's Navy driver who was 87 years old at the time. Spalding told us that when For-

pressed a very different view of Forrestal. Here are the words of the fervent Zionist James G. McDonald, America's first Ambassador to Israel.

> He was in no sense anti-Semitic or anti-Israel nor influenced by oil interests. He was convinced that partition was not in the best interests of the U.S., and he certainly did not deserve the persistent and venomous attacks on him which helped break his mind and body. On the contrary, these attacks stand out as the ugliest examples of the willingness of politician and publicist to use the vilest means—in the name of patriotism—to destroy self-sacrificing and devoted public citizens.[92]

That observation by McDonald finds an echo from Forrestal's close friend, Ferdinand Eberstadt. Reacting at the time to what he considered to be very unfair press charges of anti-Semitism and suggestions that Forrestal harbored sympathy for fascism, Eberstadt wrote, "I know of no more truly democratic or unprejudiced man than he is."[93]

Hoopes and Brinkley address the "anti-Semitic" question head on, declaring the charge to be absurd. "No man had less race or class consciousness," they quote from *Washington Post* editor Herbert Elliston writing in 1951. That is certainly the impression that we got of the man from our extensive interview of Forrestal's Navy driver, John Spalding. He was one to side with the little guy against the admirals, according to Spalding, and, as noted previously, regularly called upon a prominent rabbi out of friendship upon his visits to New York City. Hoopes and Brinkley also remind us of Forrestal's long, close working relationship with Jewish people throughout his Wall Street career. The anti-Semitism

---

restal visited New York City he often called upon a prominent rabbi, whose name Spalding could not recall. The interview is at https://www.youtube.com/watch?v=GU5MDsgvfzg&t=1335s. Spalding also informed us that upon the news of Forrestal's death, he was ordered not to speak to anyone about his service with Forrestal and was given his choice of assignments outside the country to which he would be immediately reassigned. He chose the base in Guantánamo, Cuba. This development fits with what Simpson reports on page 42 of *The Death of James Forrestal*, that is, that the nurse in charge of the 16th floor that night was immediately transferred to Guam, far out of the reach of most U.S. reporters.

[92] Quoted by Alfred M. Lilienthal in *The Zionist Connection II: What Price Peace?*, p. 424. Lilienthal's reference, in turn, is James G. McDonald, *My Mission to Israel*, Simon and Schuster, 1951, p. 17.

[93] Dorwart, p. 157.

charge, according to these authors, originated completely with the Zionists to tar Forrestal over his principled opposition to their fanatical ambitions in Palestine, ambitions that he felt were contrary to the long-term interests of the United States. [94]

Ironically, for their rather bizarre theory that the word "nightingale" awakened feelings of guilt in Forrestal and may have prompted a sudden decision to end it all they reference Loftus, an arch-Zionist who we have seen deploys the "anti-Semitism" slur against Forrestal perhaps more recklessly than anyone. One wonders why they should think that he was someone they could rely upon on the crucial question of what could possibly have motivated Forrestal to rush across the hall and attempt to hang himself from a 16th floor window.

Around the same time as our exchange with the Forrestal-hating Georgetown professor, we ran across an article by Rabbi James Rudin on the web site of The Center for Catholic-Jewish Studies at St. Leo University in St. Leo Florida. That article, addressing a matter that was in the news the year before was entitled "Truman's Anti-Jewish Sentiments Revealed in Diary." [95] One passage in the article, we felt, was nothing short of slanderous toward Forrestal, "While some historians believe both Marshall and Forrestal harbored anti-Jewish sentiments, that character stain had never touched Truman."

I quickly sent an email to the executive director of the center telling him how inappropriate it was for an organization purportedly devoted to improving relations between Christians and Jews to publish some-

---

[94] Hoopes and Brinkley, pp. 390-391.

[95] Harry Truman's offending passage, newly discovered at the time by a librarian at the Truman Library was, "[The Jews] I find are very very selfish. They care not how many Latvians, Finns, Poles, Estonians and Greeks get murdered or mistreated as DPs [displaced persons] as long as Jews get special treatment. Yet when they have power, physical, financial or political, neither Hitler or Stalin has anything on them for cruelty or mistreatment for the underdog." Truman had also added, "the Jews have no sense of proportion, nor do they have any judgement on world affairs". See https://www.independent.co.uk/news/world/americas/truman-diary-reveals-anti-semitism-and-offer-to-step-down-95825.html.

thing that was so slanderous of the great Catholic public servant, Forrestal, and that it was unscholarly, to boot, to support the charge with what "some" unnamed historians say. I then set the director straight on Forrestal with the information that we have provided here from a number of named sources.

I received no response, but at least the center took the article down not long after receiving my email. From what I had seen in the attitude of that Georgetown professor and much else that I have read, I imagine that Rabbi Rudin was writing what he felt was an accepted fact about Forrestal's attitude toward Jews, either that, or he is simply part of an ongoing propaganda operation to make us believe that it is an accepted fact.

What Is "Anti-Semitism?"

Please notice that Rabbi Rudin did not even use the dreaded "anti-Semite" charge against Forrestal and Marshall, only that some historians thought he "harbored anti-Jewish sentiments," whatever that might mean, and yet he feels free to characterize such an attitude as a reflection of a "character stain." Having grown up in a rural Southern Baptist environment in which almost everyone I knew harbored anti-Catholic sentiments—although very few of them even knew a Catholic—I know that it would never have occurred to anyone, including Catholics, to suggest that this showed a character stain on their part. What is it about being critical of Jews that is so special and different that it could get Forrestal labeled an awful anti-Semite by a wide range of scholars and to be called by a couple of them a "bigoted lunatic," based upon the flimsiest of evidence?[96]

---

[96] The authors of the book with that and many other reckless charges against Forrestal seemed to have gotten by with it. As of this writing, *The Secret War against the Jews* has 95 reviews on Amazon.com with an average rating of 4.5 out of 5 stars.

The late Catholic journalist and author, Joseph Sobran, has some very useful insights on the subject in his classic 1995 article, "The Jewish Establishment."[97]

> Nobody worries about being called "anti-Italian" or "anti-French" or "anti-Christian"; these aren't words that launch avalanches of vituperation and make people afraid to do business with you.
>
> It's pointless to ask what "anti-Semitic" *means.* It means trouble. It's an attack signal. The practical function of the word is not to define or distinguish things, but to conflate them indiscriminately — to equate the soberest criticism of Israel or Jewish power with the murderous hatred of Jews. And it works. Oh, how it works.
>
> ----
>
> The word has no precise definition. An "anti-Semite" may or may not hate Jews. But he is certainly hated *by* Jews. There is no penalty for making the charge loosely; the accused has no way of falsifying the charge, since it isn't defined.

The accused especially has no way of falsifying the charge if he is dead.

"'Anti- Semitism' says Sobran, "is therefore less a charge than a curse, an imprecation that must be uttered formulaically."

In recent years, the anti-Semitism charge has been used ever more promiscuously.

> Anyone critical of Israeli policies is now routinely portrayed as an anti-Semite. Even the survivors of Israel's attack on the *USS Liberty* are labeled anti-Semitic for urging a Congressional investigation of the circumstances surrounding the killing of 34 U.S. servicemen by Israel Defense Forces in 1967. The survivors ask: "How does seeking an inquiry become 'anti-Semitism'?"

---

[97] http://www.sobran.com/establishment.shtml. Sobran's temerity in taking on Jewish power in the country earned him obituaries of unseemly viciousness in *The Washington Post* and *The New York Times* when he died in 2010. See David Martin, "A Tale of Two Obituaries," http://dcdave.com/article5/140820.htm and "Death of a Giant," http://www.dcdave.com/poet15/101003b.htm.

> In February 2006 the Church of England voted to review its investment in Caterpillar, Inc. when the church discovered that Israel uses Caterpillar equipment to destroy Palestinian homes. Concerned at the ethical implications of profiting from that policy, the church resolved to study the issue. Even that expression of moral concern was quickly portrayed as "anti-Zionist—verging on anti-Semitic."[98]

When we see the anti-Semite charge being thrown around so indiscriminately, we must wonder if something deeper might be involved than just political tactics. For a psychological exploration of that question, we turn to the philosopher-longshoreman, Eric Hoffer. Perhaps it is a matter of self-contempt:

> Self-contempt produces in man "the most unjust and criminal passions imaginable, for he conceives a mortal hatred against that truth which blames him and convinces him of his faults."
>
> That hatred springs more from self-contempt than from a legitimate grievance is seen in the intimate connection between hatred and a guilty conscience.
>
> There is perhaps no surer way of infecting ourselves with virulent hatred toward a person than by doing him a grave injustice. That others have a just grievance against us is a more potent reason for hating them than that we have a just grievance against them. We do not make people humble and meek when we show them their guilt and cause them to be ashamed of themselves. We are more likely to stir their arrogance and rouse in them a reckless aggressiveness. Self-righteousness is a loud din raised to drown the voice of guilt within us.[99]

The Israeli populace, by and large, surely displays a vicious animus towards the Palestinians, and those once large majority residents of the land to whom the residents of the Jewish state of Israel have dealt a grave injustice. One might say the same thing for the men of the *USS Liberty* and also of James Forrestal.

---

[98] Jeff Gates, *Guilt by Association: How Deception and Self-Deceit Took America to War*, State Street Publications, pp. 131-132. His reference on the charges against the Anglican Church is Helen Nugent, "Chief Rabbi Flays Church over Vote on Israel Assets," *Times* (London), February 17, 2006.

[99] Eric Hoffer, *The True Believer,* Harper and Row Publishers, Inc., 1951, p. 89. Hoffer's quote in the first paragraph is from *Pensées*, by 17th century Christian mathematician and philosopher, Blaise Pascal. His entire book makes useful reading for a better understanding of Zionist political fanaticism.

The "Suicide" Peddlers

We have detected a thread connecting those who would convince us that Forrestal committed suicide and those whom we have identified as the prime suspects in his murder. The dust jacket to Arnold Rogow's book says that he is the author of four other books. It does not name them. Maybe that is because this biographer who strongly suggests that Forrestal's opposition to recognizing the state of Israel was based upon Forrestal's personal anti-Semitism had previously edited the collection entitled *The Jew in a Gentile World: An Anthology of Writings about Jews by Non-Jews.* His dangerously paranoid, ethnocentric orientation is well summed up by this sentence from the preface: "Jew-baiters and anti-Semites of one variety or the other–Greek, Roman, and Christian–have largely dominated the Gentile world, and as a result that world has been one in which the Jew has always had to move cautiously and, more often than not, live dangerously."

Later he wrote a chapter on anti-Semitism in the *International Encyclopedia of Social Science.* His is the sort of thinking that gave rise to the modern state of Israel, that is, that Jews can never be safe living in majority gentile populations, so they must have a state of their own. In this view, one might say, Jews are in a more or less permanent state of war with the rest of mankind.

As for Pearson, at the bottom of the article by John Henshaw entitled, "Israel's Grand Design: Leaders Crave Area from Egypt to Iraq," which appeared in *The New American Mercury* in the spring of 1968, we find the following:

> The late John Henshaw was chief legman for columnist Drew Pearson, who later broke with Pearson. At that time, Henshaw's expenses were paid by the Anti-Defamation League, a lobby for Israel, which had a "special relationship" with Pearson. Thus Henshaw's Middle East insights are unique.[100]

---

[100] https://theamericanmercury.org/2011/01/israels-grand-design/.

As we have seen, the other powerful columnist and radio commentator slandering Forrestal over his Israel opposition, Walter Winchell, also had a very special relationship with the ADL and its domestic spying and eavesdropping operation.

Journalist Eliot Janeway, the man who according to Hoopes and Brinkley told Ferdinand Eberstadt that Forrestal had attempted suicide at Hobe Sound, had more tenuous Jewish connections. Though born Eliot Jacobstein of New York Jews of Lithuanian origin, he changed his last name in his teens and concealed his Jewishness from everyone around him, including his children. If he plumped for Israel, it would more likely have been on behalf of his employer, *Time* magazine, than out of a sense of ethnic or religious solidarity. What little he might have written in favor of Israel, writes his son, Michael, it was done only for geopolitical reasons at the behest of *Time* publisher, Henry Luce, and was never on account of personal Jewish leanings.[101]

And if Janeway was quite consciously lying when he relayed what the safely dead Eberstadt had supposedly said about that Forrestal suicide attempt to Doug Brinkley, it would have been for the same reasons. It would also have been completely in character. Janeway regularly did flack work and wrote speeches for New Deal Democrats while on the Luce payroll as a supposedly objective reporter on these same Democrats who were running the country. He had a taste for power and influence and a nose for seeking it out. In spite of having been expelled from Cornell, probably for selling stolen library books and having been such an active Communist that he wrote for the *Moscow Daily News* for a time in Russia, he had been able to use his connections to avoid service in the military in World War II. All of this we learn from Michael Janeway in his very revealing book.

---

[101] Michael Janeway, *The Fall of the House of Roosevelt, Brokers of Ideas and Power from FDR to LBJ*, Columbia University Press, 2004, p. 124. The younger Janeway also parrots the Forrestal suicide line, telling us on page 59 that Forrestal's friend, the liberal Supreme Court Justice William O. Douglas, felt some guilt when Forrestal "jumped out of a sixteenth story window of Bethesda Naval Hospital," because he had just been planning to visit him, implying that he might have eased his troubled mind in some way.

In sum, the sources of the stories that Forrestal had previously attempted suicide are of a highly questionable, biased quality. They are as questionable as the stories, themselves, which lack any details, whatsoever. Pearson's stories, in particular, are undoubtedly fabrications. The fact that someone felt the need to make up such stories suggests very strongly, just by itself, that Forrestal did not commit suicide. Furthermore, it is very unlikely that Pearson made up these stories himself. What is more likely is that they originated with the people who were responsible for Forrestal's death. And the blame for the long-lived undefined and unsupported charge that Forrestal was an "anti-Semite" is not very far removed from these allegations of Forrestal suicide attempts.

The Diary's Revelations

In Chapter One, we saw that Forrestal had become something of a lightning rod for the hostile emotions of the partisans for Israel. For his part, he was absolutely sure that the consequences of our sponsorship of this alien entity in the midst of the Arab world would ultimately be disastrous for us. Two February 3, 1948, meetings recorded in the version of his diary edited by Walter Millis and published in 1951 capture well his principled position and the risk he was running in propounding it:

> Visit today from Franklin D. Roosevelt, Jr., who came in with a strong advocacy of the Jewish State in Palestine, that we should support the United Nations "decision," and in general a broad, across-the-board statement of the Zionist position. I pointed out that the United Nations had as yet taken no "decision," that it was only a recommendation of the General Assembly, that any implementation of this "decision" by the United States would probably result in the need for a partial mobilization, and that I thought the methods that had been used by people outside of the Executive branch of the government to bring coercion and duress on other nations in the General Assembly bordered closely onto scandal. He professed ignorance on this latter point and returned to his general exposition of the case of the Zionists.
>
> He made no threats but made it very clear that the zealous in this cause had the conviction of trying to upset the government policy on Pales-

> tine. I replied that I had no power to make policy but that I would be derelict in my duty if I did not point out what I thought would be the consequences of any particular policy which would endanger the security of this country. I said that I was merely directing my efforts to lifting the question out of politics, that is, to have the two parties agree they would not compete for votes on this issue. He said this was impossible, that the nation was too far committed and that, furthermore, the Democratic Party would be bound to lose and the Republicans gain by such an agreement. I said I was forced to repeat to him what I had said to Senator McGrath in response to the latter's observation that our failure to go along with the Zionists might lose the states of New York, Pennsylvania and California–that I thought it was about time that somebody should pay some consideration to whether we might not lose the United States. [102]

The second meeting that day was with very nearly the most powerful man in America who was not in the government, the Jewish financier, elder statesman, and adviser to presidents:

> Had lunch with B[ernard] M. Baruch. After lunch, raised the same question with him. He took the line of advising me not to be active in this particular matter and that I was already identified, to a degree that was not in my own interests, with opposition to the United Nations policy on Palestine. He said he himself did not approve of the Zionists' actions, but in the next breath said that the Democratic Party could only lose by trying to get our government's policy reversed, and said that it was a most inequitable thing to let the British arm the Arabs and for us not to furnish similar equipment to the Jews. [103]

Baruch clearly did not know his man when he attempted to influence him by appealing to Forrestal's own self-interest. He might have known more than he was telling, though, when he hinted at the danger that Forrestal faced for the courageous position he had taken.

In Chapter One we speculated that among the important things that might have been censored out of the Walter Millis version of the Forrestal Diaries was a detailed revelation of the dirty tactics, alluded to in the Loftus-Aarons book, that the Zionists had used to get U.S. and U.N. support for creation of the state of Israel. A hint that that is the case is found on pp. 507-508 in Millis:

---

[102] Millis, pp. 362-363.

[103] Ibid., p. 364.

> At the National Security Council meeting that day (October 21, 1948), Forrestal spoke with apparent asperity of another disconnection in our policy-making. According to an assistant's note, "Mr. Forrestal referred to the State Department request for four to six thousand troops to be used as guard forces in Jerusalem in implementation of the Bernadotte Plan for Palestine. This unexpected request was an example of how the Palestine situation had drifted without any clear consequent formulation of United States policy by the NSC. Mr. Forrestal said that actually our Palestine policy had been made for 'squalid political purposes.'... He hoped that some day he would be able to make his position on this issue clear."[104]

One must wonder how much elaboration has been cut after the word "purposes." Might he have delved into the squalid methods as well, or was that elsewhere in his diaries, or was he leaving that to that future day when he hoped he would be able to shed more light on the subject.

As of the end of October 1948, he hardly sounded like a man who had given up on having an effect on the direction of his country, whether he was in the government or out of it. Instead, he sounds exactly like the man with the unfinished agenda that brother Henry described from his last visit with him in the hospital. Insofar as he was looking back instead of into the future, it was not to lament any mistakes that he had might have made but to deplore the errors of the national leadership, manipulated, as it had been, to pursue policies that were contrary to the interests of the American people. He comes across, in short, not as a prime candidate for suicide, but for assassination.

---

[104] Ibid., pp. 507-508.

CHAPTER 3

Who Was Cornell Simpson?

The Double Game

Here's how our operatives have their way,
And the populace dupe and confuse:
All the contestants are in their pay,
But most are competing to lose.

In 2003, the year after we posted our first long essay on the death of James Forrestal on the Internet, we received several emails from J. Bruce Campbell, the man widely credited for having founded the militia movement in the United States. He had once been a high-ranking member of the conservative, fiercely anti-Communist John Birch Society, he informed us. He also told us flatly, confirming our initial suspicions, that "Cornell Simpson" was a *nom de plume*, although he did not say how he knew that. It was also from him that we learned that the publisher of Simpson's *The Death of James Forrestal*, Western Islands Press, was a Birch Society company.

In 2006 we had the opportunity to give a presentation about our Forrestal findings to a small audience at the National Press Club in Washington, DC, called the Sarah McClendon Study Group, created by the late longtime head of her own independent news organization and member of the White House press corps, McClendon. After the talk, an older member of the audience who seemed to have a great familiarity with the John Birch Society told me with a great air of authority that the man using the pseudonym, "Cornell Simpson," was actually Medford Evans, the father of the notable conservative journalist and author, M. Stanton Evans. Shortly after that we finished the fourth part of our series of essays bearing the same title as this book and we took the occasion to announce at the end with a footnote what we had been told by our informant at the press club, that is, that "Cornell Simpson" was, in reality, the late Medford Evans.

That is how things stood in my mind and for anyone reading that essay for a little more than five years, when I received an email from Mark LaRochelle, M. Stanton Evans' research assistant, informing me that I was wrong. As it turned out, the efforts that I made to confirm his charges tended to confirm some of the other suspicions I had about *The Death of James Forrestal* besides the fact that it had an anonymous author.

In his email, he said that it was he who had made the discovery of our assertion that Medford Evans was "Cornell Simpson" and that he had brought it to the attention of the younger Evans, Medford's son, who was quite old by that time, and Evans had immediately expressed surprise. He said that he had never even heard of the book and requested that LaRochelle get a copy for him to read. After reading it, he offered four reasons why it could not have been the work of his father:

1. At one point, the writer says "data is," when Medford, like his son, a Yale English major, would always have rendered it with the correct plural verb, "data are."

2. Cornell Simpson has the employment of Ben Mandel wrong, a man whom both Evanses knew well. Simpson has him working for the Permanent Subcommittee on Investigations of the Senate Government Operations Committee, when, in fact, he worked for the House Committee on Un-American Activities and the Subcommittee on Internal Security of the Senate Judiciary Committee.

3. At the time the book came out, 1966, the younger Evans was already a practicing journalist and was in frequent contact with his father and would surely have known about any project as important as this.

4. Medford Evans never used anything but his own name for any of his published work.

We had surely erred in proclaiming publicly that the elder Evans was the actual author of the book in question based upon the word of only one person. The John Birch Society has a web site, so we lodged a query with them—which we should have done in the first place—asking them what they could tell us about "Cornell Simpson's" identity. On April 25, 2011, an email arrived from Bonnie M. Gillis of the John Birch Society research department. Citing an April 1967 review article in the Birch Society magazine, *American Opinion*, she confirmed our original suspicion that "Cornell Simpson" was a pen name and that everything about the man had been kept secret for the man's protection, in support of which she provided this quote from the review's text:

> Cornell Simpson for reasons best known to himself, disappeared. I could not blame him too much. He knew too much—as you will see for yourself—and the wrong people knew him. The only reason I can be so frank now is that I honestly haven't the slightest idea where he is today, or whether he is alive. It would be impossible to imagine a more devastating—or convincing—exposé than *The Death of James Forrestal.*

The writer of the review was none other than Medford Evans. So my informant had not been far wrong. The "Simpson" book and its subject were of such interest to the father of M. Stanton Evans that he wrote a glowing review of it. To the four pieces of evidence that the younger Evans supplied me we can now add one more that might be the clincher, that is, that Medford Evans said that he wasn't "Cornell Simpson," but that he knew who "Simpson" was.

I say that it "might be the clincher" because there is always the possibility that Medford Evans was not telling the truth. Medford, like his son, was a Yale man, and Yale is known to be a primary supplier of talent to the CIA, whose very business is lying. While Ms. Gillis had provided me with the strongest evidence yet that Medford Evans was not "Cornell Simpson," she had also undermined one of the younger Evans' reasons why he wasn't, that is, that M. Stanton knew all about Medford's writing projects in 1966.

Earlier in his email Mr. LaRochelle told us that the younger Evans had never even heard of this book, described by his father as "devastating" and "convincing" and about a topic so important and sensitive that the author, though protecting himself with a pen name, had still found it prudent to go into permanent hiding. The book is also right down the younger Evans' research alley (more on that later). I suppose that it's possible that the father never mentioned the book or its subject to his son, but it does strain credibility quite a bit.

Maybe one can find clues in the book review as to authorship. *American Opinion* is no longer published, and when it was, not many libraries carried it. The Birch Society will provide an electronic copy of the 8-page article for $20 or will mail it to you for $1 a page plus $4.95 for shipping and handling. I passed on that and got my copy at the Library of Congress. Here's how it starts:

> Cornell Simpson is not, of course, the author's real name. Nobody would publish a book like this under his real name. I happen to know who the author is, and that makes me a bit nervous myself. I read this book five years ago, in manuscript. A friend of mine was going to raise the money to publish it (Western Islands was not then publishing new works) but "Cornell Simpson," for reasons best known to himself, disappeared. I could not blame him too much. He knew too much—as you will see for yourself—and the wrong people knew him. The only reason I can be so frank now is that I honestly haven't the slightest idea where he is today, or whether he is alive. It would be impossible to imagine a more devastating—or convincing—exposé than *The Death of James Forrestal.*
>
> I was living in metropolitan Washington at the time of the defenestration of Forrestal. I remember being convinced immediately that he had not committed suicide—which was the official story—but had been murdered. My reason was simple, but for myself, conclusive. The first report I read, in the *Washington Post,* said that Forrestal's body had been found on the hospital roof below the open sixteenth-story window of the tower, clad in pajamas and robe, with the bathrobe cord knotted

> about his neck. The theory was, said the *Post*, that he had hanged himself out the window, and then the cord had slipped from the radiator or whatever it was tied to inside the window.
>
> I didn't believe it. I believe that men hang themselves, or that they jump out sixteenth-story windows. But I don't believe that they hang themselves out sixteenth-story windows.
>
> On the other hand, it is no trouble at all to imagine a murderer in orderly's habit garroting a man with his own bathrobe cord, then heaving him out the window—perhaps with semi-maniacal haste and strength on hearing or thinking he heard approaching footsteps.
>
> Well, it made not the slightest difference what I thought. It still makes no difference. I could prove nothing—can prove nothing now. But there were others with similar suspicions, and one of those others—who here calls himself Cornell Simpson—decided to research the thing out to the end. He was an experienced researcher of the kind. In 1912 he would have been called a muckraker. He had written exposés for national magazines. He knew how to make contacts, he knew how to evaluate reports, he knew how to analyze.
>
> But he had never tackled a thing like this before. I suppose that at the outset he had dreams of fame and fortune—as the man who *proved* that the first U.S. Secretary of Defense had been murdered! What a sensation! The book would be a smash hit for sure! A million copies—movie rights—the works! "Cornell Simpson" was—is, if he is still alive—a professional. He liked to make money. He thought he could make a mint if he came up with a good enough product.
>
> He came up with a product that was virtually perfect—and suddenly realized that he would be lucky to escape with his life.

Evans continues in this vein throughout his long review, which is not so much a critique as it is a touting synopsis. The review, therefore, can be said to have virtually all of Simpson's strengths and weaknesses when it comes to matters of substance. Particularly for the weaknesses, I would refer the reader to the section entitled "The First Ruddy?" in Chapter One.

Careful readers of that section and the quoted beginning of the Evans review above will notice that Evans reinforces Simpson's claim that the book he finally got published in 1966 was unchanged from the manuscript that he had finished many years previously when he says that he read the manuscript "five years ago." He thus provides cover for Simpson having ignored completely Arnold Rogow's very influential 1963 book, *James Forrestal, a Study of Personality, Politics, and Policy.* The Rogow book is full of claims about matters related to Forrestal's death that are in direct contradiction to what Simpson writes. Most notably, Rogow wrote that Forrestal was witnessed copying something out of a book just before he died, presumably the Sophocles poem that the press used as a surrogate for a suicide note, and Simpson says that that would have been impossible.

Simpson's book would have been ever so much stronger had he taken Rogow to task for his many inaccuracies and omissions, but he has this convenient excuse for not having done so, saying in his foreword that he completed it in the mid-1950s and then set it aside because his prospective publisher had rejected it as too "dangerous." He then says that he brought it out unchanged a decade later to preserve the flavor of the period.[105]

That may be Simpson's excuse for ignoring Rogow, but what could be the excuse of the reviewer of Simpson's book? One would think that he had an obligation to bring matters up to date in the many pages permitted him by the Birch Society house magazine by resolving the contradictions between the two books. But Evans also ignores Rogow's book. One can hardly escape the conclusion that his reason for doing so is the same as Simpson's. Cornell Simpson, Medford Evans, and the John Birch Society would all have us believe that if Forrestal was murdered, it was certainly the work of the Communists. Rogow is dead accurate on one point, though, and neither Simpson, Evans, nor the Birch Society could begin to contradict him on that one. That is, that Forrestal was at least as much if not more hated and feared by the Zionists. Furthermore, they have had a similar assassination record as the Communists and their leverage over the Truman administration and the American press was and certainly is now much greater than that of the Communists. (One

---

[105] Simpson, p. viii.

particularly ugly secret is that in many instances the Communists and the Zionists were the same people well up to the time of Forrestal's death.)

Mr. LaRochelle's email provides fresh circumstantial evidence that the story about the unchanged manuscript is simply a ruse, and it is a ruse in which Medford Evans participated. Take the matter of the misidentification of the employment of Ben Mandel. To be sure it's possible that Evans could have simply missed that error when he read the manuscript. One can assume, though, that, as is usually the case, the manuscript was shared—if, indeed, there was such a manuscript at the time—with a knowledgeable person like Medford Evans for the precise purpose of editorial review and fact checking. Easier to believe is that Evans participated in the ruse of the publication of the unchanged manuscript in order to sidestep the Zionist angle in Forrestal's death that is inescapable in the Rogow treatment.

M. Stanton Evans and His Book

So what about the statement by M. Stanton Evans to his research assistant that he had no knowledge of the Cornell Simpson book? Let's have a look at his powerful and persuasive 663-page opus, *Blacklisted by History: The Untold Story of Senator Joe McCarthy and His Fight against America's Enemies.*[106] We can certainly say with some confidence that if he had been informed by what is in the Simpson book, he has certainly covered his tracks well. If it is really true that he knew nothing of the Simpson book, it is truly a shame.

On page 413 he quotes from McCarthy's famous Senate floor speech in 1951 attacking General George C. Marshall: "If Marshall were merely stupid, the laws of probability would dictate that part of his decisions would serve this country's interest." As we have seen, though, this is an observation of Forrestal's about Roosevelt-Truman policy makers in

[106]Crown Forum, 2007.

general related by Forrestal to McCarthy as recorded on page 53 of the Simpson book.

It could not be more obvious that McCarthy was simply paraphrasing what he had been told by Forrestal and applying it specifically to Marshall.[107]

Evans, in perhaps the only part of his book in which he is strongly critical of McCarthy, would have us believe that that speech was really someone else's work. He tells us that it was an "open secret" that the real writer of that speech was Forrest Davis, a well-known journalist at the time, offering as evidence that it was in Evans's opinion that it was in Davis's style, that it used the word "malediction," a rare word favored by Davis, and it covered topics with which Davis was very familiar.

Compare this with what we learn from Simpson:

> When Senator Joseph R. McCarthy first came to Washington in December 1946, Navy Secretary Forrestal not only personally opened McCarthy's eyes to the mass infiltration of Communists into our government,

---

[107]We don't have to guess about this, and neither would Evans have had to have done so to acknowledge the Forrestal provenance for the quote. We know that he has read McCarthy's book, *The Fight for America,* and the following is from page seven of that book: "Many of [the Communist subversives' names] I heard discussed for the first time by a man who was later to be hounded to his death by the Communists. I arrived in Washington in December, 1946, about two weeks before being sworn in as a senator. Three days later my administrative assistant and I received an invitation to have lunch with Jim Forrestal.

"I have often wondered how the extremely busy Secretary of the Navy discovered that a freshman Senator had arrived in town and why he took so much time out to discuss the problems which were so deeply disturbing him. More than an equal number of times I have thanked God that he did.

"Before meeting Jim Forrestal I thought we were losing to international Communism because of incompetence and stupidity on the part of our planners. I mentioned that to Forrestal. I shall forever remember his answer. He said, 'McCarthy, consistency has never been a mark of stupidity. If they were merely stupid, they would occasionally make a mistake in our favor.' This phrase struck me so forcefully that I have often used it since. (The Devin-Adair Company, 1952)

but actually named names. (See the senator's book *McCarthyism, The Fight for America,* Devin-Adair, 1952.)

> When asked by this writer if those individuals Forrestal had named as Communists or pro-Communists had included Marshall, and if so whether this had inspired his own devastating, thoroughly documented attack on Marshall from the Senate floor (published as the book *America's Retreat from Victory,* Devin-Adair, 1952), Senator McCarthy replied, "The answer to both questions is yes. Forrestal told me he was convinced that General Marshall was one of the key figures in the United States in advancing Communist objectives."[108]

Forrest Davis might well have been the principal author of the speech on Marshall, but it certainly sounds like McCarthy had some important input into it.[109] The passage also reveals again the strong influence that the much more widely respected Forrestal had upon McCarthy and his campaign to root out subversives from the government. But James Forrestal turns up in Evans' tome only in one place in an endnote late in the book, credited only as the major influence behind the Truman Doctrine. One would think that Evans is going out of his way to deflect attention away from the man. Could it be because of our recent discoveries revealing that Forrestal was almost certainly murdered and that the Zionists, not the Communists, are the most likely suspects in the crime?

To that point, have another look at the list of names that Simpson calls either pro-Communist or Russian spies. Evans talks about all of

---

[108] Simpson, pp. 85-86.

[109]There might be a hidden reason why Evans and other Yale stalwarts and supposed McCarthy defenders William F. Buckley and L. Brent Bozell, Jr., whom Evans invokes, have jumped all over McCarthy for that Marshall speech. We might find here a key, as well, to McCarthy's ultimate destruction. In the book version, *America's Retreat from Victory, The Story of George Catlett Marshall* (Devin-Adair, 1951, pp.11-12) in a section omitted from the June 14, 1951 speech, McCarthy, citing information found in George Morgenstern's 1946 book, *Pearl Harbor,* claims that Marshall and others had knowledge of the impending December 7 attack as early as December 4, and they issued no warning to the garrison in Hawaii.

them repeatedly, with one exception, and that man was the most powerful Truman White House holdover from Roosevelt, David Niles. Evans draws heavily upon *The Venona Secrets, Exposing Soviet Espionage and America's Traitors*, by Herbert Romerstein and Eric Breindel, and they also have some highly incriminating information on Niles," as we site in Chapter One. How could Evans leave all mention of Niles out of his book? Could it be because Niles was also the leading Zionist in the Truman White House?

The John Birch Society

Seventeen years after James Forrestal's covered-up likely assassination, and three years after the publication of the Rogow cover-up book, the John Birch Society was concerned enough about it to publish Cornell Simpson's book. A few months later they thought it of enough importance to publish a glowing review of the book in their *American Opinion* magazine, written by the associate editor, Medford Evans.

That's at least how it looks if you take everything on its face. Another possibility is that, contrary to what they tell us, the Cornell Simpson book was written as a reaction, indeed, as a supplement to the Rogow book. The reasoning behind it would be that there would still be lots of people who would never believe that Forrestal committed suicide. These people would need to be steered away from the actual culprits. Such a book was written by someone, or a group of "someones," and the name "Cornell Simpson" was slapped on it. Who the actual author (or authors) was is really not very important. It might well have been Forrest Davis, for all we will ever likely know.

At this point, one of those emails that we received from J. Bruce Campbell, this one from December 25, 2003, is germane, and here we repeat this little Christmas present almost in its entirety:

> I have the unpleasant duty to inform you that for the entire year of 1979 I was a salaried employee of The John Birch Society. I'd been drilling oil wells for ARCO for four years when the District Governor of the JBS approached me, due to my spouting off to one of his loyal supporters. Anyway, I took a big pay cut and jumped on that sinking ship. I

was fed up with the large and small corruption of the oil business, which I actually liked for the part in which I was involved (drilling).

I met Larry McDonald, the congressman and later head of JBS, and although he was a very nice guy, I thought the whole thing was very dated and uninspiring. Larry was interested in my Rhodesian experiences. The night I took Larry to LAX after an important but boring fundraiser, I dreamed up a big billboard campaign in Southern California with the message "Indict the Trilateral Commission Now" signed The John Birch Society, Belmont – San Marino. At this time the TC was hot stuff and very sinister-sounding. This would have energized the whole thing and would have been cutting edge because of the newness of the TC.

I raised a ton of money for this thing and then was ordered by the DG (who'd authorized me to do so) to change the billboard message to a tax-reform thing, which was dishonest to say the least and cowardly for displaying a fear of Rockefeller. I sent everyone's money back and called Welch in Belmont, Mass, to say that I wanted to meet with him regarding this thing. Welch did not meet with hired help but I was pretty persuasive and he finally agreed. A month later I sat in his office and, though he was prepared to counter my pitch for the billboards, I switched subjects and tried to present my real message, which was that the JBS had forsaken John Birch, who was one very violent and action-oriented guy (for a missionary). Welch surprised me with his bitterness over the Birch name, saying he regretted ever naming it after him. I said, what difference does the name make - anything would have gotten the same treatment.

He stalked around, saying I was ignorant for trying to glamorize this guy (who had killed a whole bunch of Japanese and - realizing he'd fought the wrong enemy - was about to do the same to the Red Chinese) and said, "They can say he was arrogant toward his captors."

"You mean the Chinese Communists, who killed him with bayonets?"

"They can say he was living with a Chinese girl."

"So what? They killed him. Who cares what they say about him?"

And so it went. On the subject of religion, which is what this is about, he asked me if I were religious? I said no. He said, "Neither am I. I don't have time for all that stuff." That was surprising because of the underlying religious flavor of JBS. (Tell 'em what they want to hear!)

Ten years later I met a Birch guy who was a 33d degree Freemason, who knew the Welches. He told me that Welch's brother James was also a 33d degree. Eustace Mullins wrote in *Murder By Injection* that Robert Welch was a 32d degree Mason. Welch I think was nominally a Baptist but his Freemasonry would have neutralized that. John Birch was a Baptist missionary. Welch wouldn't let me finish my pitch for Birch and later told a mutual friend that it was the silliest idea he'd ever heard.

The Birch Society was just a corral for conservatives. Welch, who was an excellent writer in the sense that he could get people very agitated about this or that subject, from Eisenhower to Taiwan, was a promoter who told me in the car one time when I drove him to LAX that he had to raise over four million dollars a year just to keep the thing going. But he just kept the patriots bunched up and broke, writing to congressmen! There was no other point to it besides the following:

JBS was a Zionist operation and became virulently so with the hiring of John Rees... A British Zionist, Rees hated me personally for no apparent reason. Probably instinctive, maybe because of my background as an anti-Communist "mercenary" in Africa. But Welch ran JBS as a cheering section for Likud, referring to Begin and Sharon and Shamir as anti-Communist, anti-terrorist, etc. (We learned - I was in the Rhodesian police branch of the security forces - that Israel was aiding the Communist terrorists who were slaughtering so many Africans and Europeans in Rhodesia.) The ADL had a direct control over Welch and he would brook no discussion of Jewish aims or practices - or as I said before, the Jewish creation of Communism. I know because it was my duty as a staff coordinator to expel any member who discussed Jews in a political manner. I never had to do this because by 1979 the membership was thoroughly tamed and compliant. I was asked to question a guy who was no longer an active member about some remarks he'd made about Jews. I did so and we became good friends. I resigned over the billboard issue and the disturbing experience with Robert Welch - I had been authorized to raise money with the TC message and then was told to keep the money under false pretenses, so I couldn't stick with such slimy people.

My father had been a JBS life member and brought some financiers into the cult of Welch, which probably cut me some slack. I wasn't a member but would buy a lot of books from the American Opinion bookstores wherever I found them. I became a close friend of Alan Stang and the two of us were arrested in Southern California while target shooting one time. He wrote an interesting account for *American Opinion* magazine ("Police Story"), which was a problem for him due to the Birch line: "Support Your Local Police." We no longer supported the police after that nasty experience. Anyway, Stang was a big time Zionist (still is) and we went our separate ways once I wised up. Stang would become a tax rebel and go to prison for his beliefs.

> Welch turned his back on him because he demanded full compliance with IRS. Stang had been the house Jew to counter the "anti-Semitism" smear by the usual suspects. Nothing could have been farther from the truth. (I have a lot to say on this subject but won't now.)

Strong support for Campbell's assertions can be found in "The Birch Society—Exposed!" by John "Birdman" Bryant. The central message of the collection of materials on his web page is to be found in this quote from Revilo Oliver's book, *America's Decline:*

> After the conference between Welch and myself in November 1965, I determined to verify conclusively the inferences that his conduct had so clearly suggested, and, with the assistance of certain friends of long standing who had facilities that I lacked, I embarked on a difficult, delicate, and prolonged investigation. I was not astonished, although I was pained, by the discovery that Welch was merely the nominal head of the Birch business, which he operated under the supervision of a committee of Jews, while Jews also controlled the flow, through various bank accounts, of the funds that were needed to supplement the money that was extracted from the Society's members by artfully passionate exhortations to "fight the Communists." As soon as the investigation was complete, including the record of a secret meeting in a hotel at which Welch reported to his supervisors, I resigned from the Birch hoax on 30 July 1966 with a letter in which I let the little man know that his secret had been discovered.[110]

Bryant also notes, quoting from Mullins's *Murder by Injection,* that the Rockefellers were the primary financiers of the John Birch Society, having purchased Robert Welch's candy company for a good deal more than the market price.

Whatever we might say about the Birch Society goes for Medford Evans because of his affiliation with them. But what can we say about his

---

[110] http://www.thebirdman.org/Index/NetLoss/NetLoss-Oliver.html; Revilo Oliver, *America's Decline: The Education of a Conservative,* Londinium, 1982, Chapter VI. This book is even harder to come by than Simpson's *The Death of James Forrestal.* Only the Library of Congress has it in the Washington, DC, area. No library in Virginia has it. The next nearest place to find it is the library of the University of Maryland, Baltimore Campus. After that, one has to go to the NYU library in New York City or the UNC Chapel Hill library. The cheapest used copy to be found online costs $130.

son, M. Stanton? Certainly, his whiffing on James Forrestal and David Niles in his McCarthy book is not a good sign. Still, he had the excuse that he knew nothing about the Cornell Simpson book, although he certainly knew of McCarthy's own writings about his personal debt to Forrestal concerning information on Communist infiltration of the government.

M. Stanton Evans died in 2015 at the age of 80. His last major work was *Stalin's Secret Agents: The Subversion of Roosevelt's Government*, written with Herbert Romerstein, which we reviewed at http://www.dcdave.com/article5/130201.htm. Long before he died we had made sure that he knew all about the suspicious circumstances surrounding James Forrestal's death, but to our knowledge, this great anti-Communist Evans wrote nothing at all about the likely assassination of the great and important anti-Communist Forrestal.

At the close of the previous chapter we noted that the fabrication of a number of press stories that Forrestal had made several suicide attempts before his fatal plunge from that window at Bethesda Naval Hospital was a strong indicator, just in itself, that the man was murdered. Would not the publication of an entire book, purposely confined to a very small audience that exposes the crime but directs readers away from the likely perpetrators, be another very strong indicator that Forrestal was murdered?

As for the John Birch Society as it exists today in the United States, we do not profess to be experts. We do not follow their publication, *The New American*, on any regular basis. Furthermore, one might understand why, as a leading conservative, anti-Communist organization they might tend to bend over backward to avoid the poisonous "anti-Semitism" charge, when the Jewish element has undeniably been such a strong part of Communism in general and in the United States in particular. Even with all their efforts in that direction, they have not been able to stay completely out of that line of fire. This quote is from a 1967 article, just after the publication of Simpson's book:

> America's "radical right" has created "a huge patchwork blanket" of radio broadcasts, has made easier the recruitment of members by the

> John Birch Society, which "contributes to anti-Semitism," and poses "the greatest danger" to the civil rights movement, the Anti-Defamation League of B'nai B'rith was warned today.
>
> The warning came from Benjamin R. Epstein, national director of the ADL, and Arnold Forster, the League's general counsel. They presented a special report dealing with the radical right to the League's national commissioners at the closing session of the ADL's 54th annual meeting, which has been in session since Friday.[111]

Such charges persist right up at least to 2013 from the Southern Poverty Law Center:

> John F. McManus, the president of the archconservative John Birch Society (JBS) is also listed as a speaker at the Canadian conference. JBS has been dogged for decades by charges of anti-Semitism, accusations society leaders vehemently deny. Those same leaders, however, take great pride in JBS being at the forefront of the conspiracy-fueled attacks on Agenda 21, a non-binding United Nations plan for sustainable development around the world.[112]

One might gauge the genuineness and the courage of the Birch Society today in standing up to the most pernicious aspects of Zionism by their response to the publication of this book.

---

[111] *Jewish Telegraphic Agency,* "ADL Warned of Anti-Semitism in 'Radical Right' John Birch Society," January 31, 1967, https://www.jta.org/1967/01/31/archive/adl-warned-of-anti-semitism-in-radical-right-john-birch-society.

[112] *Hate Watch,* "Ron Paul, Birch President to Speak at Anti-Semitic Conference," August 20, 2013, https://www.splcenter.org/hatewatch/2013/08/20/ron-paul-birch-president-speak-anti-semitic-conference.

CHAPTER 4

The Cover-up Collapses

Willcutts Report Released

Secret Forrestal Investigation

Did James V. Forrestal murder himself,
Or was he assassinated?
To examine the Navy's official report,
For more than a half-century we waited.

Is there official skulduggery here?
We'll let the readers decide,
But usually when someone keeps something hidden,
It's because he has something to hide.

Signs of a Struggle?

The first person to enter former Secretary of Defense James Forrestal's fully-lighted room at the Bethesda Naval Hospital after his fatal, late-night plunge from a 16th floor window saw broken glass on his bed. The Navy photographer who took pictures of the room at some unknown time later took a picture of broken pieces of what looks like either a petri dish or an ash tray on the ornate carpet in the room, but in the photograph, the bed had nothing but a bare mattress and a couple of bare pillows on it, not even the turned-back bed covering that the nurse who saw the glass on the bed described. The two photographs of the room, taken from different angles, also failed to show either the slippers under the bed or the razor blade beside it that the nurse saw. In fact, the barren room with nothing on the bed or any of the furniture, no reading or writing material, no clothing, no spectacles, no pipe, tobacco, or lighter, in short, no sign that James Forrestal or anyone else had, shortly before, been a patient there, is clearly not the room as described, as we shall see, by the nurse, Lieutenant junior grade Dorothy Turner. Nothing is supposed to be moved at the photograph of a crime scene, but in one of the photographs, a chair is at the foot of the bed, but in another it is not there. (see frontispiece)

The scene that Navy corpsman chief John Edward McClain captured was not what a proper police crime-scene photographer would have captured. The room had been stripped down and scrubbed up, except that the cleaners seem to have overlooked the clear pieces of glass two feet, or so, from the foot of the bed. A suspicious police investigator, encountering this broken glass on the bed and the floor and noting the bathrobe cord tightly tied around Forrestal's neck, might well have concluded that these were signs of a struggle, quite inconsistent with the quick conclusion of suicide by the county medical examiner and the inferences drawn by the news accounts.

This new information on James Forrestal's untimely death, never reported before anywhere, is taken directly from the investigation of the review board convened by the commander of the National Naval Medical

Center, Rear Admiral Morton D. Willcutts, on the day after Forrestal's May 22, 1949, death.[113] The board, made up of five Navy Medical Corps officers junior to Admiral Willcutts and one retired Medical Corps captain had finished hearing and recording the testimony of all witnesses—all of whom were also members of the Navy Medical Corps on duty at the Bethesda Naval Hospital—on May 31, 1949. The "proceedings and findings" of the board were officially signed off on by the Commandant of the Potomac River Naval Command on July 13, 1949, but not until October 11 was a less than one page, uninformative 5-point "Finding of Facts" released to the public. Interestingly, as we have seen, that release did not conclude that Forrestal had committed suicide, but the press left us with the impression that it had. The Review Board investigation itself remained secret until April 6 of 2004 when the author, on his third Freedom of Information Act try, the first two of which were to the National Naval Medical Center, received the report from the Navy's Judge Advocate General's office.

Forrestal's body had been found on the roof of the second deck of the Bethesda Naval Hospital at around 1:50 AM on Sunday. The board met at 11:45 AM on Monday, May 23, and spent only 45 minutes total, visiting the morgue to identify the body, the site 13 stories below where Forrestal had landed, room 1618 where Forrestal had been hospitalized for some seven weeks, and room 1620, the diet kitchen across the hall out of whose window Forrestal had apparently fallen. A lunch break was taken from 12:30 to 1:30 and the board members then conferred among themselves until 2:18, when they adjourned for the day.

---

[113] Willcutts Report on Forrestal's Death, James V. Forrestal Papers, Mudd Manuscript Library, Princeton University, https://findingaids.princeton.edu/collections/MC051/c04531. The report, with some additional insightful analysis, is available in searchable htm format at http://ariwatch.com/VS/JamesForrestal/WillcuttsReport.htm.

Photographers First

The first two witnesses called when the board convened the next morning were the photographer who took pictures of the body and the photographer who took pictures around the 16th floor area. It is of some interest that two photographers were required for this task. Of even greater interest is that, quite properly, the time when the pictures of the body were taken is firmly established by questioning, but the board exhibits a very curious lack of curiosity as to when the second set of pictures, the ones inside the hospital, were taken.

After establishing that "Harley F. Cope, junior, Aviation photographer's mate first," had "been called upon recently to take some pictures" and having elicited from Mate Cope what the nature of the pictures were, this question is addressed to him:

> Q. Can you tell us at what time you arrived on the scene and at what time you took the pictures?
>
> A. Yes, the pictures - that series of pictures were taken between three and three fifteen. The last picture was taken at three fifteen as a matter of fact.

The second witness, "John Edward McClain, hospital corpsman chief, U.S. Navy," was also asked if he was "called upon recently to take some pictures" and asked to identify them, but the follow-up question establishing the important fact of when he was called upon and when he took the pictures never comes. It is apparent that enough time had been permitted to elapse for Forrestal's room to be transformed from the one that Nurse Turner described to the one that Corpsman McClain photographed. That the review board failed to establish just how much time that was looks to be more than inadvertent. When we look carefully at the windows in the photographs of the room (See frontispiece.) we see that bright sunlight is streaming in. The sun is about as high in the sky as it gets in May at the latitude of the Washington, DC, area. One can surmise that at least eight hours had passed between Forrestal's fall and Corpsman McClain's photographic work. Why was it necessary to let so much time pass?

Though they must have taken a look at the photographs and noticed the barren room and the bright sunlight in the pictures, the members of the review board failed to note the contradiction in the later testimony of Lieutenant junior grade Francis Whitney Westneat when he said that, "... the Navy photographers (plural) arrived at three fifteen and finished their work at about three twenty-five...."

Not only do the questioners fail to establish when the second photographer actually did his work, but in using the passive voice in their initial questions to each of the photographers, they also fail to inform us as to exactly who called upon these photographers to take these pictures. Who was in charge of things, of the *investigation*, if you will, from the time Forrestal was found dead until the board began its work at 11:45 of the next morning, some 34 hours later? If we could know that we might also be able to learn who was responsible for laundering the crime scene of Forrestal's room.

That Corpsman McClain was, to some degree, treating what he was shooting as a crime scene comes out in his volunteered remarks about one of the pictures he is asked to describe: "This is out of focus. We were shooting for finger prints which we were requested to get and that is what we have, sir."

The board never asks who requested the pictures of fingerprints or what those pictures turned up. Since the board never asks who that person was, that key investigator is never examined by the board.

In that same long response identifying his photographs, McClain reveals the existence of the broken glass: "The fifth picture is a picture of a rug with some broken glass on it, taken approximately two feet from the end of the bed. We were unable to get any identifying marks except the rug; couldn't pick up the bed because the glass wouldn't show. It was room sixteen eighteen."

Perhaps the mystery investigator who ordered up the fingerprints also made some effort to determine how the glass came to be broken, but the board members, none of whom, as medical men, seem to have any background in the investigation of crimes, have nothing to say about it.

Their curiosity about the broken glass was no greater when they questioned Nurse Turner next to last on the third day of the hearing, and here we skip ahead to that testimony:

> Q. What were your particular duties on the night of May twenty-first?
>
> A. Usually before quarter of two I go down to tower eight before I write the captain's log and I had left tower twelve and went down to tower eight and I asked the corpsman how everything was and he said he just gave a man a pill. I happened to look up at the clock. It was just about one fourty-four (sic). I sat there in a chair for a minute and then I heard this noise. It was a double thud and I said what was that. I said "It sounded like somebody fell out of bed you better check the wing in front" and he went to check the beds and said it was alright and so I said "I'll check the head" and sent him to tower seven to see if it was something down there. That's when I walked in the bathroom on tower eight. I looked out the window. I just remember thinking in my mind, "Oh my God, I hope he isn't mine" and I ran up to tower twelve and told the corpsman to check on Colonel Fuller's room so he walked into his room and I walked into room twelve thirty opposite his room and looked out the window from there and could see a body distinctly. It was then I really realized it was a body and I thought of Mister Forrestal. So I went up to tower sixteen and told Miss Harty there was a man's body outside the galley window and he wasn't mine. We both went into his room and he wasn't there and we noticed the broken glass on the bed and looked down and noticed the razor blade and told him he was missing (sic) and she said it was one forty-eight. Then I walked over towards the galley and noticed the screen was unlocked. That's about all.
>
> Examined by the board:
>
> Q. When you found out the body was not that of one of your patients what made you think of Mister Forrestal?
>
> A. I knew he wasn't mine and I knew that Mister Forrestal was up there and was being watched.
>
> Q. You said you saw his slippers and a razor blade beside them; where did you see them?
>
> A. The bed clothes were turned back and towards the middle of the bed and I looked down and they were right there as you get out of bed.
>
> Q. And the razor blade was lying beside the slippers?

A. Yes it was.

Q. Did you notice any blood on the bed?

A. No, I didn't see any and the razor blade was dry; there wasn't anything on that. I remember looking and there wasn't anything on the glass either.

Q. Where was the bathrobe?

A. I didn't see his bathrobe.

Neither the recorder nor the members of the board desired further to examine the witness.

The board informed the witness that she was privileged to make any further statement covering anything relating to the subject matter of the investigation which she thought should be a matter of record in connection therewith, which had not been fully brought out by the previous questioning.

The witness said she had nothing further to state.

The witness was duly warned and withdrew.

A few comments are in order.

Notice that when she first mentions them, Nurse Turner speaks of *the* broken glass and *the* razor blade as though she has told these people, or at least someone in authority, about these things before. Once again we are made to wonder who was in charge in the immediate aftermath of the death and what he learned from the witnesses. The corpsman who was supposed to be monitoring Forrestal and first noticed him missing from the darkened room, Robert Wayne Harrison, was also not called to testify until the third day of the hearing (Wednesday). Surely someone had interviewed him earlier, but it was not part of the official record.

The questioner said, "you said you saw his *slippers* and a razor blade..."

The astute reader will notice that she has said nothing about slippers. Maybe the transcriber just messed up, but at least as likely, some prior questioning had gone on that was not officially recorded. And why are they interested in the slippers and the razor blade when it is the glass, more than anything else, which should intrigue them? They don't even ask if she saw broken glass anywhere else, like on the floor, where they have already seen photographs of it. They had previously asked Corpsman Harrison if he had seen any glass on the floor, and he had responded in the negative (but he apparently never turned on the lights).

The nurse in charge of the16th floor, identified as Regina M. L. Harty, who accompanied Nurse Turner to the room, had been interviewed earlier, but she was never asked to describe what she saw in the room.

The final question about the bathrobe might have some real significance. We wonder which of the board members asked it, and if he might have been on to something. Unfortunately, we will never learn who played what role in the questioning because the individual questioners on the board are never identified. He is just a "Q."

Although the "cord" found tied tightly around Forrestal's neck is commonly referred to as his bathrobe cord, no official connection is ever made between that cord and his bathrobe. He was wearing only his pajamas when he fell from the window. The cord appears in the list of exhibits, but the bathrobe does not. This question of Nurse Turner represents the only attempt by the board to locate the bathrobe, perhaps to see if it was missing a belt.

The Key Missing Exhibits

Some much more important things than Forrestal's bathrobe were missing from the exhibits, though. Have a look at the complete list, dear reader, and see if you notice what they are:

Introduced on Page No.

Pictures of body of deceased,

Exhibits 1A through 1J 2

Photographs of Rooms sixteen eighteen and sixteen twenty and outside of building (illegible), National Naval Medical Center, Bethesda, Maryland,

That's right, there's no autopsy report, a pretty serious omission. Defenders of the investigation might respond that the autopsy doctor, as we shall see, was questioned at length and asked many key questions, revealing that in his opinion Forrestal was not choked to death before being thrown out of the window, but these are no substitute for the autopsy report itself. One can only wonder why it was left out. Possibly germane to this omission is the fact that the author's FOIA request for all materials connected with the Willcutts Report was not completely honored by the Navy JAG office. The first set of exhibits, the 10 photographs of the body as it lay on the third-floor roof were held back, as were an unknown number of photographs taken of Forrestal's external injuries taken just prior to the autopsy. The reason given was that "...the unauthorized release of this information would result in a clearly unwarranted invasion of personal privacy with respect to Mr. Forrestal's surviving family members (5 U.S.C.552 (b)(6), as amended)."

The JAG office informed me that I could challenge the ruling with a formal letter sent within 60 days, and I did so, on the basis that no family member who knew him and could be counted as a loved one or a "surviving family member" was still alive (He has one grandchild who was born many years after his death.). On September 14, 2004, I finally received a response. Here is the key paragraph:

> "Please be advised that these exhibits [1, 4, and 5] are missing from the original investigative report. Due to an administrative error you were

informed on April 6, 2004, that these exhibits were withheld out of respect to Mr. Forrestal's surviving family members."

It would appear to this humble observer that the Navy legal team's initial error was tactical rather than administrative. It is difficult to escape the conclusion that there is something in the death scene photographs that they don't want anyone to see. It must be really embarrassing for the government's suicide case or they would never have gone so far as to make up such an obvious cock and bull story as this. Further on in our analysis, we speculate as to what that something might be.

Also missing are some key props that played such an important role in convincing the public that Forrestal had killed himself. For the others, here are the key passages from the front-page article in *The New York Times* of Monday, May 23, 1949:

Forrestal Killed in 13 Story Leap
Nation is Shocked
He Was a War Casualty as If He Died at Front, President Declares
Copied a Poem on Death
Had Seemed to Be Improving in the Naval Hospital–Admiral Orders Inquiry

Washington May 22 - James Forrestal, former Secretary of Defense, jumped thirteen stories to his death early this morning from the sixteenth floor of the Naval Medical Center.

Suicide had apparently been planned from early evening. He declined his usual sleeping pill about 1:45 this morning. A book of poetry beside his bed was opened to a passage from the Greek tragedian, Sophocles, telling of the comfort of death.

....

The plunge that caused Mr. Forrestal's death occurred at 2 A.M. and hospital authorities announced it with a brief statement two hours later.

Pushed Open a Screen

The hospital said that Mr. Forrestal had left his room, No. 1618 in the white granite tower of the hospital, and had gone to a diet kitchen nearby. There, clad in a dressing gown, he pushed open a screen held only by thumb latches and plummeted to the third floor projection after hitting a narrower projection at the fourth floor.

The sound of the fall was heard by Lieut. Dorothy Turner, the nurse on duty on the seventh floor almost immediately after a Medical Corpsman's check of Mr. Forrestal's room disclosed he was missing. An investigation led to the discovery of the body on the roof of the passageway leading from the third floor of the main building.

There were indications that Mr. Forrestal might also have tried to hang himself. The sash of his dressing-gown was still knotted and wrapped tightly around his neck when he was found, but hospital officials would not speculate as to its possible purpose.

Mr. Forrestal had copied most of the Sophocles poem from the book on hospital memo paper, but he had apparently been interrupted in his efforts. His copying stopped after he had written "night" of the word "nightingale" in the twenty-sixth line of the poem.

The book was Anthology of World Poetry, bound in red leather and decorated in gold. A red ribbon bookmark was between Pages 278 and 279 where "Chorus from Ajax" appears.

....

He was widely denounced by persons who felt that he favored the Arabs over the Jews, and Mr. Forrestal was said to be particularly distressed by a statement that "he cared more for oil than he did for the Jews."

Rear Admiral Leslie Stone

Adm. Stone gave this account of the circumstances that enabled Mr. Forrestal to elude the attendant early this morning.

Commander R.R. Deen, a staff psychiatrist, was asleep in the room next to that of Mr. Forrestal. The attendant, Hospital Apprentice R.W. Harrison made his visit to Mr. Forrestal at about 1:30 and found him apparently asleep. On his 1:45 check he found Mr. Forrestal awake. Asked if he wanted a sleeping pill, Mr. Forrestal said he did not.

Apprentice Harrison then went to Commander Deen's room to report that Mr. Forrestal had declined to take a sedative. Back at 1:50, he found that his patient was not in his room.

> Commander Deen was immediately roused and a check of the room begun. A few minutes later the seventh floor nurse, Lt. Turner, reported the sound of Mr. Forrestal's body striking the third floor roof.
>
> Admiral Stone said that Mr. Forrestal had improved to the point where he was being allowed to shave himself and that belts were permissible on his dressing gown and pajamas. It had been accepted that continued treatment would have brought Mr. Forrestal to complete recovery in a matter of months.

So where were the poetry anthology and the memo page with the transcribed lines from "Chorus from Ajax" in the list of exhibits? Actually, the handwritten page was included among the materials that the author received from the Navy, but none of the witnesses mentions having discovered it or the book in Forrestal's room, and no one on the review board asks anything about the circumstances of their discovery. Nurse Turner, the most likely candidate to have seen them first, if, in fact, they were ever in the room, mentions only the broken glass, the turned-down bed clothes, the razor blade, and, with prompting from the board, Forrestal's slippers. The book and the transcription were absolutely vital in the selling of the story that Forrestal took his own life, but they seem to have materialized out of the ether (Speaking of ether, another thing we learn from the Willcutts Report, for what it is worth, is that Forrestal complained on a number of occasions of a strong ether smell in his room.). On the other hand, broken glass was most assuredly discovered in the room by two separate individuals, one of whom captured it photographically, and it has taken 55 years for that fact to reach the American public (Actually it remains to be seen whether the salient facts surrounding Forrestal's death will ever reach any significant portion of the American public. Those who were content for the Report to remain secret all these years will hardly be inclined to publicize its findings and its shortcomings.).[114]

Something else that is notable about the account in *The Times* is the degree of detail about the goings on in the hospital in the minutes before and after Forrestal's fatal plunge. This is information that could only

---

[114] Unfortunately, that last sentence, written first on the author's web site in 2004, has proved to be all too prescient, as we shall see in subsequent chapters.

have come from Apprentice Harrison, Commander Deen, and Lt. Turner. Someone had clearly taken charge of the investigation right off the bat to elicit this information from them. For lack of any other name, that of the commanding medical officer of Bethesda Naval Hospital, Rear Admiral Leslie Stone, the man who gave the information to the press will have to do. Yet, as we shall see, when the board questions him they ask him nothing about his actions in the wake of the Forrestal death.

Forrestal's Guard Queried

Apprentice Harrison played such an important role in Forrestal's last few minutes among the living that his testimony is produced here in its entirety:

> Examined by the recorder (Lieutenant Robert F. Hooper, Medical Service Corps, U.S. Navy):
>
> Q. State your name, rate and present station.
> A. Robert Wayne Harrison, junior, hospital apprentice, U. S. Navy, Naval Medical Center, Bethesda, Maryland.
>
> Q. Harrison, what were your specific duties on the night of May twenty-first?
> A. My specific duties were to take care of Mister Forrestal.
>
> Q. What time did you go on duty?
> A. I went on duty at eleven forty-five p.m.
>
> Q. Whom did you relieve?
> A. Price, hospital corpsman?
>
> Q. Would you tell the board what happened from the time you took over the watch at eleven forty-five until the time that you discovered Mister Forrestal was missing?
> A. When I took over the watch at eleven forty-five Price whom I relieved told me that Mister Forrestal was still up in his room and that he had been walking around; that he had been reading. Since I didn't know Mister Forrestal personally, (I had been on the night before, and when he woke up the next morning I didn't get to talk to him very

much, I didn't know him personally), he introduced me to him and he was very friendly and said "Hello" to me.

Q. How many times did you speak to Mister Forrestal between the time you took over the watch and the time he was missing?
A. Approximately three or four times.

Q. Did you notice anything unusual about Mister Forrestal's behavior during that time?
A. No, sir, I didn't.

Q. Did he say anything to you that would lead you to believe that he was in any way disturbed?
A. No, sir, he didn't.

Q. At what time did you last see Mister Forrestal?
A. It was one forty-five, sir.

Q. Where was he then?
A. He was in his bed, apparently sleeping.

Q. Where were you at that time?
A. I was in the room when I saw him.

Q. Did you leave the room at that time?
A. Yes, sir, I did.

Q. Where did you go?
A. I went out to the nurse's desk to write in the chart, Mister Forrestal's chart.

Q. At what time did you become aware of the fact that Mister Forrestal was missing?
A. At approximately one-fifty a.m.

Q. Had you previously spoken to the doctor regarding Mister Forrestal?
A. Yes, sir, I had.

Q. At what time was that?
A. That was just before one forty-five before I went back into his room to check to see what he was doing, to see if he was asleep or resting.

Q. And then you left the room and went out to the nurse's desk?
A. To write in the chart, yes, sir.

Q. What did you do when you discovered Mister Forrestal was missing?
A. When I went back into the room after I had finished writing in the chart, I went over to my chair where he had been sitting while I was in the room before and since it is dark in the room, very dark, my eyes had

to become accustomed to the light before I could see anything. There is a chair sitting directly in front of the night light and it is very hard to see anything at all when you first walk into the room so I went over and started to sit down in the chair; by that time I could see enough to see that he wasn't in his bed. The first thought that came to my mind was maybe he had gotten up and gone into the head and at the same moment the corpsman on duty, Utz, came to the door and told me I had a phone call out at the desk. I told him Mister Forrestal was gone. I went out to the desk and answered the phone call. It was Bramley, the night Master-at-arms of the Neuropsychiatric service. Bramley asked me if Mister Forrestal was alright. I said that I didn't know, that he wasn't in his bed and he told me to make a thorough check and to find out for sure where he was. So I went back into the head, looked in the closet, any possible place in the room, and on my way back out in the hall back to the phone I looked into the galley and I didn't see him in there, either. So I went back to the phone and told Bramley that he was not there.

Examined by the board:

Q. Just prior to discovering that Mister Forrestal was missing did you hear any unusual noises coming from the vicinity of the diet kitchen?
A. No, sir, I heard nothing.

Q. Were you close enough to the diet kitchen to hear if there had been any unusual noises?
A. Yes, sir, I definitely would have.

Q. What is your regular assignment in the hospital?
A. I was on night duty on ward 6-D, a neuropsychiatric ward.

Q. How long have you been there?
A. Approximately two months, a little over two months, sir.

Q. How long have you been assigned to the neuropsychiatric service?
A. A little over two months, sir.

Q. How many times did you say you stood watch on Mister Forrestal?
A. Part of Friday night and I took the regular watch on Saturday night.

Q. Did Mister Forrestal do very much wandering about his room or corridor Saturday night?
A. He was walking around his room and he did follow me out to the diet kitchen when he asked me for some orange juice and then once after that he was out of his room to drink a cup of coffee.

Q. Did he go to the diet kitchen for the coffee?
A. Yes, sir, he did.

Q. Were you with him then?
A. No, sir, I was not.

Q. He served the coffee himself?
A. No, sir, the corpsman on duty, Utz, was bringing coffee up in a coffee pot at that time. I was out writing my chart and he went past the desk where I was sitting and entering in the chart. He went out towards the galley with his pot of coffee and I heard him mention Mister Forrestal's name and say something to him and ask him if he would like a cup of coffee. Mister Forrestal said "Yes" and then I heard a noise which would signify he was giving him a cup of coffee and right after that I got up and went out to the diet kitchen. He was coming out with his coffee in his hand. He handed me the cup of coffee and said he was all finished with it. He said I could put it in the galley.

Q. About what time was that?
A. That is one time I don't remember.

Q. How was he dressed?
A. He was in his pajamas, sir.

Q. Did he have a bathrobe on or not?
A. No, sir.

Q. Did you give Mister Forrestal any medication at all that night?
A. No, sir, I didn't.

Q. Did he talk to you very much that night?
A. No, he didn't.

Q. Didn't he ask you about yourself and where you came from and so on?
A. No, sir, he didn't say much except when I first came in and was introduced to him. That was when he said "Hello" to me. When I asked him if he wanted his sleeping tablets he told me no, he thought he could sleep without them.

Q. Was your station inside Mister Forrestal's room or was it outside the door?
A. I don't exactly understand what you mean by that, sir.

Q. Were you directed to sit in his room while you had the watch most of the time or could you sit at the nurse's desk?
A. I was supposed to be in the room except when I went out to make entries in his chart or get something for Mister Forrestal.

Q. Were the lights on in Mister Forrestal's room when you took over the watch - the overhead lights?
A. No, sir, not the overhead lights; just the night light.

Q. Did you notice a broken ashtray any time during your tour of duty in Mister Forrestal's room?
A. No, sir, I didn't.

Q. When you were at the nurse's desk is it possible for a person to go into the diet kitchen without your observing him?
A. I couldn't have seen him.

Q. Did Mister Forrestal appear cheerful or depressed in the time that you observed him?
A. He appeared neither, sir.

Q. Did Mister Forrestal do any reading?
A. Not while I was on watch, sir.

Q. After you discovered Mister Forrestal was gone did you go into the galley?
A. About fifteen or twenty minutes afterwards, yes, sir.

Q. Would you describe the condition of the window in the area at the time that you were in there, in particular whether the screen was locked or unlocked?
A. The screen was unlocked at that time, sir.

Q. Were there any attachments to the radiator?
A. I saw none if there were.

Q. Did you notice any marks on the window sill?
A. Sir, at that time I was in such a state that I didn't notice any marks on the window sill.

Q. You did state earlier that you had looked into the galley but no one was there?
A. Yes, sir.

Q. You had no reason to examine the galley further?
A. No, sir, I didn't.

Q. Did you see Mr. Forrestal's body at any time later?
A. Yes, sir, I did, in the morgue.

Q. Did you recognize the body as that of Mister Forrestal?
A. Yes, sir.

> Neither the recorder nor the members of the board desired further to examine this witness.
>
> The board informed the witness that he was privileged to make any further statement covering anything relating to the subject matter of the investigation which he thought should be a matter of record in connection therewith, which had not been fully brought out by the previous questioning.
>
> The witness said he had nothing further to state.
>
> The witness was duly warned and withdrew.

Notice, first, that there is a difference in the explanation Admiral Stone gave to *The New York Times* from that of Apprentice Harrison for the latter's absence from the room at the time of Forrestal's disappearance. According to Stone, Harrison had left the room to inform Dr. Deen that Forrestal had declined his usual sleeping pill. Harrison's explanation here, though, is that he had simply gone down the hall to make routine entries in the logbook at the nurse's desk. Actually, Dr. Deen in his testimony did say that Harrison had awakened him a few minutes before to report that Forrestal was not sleeping and that he had told Harrison that he should remind Forrestal that he should take a pill if he was having trouble sleeping. Harrison had then returned to Forrestal's room before his last trip down the hall to make his log entries.

Second, the account given by Townsend Hoopes and Douglas Brinkley is seen to have some serious flaws. Using Arnold Rogow as their source, they describe an unnamed "new corpsman" looking into the room at 1:45 and noticing Forrestal busily copying something from that leather-bound book of literature, which they later learned was the translation of a morbid poem by Sophocles. Shortly thereafter Forrestal sent the corpsman away on some odd errand, presumably to get him out of the way so that Forrestal could do himself in unmolested.[115]

According to Apprentice Harrison, only the dim nightlight was on in Forrestal's room from the time that he went on duty at 11:45 p.m. until the patient turned up missing at 1:50 a.m., and Forrestal did no reading.

---

[115] Hoopes and Brinkley, pp. 464-465.

Hoopes and Brinkley do prove to be correct with their revelation—not found in any previously published account of which the author is aware—that the guard on duty was new to the job. Here we find that he was spending his first full night on the Forrestal detail, having spent part of Friday night on duty. The significance they read into that fact, however, that it made him easily manipulated by a suicide-bound Forrestal, proved to be off the mark. If, on the other hand, Forrestal was murdered on orders of the powers that be, Harrison's newness to the job might indicate that he was part of the plot, brought in from outside to help carry out the deed during the hours when Forrestal was most vulnerable. To allow the accomplice time to get to know Forrestal as a person would have jeopardized the mission, and it would have looked really bad if the deed had been pulled off within a few days of Forrestal's admission into the hospital when he was ostensibly under heavy guard, expressly to prevent suicide.

The timing of the board's question, giving Harrison the opportunity to establish that he had worked previously in neuropsychology elsewhere in the hospital, seems almost to have as its purpose the forestalling of speculation as to the possibility that he was a ringer. We don't know if Harrison was, in fact, telling the truth on this point. Furthermore, he could have been an operative all along, working for one of the more clandestine branches of the government. It would have been helpful if the board had established why the regular night-shift attendant was not there. Hoopes and Brinkley say that he had gone AWOL on a drunken bender, but this is neither corroborated by the official inquiry nor is it contradicted.

We learn from the Nurse's Notes accompanying the witness testimony in the Willcutts Report that the person that Harrison relieved was one C. F. Stuthers. He is one of a number of people who should have been called as witnesses by the board, but were not. We could have learned from him if the Hoopes and Brinkley account is true, for what it's worth. The board also should have also been interested in his observations about Forrestal's normal demeanor at that time of night in comparison to that final night.

A couple more revelations in the Harrison testimony are of interest. We find out that the regular station of Forrestal's attendant was not just outside the door of his room, as one might assume, but in the room itself. Dr. Raines and the other psychiatrists in their testimony make a big deal out of relaxed restrictions on Forrestal being an important part of his "recovery" process. At the same time, they have a person violating his privacy on an almost permanent basis. The picture that comes across is more of Forrestal as a prisoner than as a patient. We discover further that those detailed periodic log entries that make up most of the bulk of the exhibits to the Willcutts Report were made at the nurse's desk down the hall and that from that location one could not see anyone going from Forrestal's room to the kitchen across the hall with its unprotected window. It almost makes a farce of the story that when Forrestal was first admitted and his mental state was bad, precautions against suicide were tight, but were loosened only as his condition improved. Furthermore, we learn from other testimony that immediately upon admission to the hospital, Forrestal was sent immediately to the 16th floor room even though "security screens" would not be installed on the room's windows for several more days. Recall, as well, the one clear picture that we have of one of these "security screens" and we must really wonder how much of a hindrance they would have been to anyone bent on suicide. The screen is already half out of the window. The room pictures also reveal Venetian blinds on the windows with long cords hanging down from them and radiators beneath the windows. The cords as a noose and the radiator as a perch from which to jump look to be almost tailor-made for suicide by hanging. One must really wonder whether the good doctors at Bethesda ever really considered Forrestal much of a suicide threat or if they did, whether they were expected to make much of an effort to prevent it.

The authorities also didn't seem to have a problem letting us know that he was the corpsman on duty when Forrestal went out the window. The newspapers name him freely, as does Cornell Simpson, who presumably got his information from the newspapers. They never name the person who preceded him, though, and go even further to reduce that person's significance by telling us erroneously that Harrison's shift began at 9:00 p.m. rather than at midnight, a falsehood that Simpson repeats.

A Misnamed Witness

The testimony of the witness who followed Harrison on the stand, but was relieved by him on the night of Forrestal's death, Edward Prise, is perhaps even more intriguing than Harrison's, and it is also reproduced here in full:

> Examined by the recorder:
>
> Q. State your name, rate and present station.
> A. Edward William Price, hospital apprentice, 339 78 55, U.S. Naval Hospital, National Naval Medical Center, Bethesda, Maryland.
>
> Q. What are your regular duties at the Naval Hospital?
> A. Taking care of neuropsychiatric patients.
>
> Q. How long have you been taking care of neuropsychiatric patients?
> A. Fifteen months, sir.
>
> Q. What were your specific duties on the night of May twenty-first?
> A. I had the watch on Mister Forrestal from four until twelve o'clock midnight.
>
> Q. During the time that you had the watch on Mister Forrestal did you notice anything unusual about his behavior.
> A. Yes, sir.
>
> Q. Will you tell the board what this unusual behavior was during the watch?
> A. Well, sir, at twenty-one ten he started walking the room and it didn't seem odd at twenty-one ten but when he was still walking the floor at twenty-two hundred that was the first time he had ever walked the floor that long and he was walking the floor for a period of two hours and fifty minutes before I went off watch at twenty-four hundred. And another thing was he went into the doctors' room adjoining his room and he raised the blinds, I would say that was–I don't know exact time–

around twenty hundred and he raised the blinds and raised the window and at the time I was at the desk. We had orders we could stay at the desk until twenty-one hundred so long as we checked on him; so I went back to the doctors' room and the patient was standing at the window. He had raised the bottom part of it as far as it would go. When I walked in the room he jumped aside. He said "Price, I raised that window. If it gets you in any trouble close it" so he went back through the head and closed the door so I let the blind down and walked out of the room. Just as I got to the door I heard the door to the head open again. He stuck his head out so I went back and closed the head door and locked it and I went back to the desk. I didn't make any note of it because he has opened windows several times in his own room and the doctors' room. Only difference was I am usually there with him when he does it. Other than that there was nothing odd that he done that I can think of.

Q. How long had you stood watch on Mister Forrestal previous to this particular night?
A. Well, sir, I took over the watch the third day he was up there.

Q. Do you know the date that was.
A. I'd say it was the fifth of April.

Q. And you had stood watches continuously on him since that date?
A. Yes, sir, I had eight in the morning to four in the afternoon, then I went from there to twelve to eight, stood that for two weeks, then went on four to twelve. I have been on four to twelve for a little over three weeks.

Examined by the board:

Q. These occurrences that you have just related in regard to Mister Forrestal's behavior on that night, did you consider them sufficiently unusual to report them to the doctor?
A. No, sir, I reported his walking the room to Doctor Deen and I put it in the chart and then Doctor Deen asked me how come the door was locked back there and I told him I thought I better lock it being as he raised the blind.

Q. Did you attach any particular significance to this type of behavior?
A. No, sir, I didn't at the time.

Q. Had you seen him in the past do things similar?
A. Well, sir, he several times did walk the room. He hated light and walked over to the window shades and if they were open a little too far he would pull it closed.

Q. Did Mister Forrestal seem friendly on that night?
A. Yes, sir, he seemed very friendly. I introduced Harrison to him as I

left the watch and he shook hands with Harrison and said he was glad to meet him.

Q. Did he meet him the night before?
A. No, sir, he was sleeping when Harrison came on watch and hadn't awakened by the time Harrison went off.

Q. Other than the conversation you have given with Mister Forrestal did he say anything else to you on that night?
A. No, sir, he asked me if I thought it was stuffy in the room and he asked that several times since I have been on watch; he liked fresh air. When I was on night watch, twelve to eight in the morning he always got a blanket out for us to wrap around us because he had the windows wide open.

Neither the recorder nor the members of the board desired further to examine the witness.

The board informed the witness that he was privileged to make any further statement covering anything relating to the subject matter of the investigation which he thought should be a matter of record in connection therewith, which had not been fully brought out by the previous questioning.

The witness made the following statement:

He started reading a book at about twenty hundred and whenever the corpsman would come in the room he would turn the bed lamp off and sit down in the chair and so far as the writing I don't know. It appeared that he was but I couldn't say for sure.

Neither the recorder nor the members of the board desired further to examine this witness.

The witness said he had nothing further to state.

The witness was duly warned and withdrew.

This rather matter-of-fact testimony may be contrasted with the account derived from that undated outline of an unpublished manuscript by John Osborne, as relayed by Townsend Hoopes and Douglas Brinkley that we saw in Chapter One.

The corpsman, by his own testimony, did *not* consider Forrestal's behavior, even the window raising, sufficiently unusual that he should alert the doctor, though he did routinely inform him of the patient's restless pacing. He also says nothing about Forrestal declining a sleeping pill because he wanted to stay up to read nor does he volunteer anything about hanging around for an additional half hour out of anxiety. Tellingly, in neither account, nor in the testimony of corpsman Harrison, do we hear of his passing any sort of warning on to his successor for the evening. In short, neither in word nor in deed did he give the impression that there was anything really amiss.

Still, from our vantage point, it does appear that Forrestal that evening was behaving somewhat peculiarly, or, at least, showing some signs of anxiety. Recall that it was reported by Simpson that Forrestal's brother, Henry, was coming the very next day to take him away from the hospital (This allegation is corroborated in no way by testimony before the Willcutts Review Board. Dr. Raines says at one point that he thought Forrestal would be ready for release in another month or so.). Recall, further, that Hoopes and Brinkley reported that Forrestal had said that he did not expect to leave the hospital alive.[116] If, in fact, Forrestal did expect that his brother was going to make an attempt the next day to get him out of the hospital and he thought that his life was, indeed, in danger as long as he was there, he had every reason to be extremely anxious that night, especially with a new attendant whom he did not know handling the graveyard shift. That might explain why he would have "jumped aside" from the open window of the doctors' room when the corpsman entered the room. As for the opening wide of the window and the raising of the blinds, the corpsman clearly didn't take it as an indication that Forrestal was on the verge of jumping out, so there's no real reason why we should, either.

The freedom with which Forrestal could open 16th floor windows, hither and yon, even those in his own room that had "security screens" between the glass and the inside of the room, further gives the lie to the notion that anyone at the hospital was ever really serious about the need for suicide prevention. We learn from Dr. Deen's testimony that For-

116 Hoopes and Brinkley, p. 454.

restal was permitted to sleep in the spare bed in the doctors' room when it got too stuffy for him in his own. Nothing would have prevented him from getting up in the night and taking a swan dive out of an unprotected window in that room.

Finally, there's the curious matter of the misspelling of the corpsman's name. No, this is not just another example of poor scholarship by Hoopes and Brinkley. In this case, their source, the undated, unpublished outline of a manuscript by John Osborne is verifiably correct and the Navy's official investigation of Forrestal's death is wrong. Every time he made an entry onto the medical chart, Exhibit 3 accompanying the Willcutts Report, he signed his name, and it is unmistakably the rare name of "Prise," not the common name of "Price." The email from his daughter, discussed in Chapter One, confirms the fact.

Clearly this is not the trivial matter that it might seem to be. There are only two possibilities, either the name was repeatedly typed wrong by the review board by mistake, or it was intentionally written wrong. If it was just a mistake, the overall competence of the work is called into question. How could they get something as simple as this wrong, and if this is wrong, how much else is wrong?

And how could the mistake happen? Corpsman Prise had been on the case from the beginning. He was well known to the higher-ups involved with Forrestal's care, and they all must have read the draft of the report. Surely, they would have known that his name was not "Price," and would have corrected the manuscript when they read it. It was hardly rushed into print, so there was plenty of time to set it right. Furthermore, the likelihood that the name would have been taken down wrong at the beginning of Prise's testimony is very small. When he was asked to state his name, he did it either pronouncing it "Prize" or "Price." In the first instance, hearing the strange name, the recorder would likely have asked him how it is spelled, if he did not volunteer it. In the second instance, the volunteering of the correct spelling would certainly have been virtual second nature to Mr. Prise. He would already have done it thousands of times in his life, knowing that the common assumption would be that the name is spelled like it is pronounced.

For some reason, the very existence of Prise was also left out of the account that the hospital gave to the newspapers in the wake of Forrestal's death. As we have noted, the newspapers reported at the time that Harrison's watch began at nine p.m. and lasted until six a.m., which the author, Simpson, repeated in his version of Forrestal's last hours.

That leaves us with the greater likelihood that the name was misspelled intentionally, and the implications of that are quite sinister, indeed. The email we received from Prise's daughter in 2017 virtually seals that conclusion in stone. It is a technique that is used by corrupt investigative authorities when they want to make it difficult for others to track down witnesses, witnesses whose testimony has been misrepresented. There was a classic example of it, among others, in the case of the death of Deputy White House Counsel Vincent Foster in the Bill Clinton administration. Investigators reported that a Patrick Nolton from Washington, DC, saw Foster's car in the parking lot of Fort Marcy Park, Virginia, when Nolton stopped off for an impromptu urination. It took a foreign reporter, Ambrose Evans-Pritchard of the *Telegraph* of London to get past the obfuscation:

> I grabbed the Fiske Report and flicked to page 28.... The key passage had been expurgated...
>
> Finding this witness was no easy matter. His name was redacted in the FBI documents. There was a brief mention of him in a Park Police "incident report": a Patrick Nolton, with a Washington telephone number 296-2339. But nobody at the number had ever heard of him–it appeared to be a doctor's clinic—and it soon became clear that there was no such person as Patrick Nolton in the District of Columbia, and never had been. The Park Police had done a first-rate job of "laundering" the identity of the witness... [117]

---

[117] Ambrose Evans-Pritchard, *The Secret Life of Bill Clinton: The Unreported Stories*, Regnery Publishing, 1997, p. 159. We see the technique employed again in the case of the curious death in Thailand of the famous Catholic monk, Thomas Merton. In the translation of the Thai police report, furnished by the U.S. Embassy in Thailand, the names of all the witnesses are wildly misspelled. Even the name of the lead investigator is misspelled. See Hugh Turley and David Martin,

But Evans-Pritchard, using a bit of detective work, managed to find Patrick *Knowlton* and interview him. It turned out that he had seen a reddish-brown, older model Honda than the light gray Honda that belonged to Foster, and he was quite sure of the matter, and other parts of what he had told the FBI were also misreported.

> "Patrick Knowlton is convinced that the FBI did not misunderstand him when they wrote up his 302 statement the next day. He believes they knowingly falsified it."[118]

If any part of Prise's testimony is knowingly falsified, what part might it be? My candidate is that last volunteered part about Forrestal reading a book and perhaps writing. The passage doesn't make much sense, but it did manage to get the suggestion on the record that Forrestal might have been doing some transcribing from a book at some time on that fateful evening—although the book seems to have disappeared.

Whether or not this speculation is correct, the failure of the poetry book to turn up anywhere in the testimony of the review board witnesses suggests strongly that the author Simpson is correct, that is, that the whole poem transcription business was a red herring to distract people away from the fact that the almost compulsive writer Forrestal wrote no suicide note.[119]

Having employed this trick successfully in 1949, the authorities would use it once again in 1993, making a big fuss over the torn-up note supposedly belatedly found in Vincent Foster's briefcase. In that note, the writer expresses displeasure at how various things are going, but nothing mentioned is nearly serious enough to make a person want to kill himself, but as far as the press was concerned it might as well have been a suicide note.

The Martyrdom of Thomas Merton: An Investigation, McCabe Publishing, 2018, pp. 25-28.

[118] Ibid., p. 162.

[119] Simpson, p. 18.

In light of what we learned from Prise's daughter as described in Chapter One, he knew a lot more than what was elicited from him in this testimony. That obviously explains the lengths that were gone to to conceal his identity from the public.

Another Misnamed Witness

Sometime after we posted our analysis of the Willcutts Report in 2004, we received a communication from an elderly military veteran whose wife, a former Navy nurse, was acquainted with several of the Navy nurses who had been on duty on the night of Forrestal's death. He said that she had told him that none of them believed that Forrestal had committed suicide. Most intriguingly, he also told me that the head nurse on duty that night covering the floors from 12 to 17, starting at 10 p.m. and continuing until 7 a.m., identified as Lieutenant Regina M. L. Harty, was really one Margie *Hardy*. That "M" probably stood for "Marjorie," the name for which "Margie" is most commonly the short form. When the pen-named "Mark Hunter," whose real name I do not know, did his htm version and analysis of the Willcutts Report, I put him in touch with my informant, and you can see his reflection on this misnamed witness on his web site.[120]

We learn from her testimony, which came right after Prise's late on the third day, that while making her rounds, she encountered Forrestal twice, the first time a little after 11 p.m. and he was with Prise across the hall in that fateful kitchen, drinking a glass of orange juice.

"I spoke to him then and he was very calm and self-assured and quite pleasant," she stated. If he had been wrought up earlier, as the testimony of Prise suggests, he would appear to have been completely calmed down by this time. As we saw, there was nothing in Prise's testimony about that little late orange juice social. She checked his room again at approximately 1:30 a.m. Only the nightlight was on, and she assumed

---

120 http://ariwatch.com/VS/JamesForrestal/WillcuttsReport.htm#ObscuredWitness1

that he was sleeping, and returned to her desk down the hall around a corner. Harrison, who was on duty by that time, promptly informed her that Forrestal was not sleeping, because, she says, Harrison said that Forrestal had asked who it was that had come to the door. She was at that desk at the time that Forrestal would have gone out of the window, and Harrison says that he was there, too, making routine entries in the log.

Altogether, she was asked only twelve questions by the board.[121] Although from her desk she could not see to the door of Forrestal's room or the kitchen across the hall, she was only a short distance away, and she was never asked if she had heard anything unusual. One would think that, at the very least, the breaking of that glass found on the bed and on the carpet at the foot of the bed would have produced a sound that she would have heard. The lack of curiosity of this board of Navy medical doctors is really quite stunning.

Considering the falsification of her name and, if we are to believe Cornell Simpson's report that her name was withheld from the public at the time and that she was promptly transferred to Guam to keep her out of the reach of prying reporters (as if there were any such creatures when it comes to Deep State shenanigans such as this), we must wonder what she really knew. Perhaps one day I will receive an email from one of Margie Hardy's offspring.

---

[121]The most fruitful question was probably #11, one very similar to what was asked of Prise, "On that particular night in question did you notice that he appeared unusual in any way or more agitated, more disturbed, more distraught than usual?" Her answer contrasts not only with Prise's but with the assumption behind the question, that is, that it might have been usual for Forrestal to be agitated, disturbed, or distraught: "At the time I saw him in the galley close to eleven thirty he appeared his usual self; very cheerful, pleasant but *no different than at any time that I had ever seen him*." (emphasis added) One may be virtually certain that Margie Hardy was among the nurses at Bethesda who did not believe that Forrestal committed suicide.

The Officer in Charge

When Forrestal's death occurred, Captain Raines, and the number two psychiatrist at the hospital who was also the number two man on the Forrestal case, Captain Stephen Smith, were both off to a psychiatric conference in Montreal, Canada, so neither was in a position to have taken charge of matters in the wake of the death. Commander John Nardini was the doctor in charge of the care of Forrestal in their absence. The board interviewed him at length, but they asked him no questions about his actions in the wake of the death. As a purely medical man, he would have hardly been the person to take charge of the "crime scene," at any rate.

That would leave either Rear Admiral Morton C. Willcutts, the Medical Officer in Command of the National Naval Medical Center and the man who convened the review board, itself, or Rear Admiral Leslie O. Stone, the Medical Officer in Command of the Bethesda Naval Hospital and the man who gave the detailed statement to the press on the day of the death, to provide an explanation for the initial conduct of the investigation. If anyone was in a position to explain why Forrestal's room was "laundered" before it was photographed, why many hours were allowed to elapse before the room was photographed, why the regular graveyard shift attendant had been replaced, and who discovered the book and the transcription that played such a large role in supporting the suicide conclusion, it would be either Willcutts or Stone. According to the aforementioned testimony of Lieutenant junior grade Westneat both of them arrived on the scene in the wee hours of Sunday morning and began giving orders.

Even though Willcutts had had dinner with Forrestal on Friday night and was one of the last people to see Forrestal alive, he was not called to testify. Stone *was* called. As you read his entire testimony below, including all the questions directed to him by the board, you will gain an appreciation for the fact that all of the members of the board (and the recorder) were his subordinates:

Examined by the recorder:

Q. State your name, rank and present station.
A. Leslie O. Stone, Rear Admiral, Medical Corps, U.S. Navy; Medical Officer in Command, U.S. Naval Hospital, Bethesda, Maryland.

Q. Admiral Stone, as Commanding Officer of the U.S. Naval Hospital what was your connection with the handling of Mister Forrestal's case?
A. I was aware that he was going to be admitted on April second of this year, the afternoon of the second of April.

Q. At that time, Admiral, did you leave?
A. No, sir, I was detached Sunday, April third, and left here at three p.m., checked out with the Officer-of-the-Day the morning of April third.

Q. What time did you return?
A. I returned Friday, April fifteenth.

Q. From that time on would you tell the board your connection with Mister Forrestal's case, if any.
A. Well, I was in constant contact. Captain Raines, the Medical Officer in charge, kept me daily informed about his progress and his condition and on numerous occasions, on two occasions, I was up with the Defense Secretary, Mister Johnson, for a visit and also with President Truman when he was out to visit with him and I daily was on the floor but not in the room with Mister Forrestal.

Examined by the board:

Q. What are your feelings in regard to the type of handling and treatment Mister Forrestal received during the period after your return and resuming command of the hospital?
A. I feel that Mister Forrestal had nothing but the best of care; that I have all the confidence in the world in the psychiatric staff of this hospital and I feel that the statement that Captain Raines has made publicly is what he believes and I believe that Mister Forrestal had as good care as he would have received in any institution.

Neither the recorder nor the members of the board desired further to examine this witness.

The board informed the witness that he was privileged to make any further statement covering anything relating to the subject matter of the investigation which he thought should be a matter of record in connection therewith, which had not been fully brought out by the previous questioning.

The witness said he had nothing further to state.

> The witness was duly warned and withdrew.

So much for that. RHIP. Rank has its privileges, as they say.

The Suspicious Cord

The general approach of the review board from the beginning seems to be to take it as a given that Forrestal took his own life and that it is their job to come up with some explanation as to how he was able to get away with it. The exception to that rule is in their treatment of the bathrobe cord that was tied around Forrestal's neck. They certainly knew that this had to look very, very suspicious, that someone might have used it to throttle Forrestal in his bed and then throw him out of the window. If Forrestal was bound to kill himself, was he so addled that he did not realize that throwing himself out a 16th floor window, by itself, would do the job?

The first person to testify about it was Hospitalman William Eliades:

> When the doctor shone the light you could see one end was tied around his neck and other end extended over toward the left part of his head. It was not broken in any way and didn't seem to be tied on to anything. I looked to see whether he had tried to hang himself and see whether a piece of cord had broken off. It was all in one piece except it was tied around his neck.

Eliades and several succeeding witnesses are asked how tight the cord was, and the consensus seems to be that it was tight, but not all that tight. One of the doctors who saw the body when the cord was still on is asked if he saw any signs of asphyxia, and he responded in the negative. Finally, Captain William M. Silliphant, the autopsy doctor, is called upon to lay to rest all speculation that Forrestal was first choked to death and then thrown out of the window:

> Q. Was there any evidence of strangulation or asphyxia by strangulation?
> A. There was absolutely no evidence external or internal of any strangulation or asphyxia.

That still leaves open the possibility that Forrestal was subdued and quieted by use of the cord and then thrown out of the window. If both carotid arteries taking blood to the brain are blocked, unconsciousness can occur within ten seconds. Maybe this is what happened in Forrestal's case, with insufficient bodily evidence remaining for the autopsy doctor to notice. There is also the possibility that Captain Silliphant was not telling the truth. Those of us familiar with the performance of the autopsy doctor in the aforementioned Foster case, and in the John F. Kennedy case by Navy doctors in that same Bethesda Naval Hospital, are not inclined to believe autopsy doctors implicitly.

It would have helped if someone had gone to the trouble to determine if there was enough cord left over after "one end" was tied around Forrestal's neck for the other end to have been tied to the radiator below the window for the man to hang himself out the window. And if an attempt had been made to so attach it, the cord might have left telltale creases where the failed knot had been. This avenue of inquiry, needless to say, was not explored.

The death scene photographs that we were initially told we couldn't see on account of the sensitivity of surviving Forrestal family members and were later told were simply lost doubtless would have shown the cord around Forrestal's neck. Might it have been obvious that there was not enough of the long end left over to stretch all the way to the radiator and to tie a knot attaching it to the radiator?

Another possibility is that there wasn't any "long end" of the bathroom belt and that the witness or the preparers of the written report embellished the testimony to make it accord more closely with the preferred suicide conclusion. If the belt had been used to throttle Forrestal, what is most likely is that his assailant would have naturally held the belt near the middle with about an equal amount left over at each end, and that might well have been obvious from the never-to-be-seen photographs. Whatever the case, it is highly likely that the photographs would have rendered the radiator-tying theory even more absurd than it appears on its face.

The Doctors' Perspective

A substantial part of the testimony before the Willcutts Review Board, which altogether filled 61 legal-sized pages and required four days to accomplish, dealt with Forrestal's psychological condition. It was, for the most part, a defense case against any possible charge of negligence against the Navy and hospital officials. The theme followed—and never challenged by the board—was that the patient was in pretty bad shape when he was admitted, and during that early period security precautions were stringent. The patient improved, though fitfully, and eventually he had improved to the point that hardly any security precautions were necessary. Indeed, medical necessity required that security be relaxed to the point of virtually inviting the patient to take a fatal leap from a high level, although it was never stated in just these terms, of course. The idea, according to the doctors, was that the patient had to be re-acclimated to real-world dangers in order to get used to returning to normal life.

Five doctors were responsible for Forrestal's care, but the name of only one, Captain George Raines, appears in the two popular biographies of Forrestal, the ones by Hoopes and Brinkley and Rogow. There was a definite hierarchy among the doctors, corresponding, to a degree, to their military rank. Captain Raines was the Chief of Neuropsychiatry at the Bethesda Naval Hospital. He was primarily responsible for Forrestal's therapy, prescribing medication and engaging in one to three hour therapy sessions on an almost daily basis until he ceased them early in May. Captain Stephen Smith was his second in command who talked less formally on a daily basis with Forrestal and provided "supportive" and "consultive" services to Dr. Raines. Commander David Hightower was a resident in neuropsychiatry and Commander Robert Deen was a resident in second year training in psychiatry. They had the babysitting duties, alternating sleeping over in the room next to Forrestal and making themselves available at all times for anything that might arise that might require a doctor's attention. Finally, there was Commander John Nardini, who was called in to be in charge of the patient when Raines and Smith left on May 18 for the psychiatric conference. He developed only a nodding acquaintance with the patient in the short period of his duties.

Some striking differences among the doctors and between the doctors and the press reports come to light with respect to Forrestal's condition. The popular notion of what was wrong with Forrestal was captured and perpetuated by Rogow in his widely-quoted and referenced biography, that is, that he was suffering from "involutional melancholia," a manic-depressive form of schizophrenia most typically occurring in middle age and manifesting itself in paranoia and "nihilistic tendencies."[122]

This assessment is contradicted by the testimony of the Bethesda doctors in almost every respect. Not once do any of the doctors speak of paranoia as one of Forrestal's symptoms, from the time he arrived until his untimely departure. The term, "involutional melancholia" is never used, nor is there any mention of manic-depression, schizophrenia, or nihilistic tendencies. They all use the term "depressed" or "depression," with respect to the patient, but they never say what they mean by that. Moreover, the consensus of psychiatric community these days is that there really is no special medical condition known as involutional melancholia, or a type of depression to which those in middle age are particularly susceptible. Rather, there is just garden variety depression which, when it strikes people in middle age, used to be given the special name of "involutional melancholia."

In his testimony, the only special sort of depression that Forrestal might have had, according to Dr. Raines, was "reactive depression," or, conveniently for the official story, one that might lie dormant until touched off by some external factor like, say, reading a depressing poem.

---

[122] Rogow, pp. 9-10.

Reading over the various doctors' use of the term "depressed" to describe Forrestal, one is struck by how fast and loose they are with the term. Virtually nowhere is it explained how the "depression" showed up or how it could be detected or measured, though it is often spoken of as something as discrete and measurable as heart rate or blood pressure. The only manifestation that might possibly be separated out from simply the effects of heavy sedation are verbally expressed suicidal tendencies. Dr. Raines, though, is the only one who says that, and the testimony of the other doctors and the peculiarity of some of Dr. Raines' assertions seem to call his reliability on this matter into question.

Dr. Raines Weighs In

Dr. Raines was the third person to testify, after the two photographers, and he was the only person to testify twice. He was the only witness to appear before the board on the last two days of witness testimony. Here are some key early passages:

> Q. Would you tell the board the results of your observations and treatment of Mister Forrestal, especially in reference to his mental status?
> A. Mister Forrestal was obviously quite severely depressed. I called the hospital from Hobe Sound on the morning of the second and asked that they have two rooms available, one on the officers' psychiatric section and the other in the tower. At that time I had not examined Mister Forrestal, was not at all sure of how much security he needed. On the flight up I had opportunity to talk to Doctor Menninger at great length and to see the patient briefly. As a result, I felt he could be handled in the tower satisfactorily, provided certain security measures were taken. Consequently, he was admitted to the tower with a continuous watch when he arrived here. The history indicated that Mister Forrestal had had a brief period of depression last summer but that this had cleared very rapidly when he went on vacation. His present difficulties seemed to have started about the first day of the year, perhaps a little earlier, with very mild depressive symptoms beginning at that time and a good many physical symptoms, noticably (sic) weight loss and constipation. The depression had been rather marked from about the fifteenth of February nineteen forty-nine but had not become actually overwhelming until the week-end preceding admission which would have been approximately March twenty-fifth and twenty-sixth. At that time he became very depressed and I believe as a result of that relinquished his office some three days earlier than had been previously planned. He was seen by Mister Eberstadt on the Monday before admission and on

his advice immediately relinquished his office and went to Florida for rest. The physical examination was done by Doctor Lang immediately after admission which showed nothing remarkable except some elevation in blood pressure. The neurological examination was negative except for small, fixed pupils which, so far as I know, had no significance. Mister Forrestal was obviously exhausted physically and we postponed any complete studies until such time as his physical condition could be alleviated. He was started immediately on a week of prolonged narcosis with sodium amytal. His physical condition was so bad we had difficulty adjusting the dose of amytal because of his over-response to it. About the third night his blood pressure dropped to fifty-five systolic under six grains of amytal. To prevent any confusion in the orders on the case I selected two of the residents, Doctor Hightower and Doctor Deen, and put them on port and starboard watch to begin at five o'clock each evening. The doctor on watch slept in the room next to Mister Forrestal. On Monday after admission on Saturday security screens were provided for the room that Mister Forrestal occupied and for the head connected with it by moving them from tower five. At the same time a lock was placed on the outer door of the bathroom and strict suicidal precautions were observed. I saw Mister Forrestal for interviews daily during the morning of that first week when he was allowed to come out of the narcosis for short periods of time. These interviews were devoted primarily to history-taking. His response to that early treatment was good and he gained about two pounds during the course of the weeks' narcosis. The following week, beginning the eleventh of April we started Mister Forrestal on a regime of sub-shock insulin therapy combined with psycho-therapeutic interviews. This was continued about four weeks but his response to it was not as good as I had hoped it to be. He was so depleted physically he over-reacted to the insulin much as he had to the amytal and this occasionally would throw him into a confused state with a great deal of agitation and confusion so that at the end of the second week I had to give him a three day rest period instead of the usual one day rest period. I am not sure that that was the end of the second or third week. At the end of the fourth week again he was over-reacting to the insulin and I decided to discontinue it except in stimulating doses. From that time on he was carried with ten units of insulin before breakfast and another ten units before lunch with extra feedings in the afternoon and evening. In spite of this he gained only a total of five pounds in the entire time he was in the hospital. His course was rather an odd one, although in general it followed the usual pattern of such things. The odd part came in the weekly variation of the depression. I can demonstrate it and explain. Instead of the depression lightening, instead of straight up in a line he would come up until about Thursday and then dip, hitting a low point on Saturday and Sunday and up again until the middle of the week and down again Saturday and Sunday. Each week they were a little higher. He was moving upward steadily but it was in a wave-like form. In addition, he had the usual diurnal variation, the low point of his depression occurred between three and five a.m. so that the course towards recovery was a double wave-like motion, the daily variation being ingrafted on his weekly variation. The daily variation is very common, the weekly variation is not so common and that was the portion of the course that I referred to as "odd".

Q. Captain Raines, I show you a clinical record, can you identify it?
A. This is the nursing record of Mister Forrestal. The only portion I don't recognize is this poem copied on brown paper. Is that the one he copied? It looks like his handwriting. This is the record of Mister Forrestal, the clinical record.

In the following excerpts from the testimony of Dr. Raines, the "Q" and "A" format will not be strictly adhered to. Rather, the portions relating to Forrestal's supposed suicidal tendencies are selected from Raines' answers to various questions:

As late as the twenty-ninth of April the patient was still quite suicidal and personnel were reminded of this by an order in the chart. A week later the insulin therapy was discontinued and beginning on the eighth of May the patient was placed on the stimulating doses of insulin which I previously mentioned. He continued to improve in the irregular fashion which I have described and by the ninth of May I felt it safe for Mrs. Forrestal to make her plans to go abroad but didn't think he should go with her. My reason for objecting to his going was, ironically enough, that I knew in the recovery period which seemed at hand the danger of suicide was rather great. The son returned to his work in Paris on May thirteenth. The family was at all times kept fully advised as to the patient's progress but I didn't warn them continuously of the suicidal threat nor did I mention it to any one except my immediate colleague, Doctor Smith.

....

I first eased the regulations as a test on the twenty-sixth of April but found that the patient was not ready for it and that resulted in an order on the twenty-ninth of April that the watch was to remain in the room at all times, that the patient was still quite suicidal. The relaxation of the afternoon watch was only a few days later, on May first, which indicates how abruptly his condition would change at times in these undulating moments in the illness.

....

He was very close to well actually. When I saw him on the eighteenth I felt we could, didn't tell him, but felt hospitalization for another thirty days would probably do the trick. He was that close to the end of it. That, of course, is the most dangerous time in any depression.

Q. Did Mister Forrestal make any attempts at suicide while he was under your care?
A. None whatsoever. The matter of suicide in Hobe Sound, he told Doctor Menninger that he had attempted to hang himself with a belt. Menninger and I were very skeptical of that and both he and I were of the opinion that it was sort of a nightmare. The man had no marks on him and there was no broken belt. Very frequently a depressed person has a fantasy of dying and reports it as real. So far as I know he never made a single real attempt at suicide except that one that was successful. He was the type of individual, fast as lightening (sic), of extremely high intelligence and one reason I doubt previous attempts I knew if he decided to do it he would do it and nobody would stop him. He was a boxer in college and his movements, even when depressed, were so quick you could hardly follow them with your eye. In the course of psychotherapy he talked a great deal about his suicide; he would tell me when he was feeling hopeless and had to do away with himself. At those times we would tighten restrictions. He would tell me in symbolic language. One morning he sent me a razor blade which he had concealed. When I interviewed him I said "What does this mean?" He said "It means I am not going to kill myself with a razor blade." Of course, he had the blade and could have done it. A man of that intelligence can kill himself at any time he desired and you can't very well stop him. He is my first personal suicide since nineteen thirty-six, thirteen years ago. The last one was on a locked ward at St. Elizabeth's Hospital under immediate supervision of an attendant. He discussed, whenever he felt badly enough, he would talk about the possibilities of killing himself and I am sure that when I left here on the eighteenth he had no intention of harming himself.

Q. Had he, in the course of your interviews, either symbolically or otherwise, suggested his method if he committed suicide?
A. Yes, I am sure he didn't jump out of the window. My interviews with him were for one to three hours a day over a period of eight weeks (sic); can't go into all the material that makes me think that but by the time he had been here four weeks I was certain there were only two methods he would use because he had told me, one was sleeping pills. He said that was the one way he could do it and the other was by hanging which made us feel somewhat more comfortable about the period of risk, knowing that he wasn't going out one of the windows. I haven't gone into all the details of what happened, but personally feel he tried to hang himself. I don't think he jumped; he may have; don't think

it was out the window; think he meant to hang. For some time he had had complete access to the open windows in the residents' room and for a short period of time he even slept in there for two or three nights. There were two beds in the residents room and he would sleep in one of those until about three o'clock and then go back to his own bed. That was the one thing that puzzled me, when he called me (sic), as to what had happened; I couldn't believe it because of the window, until I got back and found out about the bathrobe cord.

....

Actually, he dealt quite well with almost everything. It is my own feeling from what I know that the period of despondency which caused him to end his life was very sudden of onset and probably the whole matter was on an impulsive basis. That was the one thing I had feared, knowing of his impulsivity. Again, I say, he moved like lightening (sic), some of those on pure impulse. That is supported by several things. I talked to Doctor Hightower last night and was glad to hear him say spontaneously and not just in agreement with me that he felt that this was an impulsive thing of sudden origin, but one of the main evidences is the complete absence of any suicidal note or expression of suicidal intent in any way. He left no message at all except this poem which I am sure was meant for me and was not a portion of the suicide. That is to say, I think he was simply writing that out to demonstrate how badly he felt.

Q. Before he came to Bethesda while he was down south, did he make any attempt to slash his wrist?
A. No, he had a small scratch on his wrist which he told me was not a suicidal attempt but he was considering it and he was wondering what he could do to himself and he took a knife or blade and scratched his wrist, so superficial it was not even dressed, and wouldn't come under the heading of "attempt" so far as I am concerned.

Now let's examine Dr. Raines's remarks. He says that he ordered two rooms to be prepared, one in the officers' psychiatric suite and the other in "the tower." After some deliberation he concluded that Forrestal "could be handled in the tower satisfactorily, provided certain security measures were taken." It's really not a matter of whether he *could* be housed on the 16th floor but, rather, *should* he be put up there. No one on the panel asks Dr. Raines or anyone else why they should ever consider putting Forrestal on the 16th floor when they claimed to have believed that he was a danger to himself. Why take the chance? We also learn that initially there were not even any security screens, such as they were, on the windows, though there was a full-time guard to keep an eye on this "fast as lightning," "impulsive" patient.

The revelation in Chapter One that the orders came from "downtown," that is, the White House, to put Forrestal up on the 16th floor, to the general consternation of the psychiatric staff, looks better in light of these revelations. The board might have known better than to ask why Forrestal was placed in "the tower," because they knew there was no good medically defensible reason that could have been given.

Dr. Raines is wrong about the reason for the advancement of the date of Forrestal's departure from office. It was not Forrestal's decision, brought on by his "depression," but President Truman's decision. Forrestal's alarming, almost zombie-like behavior, was first noticed by his assistant, Marx Leva, and called to the attention of Ferdinand Eberstadt, some hours after Forrestal had been replaced by Louis Johnson.

We also learn from Raines's testimony that constipation was among Forrestal's physical symptoms upon entry into the hospital as well as constricted pupils of the eyes, but he makes nothing of it. According to the web site on narcotics we find that these are both symptoms of someone on heroin.[123] That is not to argue that Forrestal was necessarily on heroin, but it does raise the question of whether some of Forrestal's sudden lethargic and apathetic behavior—a radical personality change for him—in the wake of his stepping down from the Defense Secretary's job might have resulted from his having been secretly drugged. Drowsiness and apathy are also heroin symptoms. At least one of the doctors on the panel should have picked up on the constricted pupils and inquired as to whether Forrestal had been tested for drugs, but the possibility is never considered by any of these medical men.

If Forrestal already had an opiate like heroin in his system, sedating him with a strong barbiturate like sodium amytal could have been dangerous, and might explain Forrestal's poor reaction to it. One might

---

[123] Prescribers' Digital Reference, http://www.pdrhealth.com/diseases/drug-abuse/symptoms.

question the wisdom of putting Forrestal on sodium amytal in any case, and it is doubtful that it would have been done given the current level of medical knowledge. This comes from *McDermott's Guide to the Depressant Drugs*:

> Like opiates, barbiturates are addictive, only more so. Taken to help you sleep, after a few days, it becomes impossible to sleep without them. Like the opiates, barbiturates produce tolerance so that you need to keep upping the dose to get the same effect, but the real hum-dinger is the withdrawal syndrome. If withdrawal from opiates is cold turkey, then withdrawal from barbiturates could be cold raven. Besides the craving, discomfort and inability to sleep, barbiturate withdrawal also causes major epileptic seizures. Nobody dies from opiate withdrawal, but it is a strong possibility with barbiturates and you should only think about it under the supervision of a doctor, preferably as a hospital in-patient. The possibility of overdose is amplified greatly if barbs are injected into a vein rather than taken orally. By and large, it is usually only those people who have had their switches set to automatic self-destruct mode who use barbiturates because the drug isn't at all pleasant or enjoyable. Barbs lack the euphoric content of opiates and the social lubricant properties associated with alcohol. They simply produce a dark, blank oblivion and as such will always remain popular with those people who hate themselves or their lives so much that their behaviour is governed by a compulsion to obliterate all possibility of thought and self-examination. Do yourself a favour. Just say no. [124]

As we noted, it is sometimes difficult to sort out what in Forrestal's behavior was a result of his presumed condition and what was caused by his medication. For example, if the description of Corpsman Prise of Forrestal walking the floor restlessly on the night he died is accurate, he might well have been simply exhibiting a case of barbiturate withdrawal. In his resistance to taking sodium amytal as a sleep aid, the patient seemed to exhibit a keener sense of what was good for him than did his doctors

Suicidal Tendencies?

Now let us look at Forrestal's "suicidal tendencies," as related by Dr. Raines. "In the course of psychotherapy he talked a great deal about his

---

124 https://www.erowid.org/chemicals/opiates/opiates_mcdermotts_guide.shtml.

suicide; he would tell me when he was feeling hopeless and had to do away with himself."

That statement, along with his two written orders in the medical chart, first on April 7, "Still suicidal - keep close watch" (underlining in original) and again on April 29, "Watch in room @ all times. Suicidal. Don't get careless," represent the strongest evidence that Forrestal was, indeed, inclined toward ending his own life and eventually succeeded.

Still, there are anomalies and curiosities in Raines's testimony and treatment. He says the only person he shared Forrestal's suicide talk with was Dr. Smith. One would think that those with the most need to know about the specifics of Forrestal's putative "suicidal tendencies" would be the people right on the front lines guarding against it, Drs. Deen and Hightower. And much of what Dr. Raines says, especially his assertion that he took the patient at his word as to what method of suicide he might use, comes across as self-serving, and just plain strange. If he really believed Forrestal was considering hanging himself because it is on his short list of preferred methods, do those Venetian blind cords in the room make any sense, or the relaxation of rules against cords and belts?

As an example of the self-serving quality of Raines's testimony, notice how he volunteers that the poetry transcription looked like it was in Forrestal's handwriting. Was there any particular reason why he would know what Forrestal's handwriting looked like, or that this sample resembled it? When had he seen Forrestal's handwriting? Does he take special note of what people's handwriting looks like? Did he place the paper with the transcription on it beside a known sample of Forrestal's writing? Is the good doctor qualified at recognizing forgeries?

As much as he talked about suicide, Dr. Raines does seem to put to rest the widely circulated reports that Forrestal had made previous attempts at it. Even today, at an Arlington Cemetery web site, one can find the following passage, based upon no known reliable evidence whatsoever, the following passage:

> On May 22, after several prior attempts at suicide, and after copying a passage from Sophocles' "Chorus from Ajax," he jumped from the 16th floor hall window. [125]

We know, of course, that it wasn't a hall window that he went out of, either.

Other Doctors

Now let us look at the observations of the other four doctors with respect to Forrestal's suicidal tendencies. Doctor Nardini, who only became actively involved in the case when he took over during the absence of Drs. Raines and Smith on May 18, can be dispensed with rather quickly:

> Q. Were you aware of the possibility of suicide?
> A. Yes, sir.
>
> .....
>
> Q. Did Mister Forrestal make any attempt at suicide while you had charge of the patient?
> A. No, sir, none that I was ever informed of, became aware of, or suspected.
>
> Q. Did Mister Forrestal indicate in any way that he might do harm to himself?
> A. None whatever.

Notice that Dr. Nardini volunteers nothing about Forrestal's lurid musings on the subject. Dr. Raines has told us that he told no one but Dr. Smith about them, and among those excluded would appear to be the doctor in absolute charge of the patient in their absence. Now we turn to the next person to testify, Dr. Hightower.

> Q. Were you fully aware of the various phases of Mister Forrestal's condition from shortly after he was admitted as a patient to the hospi-

---

[125] http://www.arlingtoncemetery.net/jvforres.htm.

tal?
A. Yes, sir, Doctor Raines, Doctor Smith, Doctor Deen and I had discussed at intervals various procedures and therapeutic efforts that were being made during the course of the entire case.

Q. During the period of his stay in the hospital did you feel that he was making some gradual improvement?
A. Yes, sir, my feeling from the first was that he was pretty overly depressed, as evidenced by his lack of interest in his surroundings, interest in personal contact with me on the brief occasions that I saw him, whereas as the case progressed, particularly during the insulin period he seemed to become more alert, more interested in his surroundings, and particularly interested in what was going on about the floor itself and the hospital.

Q. What was your feeling in regard to the possibility of suicide during the first few days of his stay in the hospital?
A. My feeling with regard to suicide during the first few days of his stay in the hospital was that it was potentially present, that being based on psychiatric experience with depressed patients. I had no actual factual evidence of any sort which would lead me to be able to say specifically that suicidal thoughts or ideas were present. However, I did feel and consider it a possibility on the basis of general psychiatric knowledge.

Q. What was your feeling in regard to the possibility of suicide at approximately the time that Doctor Raines left Washington?
A. At that time I felt that Mister Forrestal had made a definite improvement in the overall picture from the time of his admission and that the possibility of suicide was much more remote than earlier in the case. There were several observations made during the course of the case which led me to feel this. About two weeks before Doctor Raines left I went up to stand the watch one night and stopped by the room to speak to Mister Forrestal, asked him how he was feeling. He said "About as usual." We chatted briefly about my medical education and where I lived and what not; then later, when I came up to go to bed about twenty-two forty-five, he was awake and I asked him how he was feeling. He said "About as usual" but he felt his room was a little stuffy and in view of the fact that two of the windows were stuck and couldn't be opened I agreed that the room was a little stuffy. He said that he thought possibly he would be able to sleep better if he slept in the room with me, there being two beds in my bedroom and I said I thought that would be a good idea, it might be more comfortable over there. My feelings at this time were that the patient was making an effort to broaden his horizons. I felt that he was lonely and felt the need of friendly contact with other people and also felt at the time that the suicidal possibilities had lessened sufficiently to make it safe for him to remain out of

his room. The danger of suicide had been discussed with Doctors Raines and Smith on several occasions prior to this and we had been encouraging the patient to broaden his activities even prior to this particular incident.

....

Q. Did Mister Forrestal, in the times you would be with him, express anything about international affairs?
A. No, sir.

Q. Do you think he was trying to get away from such things?
A. I didn't have much feeling about whether he was or not. He never made any effort to talk along those lines when I was with him, no, sir. In fact, the basis of most of our conversations were relatively superficial, having to do with things of the moment; should he take his sleeping pills or not; was I going to sleep in the room next to him or not; how was the rose thorn in his finger getting along; or whether his constipation was being taken care of or not. Another one of my duties in the case was to write orders for his bowels and I had done that earlier in the course of the case.

So, although "The danger of suicide had been discussed with Doctor Raines and Doctor Smith" by Doctor Hightower on several occasions, he was still able to say that "[he] had no actual factual evidence of any sort which would lead [him] to be able to say specifically that suicidal thoughts or ideas were present," but that, [he] did feel and consider it a possibility on the basis of general psychiatric knowledge," at least during the early stages of the hospitalization. Once again, it is evident that the specific intimations of suicide that Dr. Raines said Forrestal communicated to him were not passed along to a doctor on the front line of Forrestal's care. Not only that, but it would appear that Dr. Raines's specific orders in the medical chart were not getting through, either. The episode in which Forrestal was permitted to sleep in a room with completely unprotected windows, at about two weeks before Dr. Raines left, would have taken place about five days after, "Watch in room @ all times. Suicidal. Don't get careless," with the Raines signature beside it can be found in the chart.

Next, we have Dr. Deen, the other doctor on periodic watch on the 16th floor.

Q. Did the matter of suicide ever occur to you?
A. It certainly occurred to me ever since the man has been there.

Q. How did you regard him from that standpoint for the first few days of his stay in the hospital?
A. Well, of course, on the first few days, it was much longer than the first few days, on admission to the hospital he was under almost continuous sedation and constant watch. After a few days they were able to get screened windows on the room and corpsmen were instructed to stay with Mister Forrestal at all times and if they needed anything from the nurse or corpsman on the outside or from Doctor Hightower or me they went through another corpsman, didn't leave the room at any time. Following that he was on sub-shock insulin therapy for a period of something like three weeks, I believe, and the man was obviously depressed and any time a man is depressed there is always a consideration of suicide to be kept in mind.

Q. How did you regard the progress of his condition from the time of admission to the hospital until the time that Doctor Raines left town?
A. Well, I think it is best to put it this way. From discussions with Doctor Raines, Doctor Smith and Doctor Hightower and from the changes in the orders which permitted Mister Forrestal to have more freedom of movement in that he could go into our bedroom and he could be in the room alone without the corpsman I presumed, I felt that improvement was going along or those measures would not have been put into effect. So far as my personal dealing with Mister Forrestal on his original entry and at the time he was on insulin therapy it was always quite difficult to talk with Mister Forrestal, quite difficult because we had been instructed to try to stay away from things that were on therapy and for a man like Forrestal you couldn't very well talk to him about the flowers and bees because he was not interested in them. I felt he was showing continually more interest in outside activities but, as I said, in the beginning the way I looked at it I felt sure things were going on in discussion with Doctor Raines probably I didn't know about but which were indications that the man was improving considerably.

Dr. Deen's impressions, as we see, are almost the same as Dr. Hightower's. Each perceived, without being very specific about it, that Forrestal was depressed, but that he was getting better. They knew from experience and training that depressed people sometimes commit suicide, but it is clear that Dr. Raines, as he said, did not share with either of them anything of substance about any actual suicidal tendencies in this patient. Both say that they conferred with Dr. Raines, but virtually nothing of what he told the board seems to have made it to these two primary-care physicians. One must wonder why not.

One thing in all the doctors' testimony to this point suggests that Forrestal might, indeed, have some psychological problem, drug-induced or not. There could not have been a man alive more interested in the world around him and, specifically of the welfare of his country than James V. Forrestal. His correspondence from 1948 alone requires five boxes for storage at the Seeley G. Mudd Library at Princeton University, and the 932 names of the list of his correspondents read like a who's who of power, money, and influence on public opinion. Winston Churchill, Bernard Baruch, Omar Bradley, Dwight D. Eisenhower, Thomas E. Dewey, W. Averell Harriman, Henry J. Heinz, Vincent Astor, Lammot DuPont, William J. Donovan, Edward R. Murrow, Estes Kefauver, Eugene Meyer, Nelson Rockefeller, John D. Rockefeller, Jr., Drew Pearson, Henry R. Luce, Walter P. Reuther, Francis Cardinal Spellman, Robert A. Taft, William S. Paley, and Frank Wisner, are just a few of the names that appear. No one had a more imposing Rolodex. Yet he comes across from the testimony of these doctors as someone who was difficult to talk to and had little interest in his surroundings. We know that he was deeply troubled about many things that were going on in the government of which he was a part. His candor and forthrightness about his concerns were what got him on the bad side of so many powerful and unscrupulous people in the first place. Forrestal would have sounded more like himself if one of these politically unsophisticated medical men had said that he sounded paranoid, rather than that he was a difficult person to carry on a conversation with.

The Man, Not Just the Patient

That brings us to Captain Stephen M. Smith, the last of Forrestal's psychiatrists to testify and the one person with whom Dr. Raines said he shared Forrestal's suicidal ruminations. It is noticeable from examining the nurse's log that, although Dr. Raines might have spent more total hours with Forrestal, Dr. Smith seemed to have visited him more frequently. From the excerpts of his testimony that we will give here, the reader can judge who got to know the patient better and who gave a more candid assessment of his condition. (The patience of the reader is begged at this point. Dr. Smith is articulate, but he is also verbose, given to big words and long sentences.)

> Q. Captain, will you please tell the board what you know relative to the treatment of the late Mister Forrestal?
> A. Perhaps I should begin by saying that the treatment was directed by Captain George Raines who is the chief of the neuropsychiatric service and my role was supportive to his therapeutic endeavors and consultive at any time when it was deemed necessary and advisable. I first met Mister Forrestal on the day of his admission to the hospital which, I believe, was April second and subsequently saw him almost daily until May eighteenth at which time I left on authorized leave and didn't return until after his demise. Through Doctor Raines and through my daily conversation with the patient I acquired some degree of familiarity with the emotional state which was responsible for his hospitalization. I found him to be a very cooperative patient and at all times quite willing to accept opinions concerning his illness and an expressed willingness on his part to avail himself of all the benefits which might be derived from his hospitalization here and the psychotherapeutic therapy which might be instituted. In the nature of our handling of his psychotherapeutic therapy it was an arrangement between Doctor Raines and myself that he would control all the therapeutic measures although I can sincerely state that we compared opinions almost daily, particularly in regard to the reactions of the patient and their import. Inasmuch as it is considered good psychiatric practice to avoid confliction and confusion in treatment, especially as it pertains to the interpretation of psychodynamics, that this rests entirely in the hands of one individual. As a result of this arrangement my discussions with Mister Forrestal were on a less personal level than would accrue from therapeutic endeavors. However, these conversations had a degree of intimacy and resulted in the establishment of a rapport with Mister Forrestal that I always interpreted as being friendly and comfortable. We talked of many diverse matters that had only a casual relationship to his illness as he was a man who not only was mentally alert but continued to maintain an active interest in all current matters on a level compatible with his broad public service and wide experience. These conversations ran a gamut from a discussion of matters of purely local interest to various philosophies and ruminations that touched on the behavior patterns of all people under various circumstances of stress and his astuteness and acumen were such that his comments and discourses were pregnant with comprehensive significance. As indicated

previously, the matter of discussion of the more intimate aspects of his personal problems was left for his interviews with Doctor Raines. This Mister Forrestal and I both understood; that this was the arrangement and for that reason our tendency was to stay on less disturbing subjects. My interviews with him usually would last from fifteen or twenty minutes to perhaps an hour. In evaluating the course of his illness as I observed it he apparently was showing a continuous improvement with moderate fluctuations which were not incompatible with the type of emotional disturbance which he showed. He was acutely aware of his depressed state of mind and at times (illegible) interpretation of his own reaction to his predicament and (illegible) which might have led up to it although he not infrequently mentioned impending disaster. They were always of vague and non-specific character and had to do with matters which had been of paramount interest to him, namely, the safety of the country. Many times he expressed uneasiness about the future possibilities and windered (sic) whether or not people were as alert to these potentialities as they should be. Each time he would reassure himself by such assertions as, "I really have no uneasiness about the future of the country, I am certain that that is assured. But the travail might be easier if people were perhaps more concerned about some of these things." We talked frequently of his recovery and the possible change in his pattern of living which would be possible with more leisure and greater opportunity for diversification of interest and a release from the tremendous pressure which his duties had imposed on him over the previous eight or nine years. He himself offered the opinion that he should have sensed that his burden had become too heavy many months previously and should have done something to correct it. He regretted that he hadn't done so. Incidentally, he, on several occasions in connection with this type of thinking had offered the opinion that all men highly placed in public life should be more concerned about their emotional health and even perhaps come to a better understanding of the benefits which would result from a more profound knowledge of the emotional concomitant of continuous tension and strain. Inasmuch as he was a man who suffered with a depression and an interpretation of his own predicament through depressive eyes the matter of his recovery or non-recovery was discussed, even including self-destruction. *He, at all times, denied any preoccupation with such thoughts* and even though his construction of the future possibilities as they affected him were nebulous he not only agreed but frequently volunteered that he was certain that he would be able to reach a level of adjustment which would bring him greater happiness, especially through more intimate contacts with his family from whom he had felt somewhat separated because of the pressure of work and also because of the opportunities for less hurried and constructive endeavors which his new freedom would permit (emphasis added). He was actively interested in sports and had participated in them to a considerable extent when he was younger, following the various sporting events, not deeply but enough to be fully informed about them. He was interested in his-

> tory, especially, and enjoyed discussions that pertained to historical backgrounds of various situations from the time of Alexander the Great on up to the present and often wove a very interesting course into the fabric of his conversation pertaining to these historical and philosophical backgrounds and would draw comparisons and analogies with recent happenings.

Dr. Smith goes on in this vein for another page or so, describing a patient who was "rather heavily sedated" in the first week but exhibited substantial improvement and was generally able to sleep without sedation after a few weeks. Several marathon sentences later Dr. Smith volunteers, "At no time did I ever hear him express any uncertainty that he would not recover nor did I ever hear him express any threat to destroy himself."

To make a long story short, something of which Dr. Smith is utterly incapable, the James Forrestal described here is the old familiar conscientious, public-spirited, learned and capable man whose tombstone bears the inscription, "In the great cause of good government." One can easily imagine that, true to their sometimes-misguided profession, it was usually the psychiatrists who steered the conversation around to what was wrong with James Forrestal. The patient, demonstrating mental health that was in important ways superior to that of his custodians, wanted to talk about what was wrong with the country. From what we can read in the surviving, published portions of his diaries and from his well-known public positions, Forrestal had demonstrated that he had a better grip on reality than almost anyone in the country. And if Dr. Smith were the only psychiatrist whose report we were able to read, we would have to conclude that Forrestal was not the least bit suicidal.

Whether it was because he was not giving the responses that were expected of him or because their eyes were glazing over, the board members had very few questions for Dr. Smith. The last person who might have vouched for Dr. Raines ended up vouching for hardly anything at all that Dr. Raines had to say about Forrestal's suicidal tendencies, and like the contradiction between the photographs showing a bed without even sheets on it and the description that Nurse Turner gave, the board members just let it pass.

Providing a tremendous reinforcement to this analysis of Dr. Smith as a strong dissenter from the expressed view of Dr. Raines that Forrestal was suicidal—or perhaps that he was in need of psychiatric help at all—is the unpublished manuscript of John Osborne. Recall that it is from Osborne that Hoopes and Brinkley made the attendant, Edward Prise, into the major supporter of the suicide claim, which we now know from his daughter's email and the hiding of his real name is probably the opposite of the truth. Osborne wrote that the doctor "second in rank and authority to the psychiatrist in charge of the case believed throughout its course that Forrestal was wrongly diagnosed and treated. But he also thought that Forrestal was recovering despite the treatment..."[126]

Osborne does not name him, but that doctor was Stephen Smith. It goes without saying that Hoopes and Brinkley chose to ignore that passage.

Another Look at Rogow

Recall now that without any source for his assertion Arnold Rogow wrote, and Hoopes and Brinkley repeated, that late on the night of May 21 Forrestal had informed the unnamed Navy corpsman on duty that he didn't want any artificial sleep aid because he planned to stay up late and read and that when the corpsman looked into the room at about 1:45 Forrestal was busy copying from that precisely described book of poetry. He then provides the 17 lines of the depressing Sophocles poem that he got from Walter Millis, telling us that Forrestal stopped after having written the "night" part of the word "nightingale" and went across the hall and tried to hang himself out of the kitchen window.[127]

Now we can see why Rogow provides no reference for any of this. It appears that he has made it all up In his effort to persuade us that Forrestal was moved by morbid lines from "The Chorus from Ajax" to stop

[126] John Osborne Collection, Library of Congress.

[127] Rogow, pp. 17-18.

his copying suddenly and go kill himself in a less-than-sudden, peculiar fashion, Rogow has told us a lot of things that are not supported by the official record. If Forrestal actually transcribed those lines, it was before Corpsman Harrison came on duty, because the room was dark the whole time he was on the job. None of the Navy officials would even speculate about the dressing-gown cord being tied to the radiator, though Dr. Raines strongly suggests that Forrestal must have tried to hang himself from something. It's an open question as to whether the poem transcriber even made it to the 26th line, the one with "nightingale" in it. A single page is included with the exhibits provided to us. It looks as though the page is torn at the bottom and the photocopier might have cut off a little of the bottom as well, but it's hard to believe that it would have cut off 11 lines. Only the first 15 lines of the poem are on the page.

Rogow's very unspecific and un-referenced assertion that Forrestal "made at least one suicide attempt" at Hobe Sound also looks pretty shaky in light of the testimony of Captains Raines and Smith.[128] Even more outrageously wrong was the assertion of the very influential columnist and radio commentator, Drew Pearson, that Forrestal had made four attempts to kill himself, three times while at Hobe Sound and once at Bethesda Naval Hospital.[129] Also called into serious question is the claim by the politically connected Wall Street journalist Eliot Janeway to biographer Douglas Brinkley that Ferdinand Eberstadt had told him privately that Forrestal had made one suicide attempt at Hobe Sound.

The report of the Willcutts Review Board reveals additional misinformation in Arnold Rogow's frequently cited book. Consider the following Rogow passage:

> In the spring of 1949 Forrestal also had evidence that he was not *persona non grata* to all Jews and Jewish organizations. Although he declined to be present, he was invited in February to attend a celebration at one of Washington's Reformed Jewish Temples. When his resignation was announced in March, he received a letter commending him for his past

[128] Ibid., p. 6.
[129] Ibid., pp. 32-33.

> services and expressing regret from Myer Dorfman, National Commander of the Jewish War Veterans. Many persons of Jewish extraction, during his stay at Bethesda, wired or wrote him expressing their hopes for an early recovery, and several added that his anti-Zionist position had by no means concealed or confused his great service to the country as our first Secretary of Defense.
>
> Forrestal, *of course,* never received these messages, and in any case it was then too late to relieve by ordinary means the guilts, fears, doubts, and anxieties that had precipitated his illness. However history may ultimately judge his opposition to the establishment of Israel, by 1949 it was clear that Forrestal was, in a sense, one of the casualties of the diplomatic warfare that had led to the creation of the Jewish state (emphasis added).[130]

Notice how, in a few lines, Forrestal is shown to have become such a basket case that he couldn't even be allowed to read his mail, and the suggestion is made that he should have been wracked with guilt over the courageous, principled, and patriotic position he took—along with virtually all the Middle East experts in the United States government—against U.S. sponsorship of a new, ethnic-supremacist, essentially European country in the heart of historically Arab territory. But we see from the testimony of Captain Raines what Rogow would have us believe was a self-evident fact was not true:

> From the very first Mister Forrestal's mail and other communications were handed to him unopened. He was allowed to see all of them on the theory no one can live in a vacuum and might just as well be exposed to whatever came along; that is the method of dealing with it; it would depend on how well he was or how sick he was. It was as simple as that. Actually he dealt quite well with almost everything.

Rogow's diagnosis of paranoia is not only undercut by the testimony of all the doctors at Bethesda, but also by a telling footnote on page 181 in his own book. First, we have the passage to which the note applies:

> Finally, [Forrestal's position on Palestine] encouraged suspicion in both gentile and Jewish circles that Forrestal personally was not merely anti-Zionist but anti-Semitic. Nor should it be overlooked that one consequence of these suspicions was that Forrestal, during his last months in office, harbored a conviction that he was under day-and-night surveil-

---

[130] Ibid., pp. 194-195.

> lance by Zionist agents; and when he resigned as Secretary of Defense in March, 1949, he was convinced that his resignation was not unrelated to pressures brought to bear on the Administration by American Jewish organizations.

Now here's the footnote:

> While these beliefs reflect the fact that Forrestal was a very ill man in March, 1949, it is entirely possible that he was "shadowed" by Zionist agents in 1947 and 1948. A close associate of his at the time recalls that at the height of the Palestine controversy, his (the associate's) official limousine was followed to and from his office by a blue sedan containing two men. When the police were notified and the sedan apprehended, it was discovered that the two men were photographers employed by a Zionist organization. They explained to the police that they had hoped to obtain photographs of the limousine's occupant entering or leaving an Arab embassy in order to demonstrate that the official involved was in close contact with Arab representatives.

So, in all likelihood, the conviction that Forrestal harbored that he was under constant surveillance was correct. And as we saw in Chapter One, intimidation and blackmail were among the uses to which such surveillance was intended. Naturally, Rogow takes the culprits' explanation at face value, putting the best possible face on it. He also conceals the name of the shadowed Forrestal associate, preventing the inquiring reader from learning even more damning information from that source. He also fails to give us the name of the guilty Zionist organization.

Missing Witnesses

As noted previously, only Navy personnel were called before the Willcutts Review Board as witnesses, and, even so, a couple of important ones were overlooked. First, and obviously, there is Admiral Morton Willcutts himself, although calling him would have been pointless if he were to receive the same deferential treatment afforded to Admiral Stone. He had eaten dinner with Forrestal on Friday before the fateful next night, and according to published reports he had described the patient as in very good shape and excellent spirits. As a medical man, his opinion as to Forrestal's emotional condition would have been worth something. More importantly, he could have answered questions about the larger picture had the board been inclined to ask them. What role, if any, did the White House and non-medical considerations play in Forrestal's hospitalization and treatment? Upon what legal authority was the private citizen Forrestal put up in the Bethesda Naval Hospital in the first place?

Admiral Willcutts also showed up at the hospital very early on that fateful, May 22 morning, and as the commander of the National Naval Medical Center, he was the officer in charge. Everything that was done from the moment he arrived, and maybe even from the moment he was notified of the death by telephone was his responsibility. He was the one for the board to ask about the laundering of Forrestal's room and the delay in photographing it and about any determinations that might have been made about fingerprints, the broken glass, and the cord around Forrestal's neck.

Along with Admirals Willcutts and Stone, there was a third important Admiral who arrived at the death scene shortly after Forrestal's plunge. That is Surgeon General of the Navy Clifford A. Swanson. He was important not for what he might have observed that night, though, but for what he might have learned from Forrestal early in the hospitalization.

From the Nurse's Notes of 10:00 a.m., April 3, the first full day Forrestal was at Bethesda, we find this: "Pt. Asked to see Adm. Swanson; Dr. Smith notified. Pt. states "It is of the utmost importance for the Navy." Slightly agitated. Five minutes later we see that he was given sodium amytal, but that he is "still asking to see Adm. Swanson."

At 10:10 we have this notation: "Pt. seen by Dr. Raines @ this time.

The next notation is at 10:40: "Pt. sleeping very soundly."

Admiral Swanson did arrive to see the patient at 1700 hours that same day, however. It would be very interesting, indeed, to know what they talked about. The nurse's notes also record several subsequent visits by Admiral Swanson, and his name appears among the Princeton library list of the 932 people who corresponded with Forrestal in 1948. He was apparently among the very few old associates who visited Forrestal while he was at Bethesda, and his observations, if candid, might have been very revealing.

There are also a number of non-Navy people among the missing witnesses. First, there is Forrestal's wife, Josephine. The nurse's notes reveal that she was her husband's most frequent visitor from outside. Although their marriage was apparently a troubled one, she would have known the man better than anyone and likely could have provided great insight into her husband's psychological condition. We learn from Rogow's book, as noted in Chaper One, that Forrestal's life insurance policy would not pay in cases of suicide and that through her lawyer she claimed that the death was accidental. Had she meekly accepted that her husband committed suicide, the press would certainly have trumpeted it, as they did with Vincent Foster's widow. The fact that they didn't suggests strongly that she no more believed that Forrestal committed suicide than did that even more important missing witness among his relatives, older brother Henry.

In Chapter One we heard, through the author Cornell Simpson, Henry's bitter denunciation of the government and the press and his claim that when he visited his brother late in the latter's stay at Bethesda that he was as normal and healthy as he had ever been. We also hear that he was planning to arrive that Sunday and take his brother away from the hospital. Did he arrive in Washington that day? Are the claims in the Simpson book true? The nurse's notes confirm Henry's one late visit to Bethesda some days before his brother's death, but, otherwise, he is not mentioned. At one point in his testimony, recall, Dr. Raines says that he thinks Forrestal would have needed *only* one more month at the hospital to be completely cured, as though he knew nothing of the brother's plans to take him away forthwith.

Not everyone who visited Forrestal got noted in the nurse's notes. One such person, who two of the testifying doctors tell us visited on the afternoon of Forrestal's last day was his personal financial manager, Paul Strieffler. So close was he to Forrestal that, along with his former secretary, Strieffler was the only non-family member to be bequeathed money in Forrestal's will. The author, Rogow, tells us that he received $10,000, a substantial sum in 1949.[131] Might not important information have been gleaned from learning what Forrestal and Strieffler talked about hours before Forrestal's death? Was he making plans like a man who fully expected to be around for quite a few more years? How normal and healthy did Forrestal appear to this long-time associate, whom Forrestal had mentioned in 1933 Congressional testimony as advising him on some questionable investments when he was president of the Wall Street investment banking firm of Dillon, Read.[132]

Another person that the Willcutts Review Board should have questioned is Dr. F. J. Broschart, the Montgomery County, Md., medical examiner. We learn from the Monday, May 23, newspapers that Dr. Broschart declared the death a suicide on Sunday. This is not the only politically charged case in which a government doctor has made a suicide ruling. Enron executive, Clifford Baxter, and former National Security executive, Gus Weiss, come to mind, but it cannot be stressed too strongly that a doctor does not have either the training or the resources to determine, alone, whether a death is the result of suicide, an accident, or of foul play. He might be able to determine the medical cause of death with an autopsy—although in this case Broschart was not even the autopsy doctor—but he cannot tell us who caused the death. This is a police matter. The police are supposed to treat all violent deaths as homicides until they have examined all the circumstances surrounding the death sufficiently to rule out that possibility. Dr. Broschart should have been sum-

[131] Ibid., p. 46.
[132] Ibid., pp. 83-85.

moned by the board and asked on what basis he made his suicide determination. Why did he do it so hastily? How could he possibly know that Forrestal was not thrown from the window? Was he aware of the broken glass in Forrestal's room? How could he know for sure that Forrestal had not been rendered unconscious by one means or another before he took his long plunge?

After we received the Willcutts Report, the name of another prime candidate for interviewing by the Willcutts board came to light. The revelation was in a June 20, 2004, *Washington Post* article on the United Press Washington correspondent, Ruth Gmeiner. She was eulogized as the first woman reporter to cover the Supreme Court, among other accomplishments. Here are the closing lines of that article:

> The night of the Gridiron Club dinner in 1949, [UP] news editor [Julius] Frandsen was alerted to get out to Bethesda Naval Hospital. He left an after-dinner party and picked up Gmeiner, his reporter, on the way. While he and other journalists hollered for information outside the hospital, Gmeiner sweet-talked her way into the 16th-floor room of former secretary of defense James V. Forrestal and found, next to his bed, a book of poetry open to Sophocles' "Ajax," (sic) which includes the lines:
>
> *When reason's day*
> *Sets rayless–joyless–quenched in cold decay*
> *Better to die, and sleep*
> *The never-waking sleep, than linger on*
> *And dare to live when the soul's life is gone.*
>
> Her soon to be husband [the editor Frandsen] made that the first paragraph in Gmeiner's story on Forrestal's suicide.

If the story is true it solves the mystery of who it was that discovered the book of poetry in Forrestal's room. The Willcutts review board, recall, failed to identify that person, and apparently made no attempt to do so. I made a telephone call to the writer of the article, Patricia Sullivan, who revealed that her source for this information was Gmeiner's family. To her knowledge, she said, the story that Gmeiner got into Forrestal's room and discovered the book had never before been published. She said that she had looked up the UP story on Forrestal's death and the allegation was accurate, that is, that those poetry lines led off the story, not that Gmeiner, herself, had found the book.

It would have been an extraordinarily unorthodox way to begin a newspaper report, and Sullivan's claim sent the author to the library to check it out. The claim is interesting, as well, because the lines quoted are toward the end of the poem and are not among the part repeated by the mainstream authors Millis, Rogow, and Hoopes and Brinkley, because they were not included in the alleged Forrestal transcription (Notice that there is no claim in the *Post* story that Gmeiner also found the transcription.).

The UP story revealing the death that the author found appears with a Washington, May 22, dateline in the morning *San Francisco Chronicle.* It starts like this:

> Former Defense Secretary James Forrestal committed suicide by jumping from the 16th floor of Bethesda, Md. Naval Hospital early today. He had been reading classical Greek poems keyed to the theme of death.

Farther down in the article the reporter gives us the lines that appear in the *Post* article, telling us that they appear shortly after the section that Forrestal had transcribed, that is, the first 26 lines, ending after the "night" portion of "nightingale" had been written.

Interestingly, Gmeiner's son, Jon Frandsen, a Washington journalist whom I called on July 26, 2004, was unaware that there was any transcript involved in the story. As the story had been related to him by his parents, Gmeiner actually brought the book back downstairs and showed it to her editor, the elder Frandsen, whom she would marry some years later. It was he, they told their son, who first recognized the significance of the quoted lines. Jon also volunteered to me what I had already discovered, that is, that *The Post*'s Sullivan had stretched the truth a bit in saying that the lines actually led off the story.

The Synthesis of News

If Gmeiner was, indeed, the poetry book discoverer, she seems to have failed to get anything resembling a scoop on UP's competitors with her intrepid action, a fact that surprised the younger Frandsen when I told him by telephone. Here's how the Associated Press article that appeared in the May 23 *Philadelphia Inquirer* begins:

> Former Secretary of Defense James Forrestal committed suicide today, plunging from a high hospital window.
>
> In his room he left a book of Greek poetry, a page opened to a quotation saying "when reason's day sets rayless–joyless–quenched in cold decay, better to die and sleep."

You'd think that Gmeiner was writing for the AP rather than for the UP, because this beginning accords even more closely to what was reported in *The Post* article than does the UP-article's beginning. Both, like *The New York Times* and *The Washington Post* and every other journalist who covered the story, use the Sophocles poem to promote heavily the suicide conclusion, not to mention the fact that they all say in a matter of fact manner that it was suicide, not even using the hedging adjective, "apparent," that we saw in the Vincent Foster case.

Two slightly different story lines emerge from careful inspection, however. The reports that were submitted earliest, apparently, emphasize the book open to the page with the morbid poem. They quote these later lines of the poem, the ones seen in the recent *Post* article, leading the reader to conclude that Forrestal had surely been reading this poem and had taken the "better to die" suggestion to heart. That's what we see in the *Los Angeles Times* AP story and in the *Chicago Tribune* story written by their reporter, Robert Young (who also wrote, with no evidence presented: "He was reported to have made at least two previous attempts to kill himself."). They make no mention of any transcription of part of the poem having been discovered as well.

The stories apparently written later, but also published in the May 23 morning newspapers, reveal that Forrestal had been actually copying "The Chorus from Ajax," stopping after "night" in the word "nightingale." At the same time, with the exception of *The New York Times*, they continue to emphasize in the first part of their stories the later lines, the ones that were not copied but seem to encourage suicide more strongly. By the time the book writers, Millis, Rogow, and Hoopes and Brinkley got around to it, all mention of the later lines had been dropped.

The addition to the story seems to have confused the reporters and editors at *The Washington Post*. Here is what they have to say a few paragraphs from the start of a front-page article:

> From a book of verse found lying open on a radiator beside his bed he had copied several verses of Sophocles' "Chorus from Ajax." In firm and legible handwriting these lines stood out:
>
> "When Reason's day sets rayless–joyless–quenched in cold decay, better to die, and sleep the never-ending sleep than linger on, and dare to live, when the soul's life is gone."

In an accompanying article, on the continuation page, they reprint the entire poem with the transcribed part, they say, in italics. The italics duly end with the first syllable of "nightingale," well before the lines appear that they had elsewhere told us stood out "in firm and legible handwriting."

The writer of the first article would have the reader believe that he was looking at the transcription as he wrote, so detailed was the description, but clearly, he wasn't, or he could never have made such a blunder.

This raises anew the question of where the story of the discovery of the transcription—and the open poetry book as well—originated. None of the newspapers attribute it to anyone with the Navy or even explicitly to an anonymous source. They just somehow know that it was "found" (It is highly unlikely that it was, as *The Post* says, lying open on a radiator "beside the bed." As we see from the photograph in the frontispiece, the nearest radiator is more than an arm's length from the bed and it is rather narrow and rounded at the top. Rogow has it more plausibly on the nightstand, at the other side of the bed.).

The mystery of the poetry transcription deepens when we consider the actual page that was included with the medical records in the Willcutts Report, the one that Dr. Raines said looked like it was written in Forrestal's handwriting. As noted previously, only the first 15 lines of the poem are there. Furthermore, as we see in the frontispiece, they include five lines cut off by the ellipsis after "yawning grave."

If what we have been provided with our FOIA request is all there is, and all there ever was, then the part about Forrestal ending his transcription in the middle of the word "nightingale," was made up out of whole cloth by someone. Upon making this discovery, we wrote the Judge Advocate General's Office of the Navy on June 8, 2004, asking them if what I was sent is all there is to the transcription, noting that the newspapers talked of 26 lines. Never receiving a response, we must assume that what we have is the full transcription and all the newspaper reports were wrong (hardly an unprecedented development).

Nightingale

If, in fact, the "nightingale" line was never in the transcription that was "found" by someone, and maybe even if it was, what with the growing emphasis placed upon it, the line might have some significance that has been overlooked up to this point. Hoopes and Brinkley, citing John Loftus as their source for the speculation, make much of the fact that "Nightingale" was the name of a secret group of Ukrainian refugees who had been recruited by the CIA in the post-war period to conduct a covert war behind the Iron Curtain, and that as a member of the National Security Council, Forrestal had been among those authorizing the action. The problem with that, from the perspective of Loftus, who also co-authored *The Secret War against the Jews: How Western Espionage Betrayed the Jewish People,* was that many of the members of the Nightingale force had been collaborators with the Nazis during World War II and, in that capacity, were guilty of a number of atrocities against the Jews in the Ukraine. Hoopes and Brinkley don't come right out and say it, but their reason for bringing it up seems to be to suggest that Forrestal might have been overcome by a sudden rush of guilt upon reaching that word in his writing, prompting him to dash out and take the poet Housman's admonition, derived from Sophocles, quite literally.

Now we have seen from the testimony of Forrestal's guard that well more than an hour had passed since Forrestal had done any reading or writing, so it couldn't have happened that way, and it is highly doubtful that the fiercely anti-Communist Forrestal ever felt the slightest pang of guilt over America's use of Ukrainian refugees, whatever their personal history, to undermine the Soviet Union.

But there is extremely bad blood between many Christian nationalists in the Ukraine and organized Jewry. The Jewish Virtual Library reports that since the fall of the Soviet Union, 80% of Ukraine's Jews have left the country. This is a truly remarkable exodus, taking place, as it has, in little more than two decades. That same Jewish web site states, "Many Ukrainian citizens still distrust Ukrainian Jews and believe that the Jews' primary loyalty is to the Jewish people and not to the Ukrainian nation."[133] "Nightingale" may not have been a particularly meaningful word to Forrestal, but it would have been heavily freighted with meaning to Forrestal's enemies in the Jewish community. Loftus, in his *Secret War* book, seems to be very closely in touch with that aggrieved group and cites many covert sources among them for the information in his book. Maybe with the "nightingale" emphasis, they mean to send the message that Forrestal's destruction and death represents the settling of an old score for them. Perhaps Arnold Rogow knew more than he told when he characterized Forrestal as a casualty of the creation of the state of Israel.

Truman Blackmailed?

In Chapter One we argued that President Harry Truman would have been too compromised by his affiliation with the Kansas City political

---

[133] Jewish Virtual Library, Ukraine Virtual Jewish History Tour, https://www.jewishvirtuallibrary.org/ukraine-virtual-jewish-history-tour.

machine of Tom Pendergast to have stood in the way of any foul play directed toward Forrestal. If Truman could have been blackmailed to look the other way while Forrestal was murdered, though, he could just as easily have been blackmailed to pursue policies that put the interests of Israel ahead of those of the United States. If Zionist leader David Ben-Gurion would employ blackmail against Nelson Rockefeller to get him to use his influence on Latin American leaders for United Nations votes, as the connected, pro-Zionist authors, John Loftus and Mark Aarons claim, why wouldn't he use it for the much bigger prize of the support of the United States? It would have been relatively easy, with the great influence over the press that the Zionists wielded. That, rather than his pursuit of the Jewish vote for the Democrats, would explain why Truman overruled his entire foreign policy establishment to recognize the new state of Israel.

Two 21st century books on the Mafia give us an appreciation of how easy it would have been to blackmail Truman over some of the things Truman would have had to have done as one owing his livelihood and career to Pendergast. From Thomas Reppetto's *American Mafia*, we have this:

> Missouri boss Tom Pendergast ran up impressive city and state totals for the party while his administration did business with Charlie Corallo, boss of the Kansas City underworld. Gambling ran wide open, nude waitresses served lunch in the 12th Street dives, and drug and prostitution rings flourished. As [U.S. Treasury investigator] Elmer Irey noted, "You could buy all the morphine or heroin you could lift in Kansas City; and the man who wanted to keep his job as a police captain...had better keep his prostitute file correct and up-to-the-minute so Tom's machine would be certain that no girl practiced her ancient art without paying full tribute."
>
> Pendergast's machine made the career of Harry Truman. During World War I, farmboy Truman had commanded a field artillery battery in France that was full of tough kids from Kansas City who hit it off with their captain. After the war Truman opened a haberdashery shop in Kansas City. When it went bankrupt, his friends persuaded the machine to elect him county judge, an administrative post equivalent to county supervisor in other jurisdictions. Though personally honest, Truman

> had to hire some patronage employees whom he later described as "no account sons of bitches."[134]

It's hard to see what's "personally honest" about knowingly putting likely criminals in responsible positions in the government—and who knows what else—at the behest of a mob boss.

This latter term for Pendergast is used advisedly. Gus Russo describes the first national meeting of the country's major crime lords that took place at the Hotel President in Atlantic City, New Jersey, May 13-16, 1929:

> Present were Albert Anastasia, Dutch Schultz, Louis Lepke, Frank Costello, Lucky Luciano, Longy Zwillner, Moe Dalitz, Ben "Bugsy" Siegel, and Al Capone.
>
> "Of particular note was the presence of the notorious Kansas City machine politician Tom Pendergast, the sponsor of Harry Truman, future president of the United States."[135]

Russo could well be mistaken that Pendergast, himself, actually attended the conference. John William Tuohy reports that he sent his right-hand man, Johnny Lazia, which seems more likely, but that hardly changes the fact that Harry Truman's mentor, the man to whom he owed his entire political career, was a big-time mobster.[136]

Secret Testimonials

Obviously, after all the witnesses had been heard and the exhibits collected, someone in authority realized that the Willcutts review board had not made anything like a persuasive case that Forrestal had killed himself or that the Navy had acted properly either in the care and protection

---

[134] Thomas Reppetto, *American Mafia: A History of Its Rise to Power*. Holt Paperbacks, 2004, pp. 194-195.

[135] Gus Russo, *The Outfit: The Role of Chicago's Underworld in the Shaping of Modern America*, Bloomsbury Publishing, 2001, p. 41.

[136] John William Tuohy, "The Meet: The Origins of the Mob and the Atlantic City Conference," March 2002, Rick Parrello's American Mafia.com, http://www.americanmafia.com/Feature_Articles_194.html.

of Forrestal or in the investigation of his death. Something more had to be done.

What that something turned out to be was the solicitation of endorsements from the prominent psychiatric community. The voice of authority had to be substituted for what anyone with adequate critical faculties could see for himself. The two short letters supporting Dr. Raines by Dr. William Menninger, President of the American Psychiatric Association and Professor of Psychiatry, Raymond W. Waggoner, M.D., of the University of Michigan, sent from Montreal on May 25 where they continued to attend the annual ASA convention, which were included among the exhibits, were apparently deemed to be insufficient. So the first thing one encounters upon opening the Willcutts file are letters of praise for the clearly inadequate work of the review board from three more psychiatrists. The first one is dated September 19, 1949, and it is from the superintendent of the federal mental hospital in Washington, DC, Dr. Winfred Overholser. After a recitation of credentials, the letter states:

> I have read carefully the report of the very thorough inquiry conducted by a Board of Investigation convened at the United States Naval Hospital, Bethesda, Maryland, on May 23, 1949 to investigate and report upon the circumstances attending the death of Mr. James V. Forrestal at that hospital on May 22, 1949.
>
> From a study of the report, it is my opinion that Mr. James V. Forrestal came to his death by suicide while in a state of mental depression. It is my further opinion that the care and treatment given to Mr. Forrestal during his stay at the Naval Hospital were entirely in accord with modern psychiatric principles, and that his death was not due to the negligence, fault, intent, or inefficiency of any of the physicians, nurses, or ward personnel concerned in his care.

The second endorsement is addressed to Rear Admiral G. L. Russell, Judge Advocate General of the Navy (the same office that furnished the Willcutts Review Board report to the author) and is dated September 13, 1949. It is from Dr. John C. Whitehorn, Johns Hopkins Hospital, Baltimore, Maryland. It begins:

> The proceedings and findings of the board of investigation in the case of the late Mister James V. Forrestal, with accompanying exhibits, were delivered to me by Lt. Cmdr. Kelly this morning.
>
> In a telephone conversation yesterday you asked me to study this material and to express my professional opinion on two essential points of psychiatric principle and practice involved.

The two points boil down to whether it is a good idea to ease up on the restrictions on a psychiatric patient like Forrestal in due time and whether that time had arrived in Forrestal's case. Dr. Whitehorn's concluding paragraph was surely everything they could have wanted from him:

> There are risks, therefore, of one kind or another, in the making of every such decision. In the case of so distinguished a person as Mister Forrestal, there would have been much incentive to follow the more conservative, restrictive regime. Dr. Raines' decisions displayed courage in the application of psychiatric principles to provide the best chances for good recovery. For this he should be commended.

So, after a quick once-over of the investigation, Dr. Whitehorn concluded that his fellow psychiatrist was not negligent, he was courageous.

The third endorsement was from the Chairman of the Department of the School of Medicine of the University of Pennsylvania, Edward A. Strecker, who was also a professor of psychiatry there. He claimed as well to have studied the proceedings of the investigation and he endorsed it, but his endorsement was couched quite conservatively. He stated only that his "considered opinion is in complete accord" with "The Findings of Facts," the review board's conclusions, the ones that were finally released on October 11 and buried away in the back pages of the nation's newspapers. Then, to make sure that there was no misunderstanding, he summarized them to conclude his letter:

> (1) The identification of the body of Mr. James V. Forrestal;
>
> (2) The approximate date of the death of Mr. Forrestal and the medical cause of death;
>
> (3) The review of the behavior of the deceased during his residence in the Bethesda Naval Hospital, and the diagnosis of the mental condition as "mental depression;"

(4) The review of the treatment and precautions in the treatment of Mr. Forrestal, and an opinion that "they were within the area of accepted psychiatric practice and commensurate with the evident status of the patient at all times";

(5) That in no manner was the death of Mr. Forrestal due to "intent, fault, negligence or inefficiency of any person or persons in the Naval Service or connected therewith".

This belated effort to lend much needed credibility to the review board's work by soliciting endorsements by prominent psychiatrists is not without its comic aspects. Anyone responding that either the care and treatment of Forrestal or the investigation of his death was faulty could have been assured that his writings would never see the light of day, and it could certainly could not have been good for that person's career. As it turned out, though, the testimonials did not see the light of day for another 55 years. They became, in effect, secret testimonials.

Spreading the Willcutts Report Around

Beginning in early August 2004, we sent the following e-mail message to a number of organizations:

> To whom it may concern:
>
> Through the Freedom of Information Act, I have obtained the report of the review board convened on May 23, 1949, by Admiral Morton Willcutts, Commander of the National Naval Medical Center, to investigate the death of former Secretary of Defense James Forrestal. The report had been secret for some 55 years. Exhibits accompany it, and there are no redactions in the text. The report reveals a number of glaring inaccuracies in the accounts of Forrestal's death by biographers Arnold Rogow and Townsend Hoopes and Douglas Brinkley. It also reveals that there was broken glass on Forrestal's bed and on the carpet at the foot of his bed and that his room had been well "laundered" before the crime scene photographs were taken several hours after his fatal fall.
>
> I have had all the materials, including photographs and my transmission letter from the Navy's Judge Advocate General's office, put on a compact disc, which I would like to mail to you. If you are interested in

receiving these materials and would give them due publicity, I would appreciate your letting me know.

Sincerely,

David Martin

Those organizations were as follows:

The Harry S. Truman Library
The Seeley G. Mudd Manuscript Library, Princeton, N.J., which houses the Forrestal papers.
The Library of Congress
The John Birch Society
The Eisenhower Center at the University of New Orleans, which was headed by Douglas Brinkley at the time.
The Ludwig von Mises Center
The Cato Institute
The Howland Library in Beacon, New York, James Forrestal's hometown.

The representative of the Mudd Library, immediately recognizing the document's historical significance, responded enthusiastically and was sent a copy of the long-suppressed report. He then pleasantly surprised us by putting the entire report up on the library's web site.[137]

Even though no one there responded to the e-mail, the Library of Congress does now have a copy of the Willcutts Report because on August 19, 2004, we personally presented the CD to the head of the U.S. Acquisitions Section of the Anglo-American Division of the library. My e-mail had clearly never reached the people at that level. Like the representative of the Mudd Library at Princeton, he and his assistant easily understood how important the document was, and they appeared to be quite pleased to get it.

Larry Greenley, director of research for the John Birch Society, responded positively on August 25, apologizing that my original e-mail had become buried in the volume of correspondence that they get. He concluded, however, "I can't promise that we'll publicize the Forrestal mate-

[137] https://findingaids.princeton.edu/collections/MC051/c04531.

rials, or if we do, how much; that is up to the editorial staff and others." I wonder who the others might be.

On Wednesday, September 8, 2004, we attended a lecture in Washington, DC, by David Eisenhower on the presidential library system. Our purpose was to publicize my Forrestal work with a question for Dr. Eisenhower relating my experiences, both good and bad, with the Truman Library. As it turned out, the head of the Truman Library was present, and we presented him with a copy of the CD. It felt like we were serving a summons.

We also gave one to Dr. Eisenhower, the well-known grandson of President Dwight D. Eisenhower and Senior Fellow at the Annenberg School of Communication at the University of Pennsylvania. In a personal discussion afterward, he volunteered that his grandfather was "tasked [by Truman] to push Forrestal out." His tone of voice hardly matched his words, but then, realizing his *faux pas,* he clarified that he meant "out of office," not "out the window." In our initial shock and then our amusement we failed to ask for further clarification of why the retired General Eisenhower might have been chosen for such a job and how he would have been expected to accomplish it. We know of nothing on the official record or in the historical literature connecting Eisenhower to Forrestal's dismissal as Defense Secretary.

CHAPTER 5

Handwriting Drives Last Nail in Cover-Up Coffin

Pravda on the Potomac

Our press supports our liberty,
We proudly like to boast,
But the stark reality
Is in The Washington Post.

On May 23, 1999, *The Washington Post* marked the 50th anniversary of James V. Forrestal.'s death with a lead cover article in its Style section. "The Fall of James Forrestal," it was titled, with *The Post's* typical inappropriately cutesy word-play, and the subtitle was as follows: "When America's first secretary of defense dove from a 16th-floor window at Bethesda Naval Hospital precisely half a century ago, he left a poem, a mystery, and 50 years to understand what he'd been trying to tell us."

A half-century later, we see, *The Post* was still playing up the transcribed poem angle for all it was worth, though we now know that the official investigators made nothing of it whatever. They also seemed to have forgotten about that cord around Forrestal's neck, which had forced them to speculate that he must have been trying to hang himself out of the window rather than diving through it. Here is how the 1999 *Post* article, written by Alexander Wooley, begins:

> His hand moved across the paper, copying Greek poetry from a thick anthology. Then, abruptly, mid-sentence, it stopped. He slipped the paper inside the book and set it aside. His room was on the 16th floor of the towering Bethesda Naval Hospital. It was 2 a.m. Sunday, 50 years ago. Exactly 50 years ago yesterday. His name was James Vincent Forrestal....
>
> For one who had lived in great wealth, his hospital room was simply furnished—a narrow bed, a straight-back chair, an Oriental carpet on the floor, a rotating fan on the wall by a closed window. Closed and locked. Three windows in the room, all securely locked.
>
> He went across the corridor to a small lab-like kitchen, with locked filing drawers, white tile walls, stainless steel and glass cabinets. There, above a radiator, an open window. He pulled out a screen, stepped onto the sill, leaped into the void.
>
> Later, after they found him broken, 13 floors below on a low roof, they searched his room for clues to his last moments. There was the book, "An Anthology of World Poetry," still open to an excerpt from Sophocles' "Ajax," (sic) still containing the paper on which he'd copied the poet's words:
>
> "'Woe, woe!' will be the cry—no quiet murmur like the tremulous wail Of the lone bird, the querulous nightingale," he'd begun, stopping short, in mid-word, "Night—"he wrote. Then jumped out a window.

And this is how the 50th anniversary *Post* article, some 70 paragraphs later, ends:

> The date was now May 22, Sunday, the day of [Drew] Pearson's weekly broadcast, which had become so agitating to Forrestal.
>
> Forrestal was reading the poetry anthology, and began to copy from "Chorus From Ajax" on Pages 277 and 278. He stopped after the first syllable of the word "nightingale" and—apparently during the guard's five-minute break—walked out of his room, across a hall, into the adjoining kitchen. He took off the sash from his robe and tied one end to the radiator under the window, the other end around his neck, undid a screen and climbed out the window.

According to the coroner's report, Forrestal likely then jumped out the window and hung for some seconds suspended. The report also notes scuff marks on the cement work underneath the window, indicating reflexive kicking, or possibly terrified second thoughts. To no avail: The sash gave way and Forrestal fell 13 floors, landing on an asphalt-and-crushed stone surface of a third-floor passageway roof. Death was instant.

The coroner noted that the sash was still wound tightly around his neck. The front of his skull was crushed, his abdomen slit, and his lower left leg severed. The report notes that his watch was still running.

Last Words

Why would a man about to kill himself copy an ancient Greek poem, but not complete it? Was there any connection between the words he copied and his last, desperate act? Hoopes and Brinkley believe that more than mere chance might be at play. They note that after the end of World War II, the National Security Council authorized the recruitment of members of former Ukrainian death squads, who had worked for the Nazis exterminating Jews and Red Army supporters, to work clandestinely within the Soviet Union assassinating communists. The name of the group was Nachtigall, or Nightingale. Ironically, while one wing of the CIA was secretly bringing Nightingale's leaders to the United States to train them, another wing of the agency was in Europe working to bring them to trial in Nuremberg. The secret program, which Forrestal almost undoubtedly helped bring about, failed, however. The biographers postulate that Forrestal, in his unsedated state, may have felt a shock of guilt—or, given his reds-under-the-bed delusions, paranoia—that may have triggered suicide.

But perhaps there is another, less strained connection between Sophocles' verse and Forrestal's tragic end. Perhaps the key was in the verse that immediately followed the one containing the word "nightingale," the verse Forrestal could not bring himself to copy:

Oh! When the pride of Graecia's noblest race
Wanders, as now, in darkness and disgrace,
When Reason's day,
Sets rayless—joyless—quenched in cold decay,
Better to die, and sleep
The never-ending sleep, than linger on.
And dare to live, when the soul's life is gone.

The problem with all this, we now know, is that it is completely made up. Someone else did the poem transcription. Captain Raines, whose credibility was brought into question by many of his other statements, as we saw in the previous chapter, was simply wrong when he said that the handwriting on the poem written on brown paper looked like Forrestal's. It doesn't look the least bit like Forrestal's handwriting, which we can see in the samples in the frontispiece.

One hardly needs an expert to tell him that the person who transcribed the poem is not the same person who wrote the various letters there that Forrestal is known to have written. The most obvious difference is that Forrestal writes his words and letters almost straight up and down, while the poem transcriber writes with a more conventional consistent lean to the right. Forrestal, on the other hand, is more conventional in how he writes his small r's, making either a single hump or an almost imperceptible double peak, while the transcriber has a very distinctive exaggerated first peak in almost every one he makes. The transcriber is a very conventional "archer" in the manner in which he makes his small m's and n's. Forrestal, on the other hand, is a typical "swagger," sagging down between peaks, as opposed to rounding over arches.

What's most amazing is the complete brazenness on display. One can truly say that the transcription of "Chorus from Ajax" is not a forgery. Not the slightest effort was made to mimic James Forrestal's handwriting. The perpetrators must have been completely confident that no attempt would be made by the Navy to authenticate the note, and, in fact, that no question would even be raised either by the press or by anyone with a public forum as to the authenticity of the handwriting in the transcription.

Now that the cat is so thoroughly and obviously out of the bag, one would have anticipated that there would have been one last, desperate effort to put it back in. It would not have been at all surprising for someone to claim that what was sent to me in response to the Freedom of Information Act request was not the actual transcription written by Forrestal, but a facsimile, obviously written by someone else. That has not happened. Instead, the press has gone with Number One of the Seventeen Techniques for Truth Suppression.[138] It has dummied up, pretending that there has never been any such revelation.

After all, the transcription was right there in Exhibit Three along with the nurse's notes, just as it was when Dr. Raines examined it and volunteered to the Willcutts Review Board that it looked like Forrestal's handwriting. Just as Raines was the only person at Bethesda Naval Hospital to testify that Forrestal was suicidal at any time, he was also the only one there, or anywhere else, to say that the handwriting in the transcription looked like Forrestal's.

But was *The Post's* reporter Wooley writing in good faith? After all, all the newspapers and books, with the exception of the obscure Cornell Simpson, had said that the transcription was Forrestal's work. There is some evidence in his article that he was not. Have another look at the second paragraph of his article. Notice the precise detail with which he describes Forrestal's room and the kitchen across the hall. To our recollection, those rooms were not described in such detail in contemporary news reports. Neither was there any such gruesome description of Forrestal's broken body. The latter is doubtless what one would have seen in the photographs that weren't sent to me—and likely a cord around the neck that would have never reached the radiator—and the former is what one sees in the photographs that we have.

It looks very much like the Willcutts Report, while secret to the general public, was shared with the Jewish-owned secret government adjunct known as *The Washington Post*. If Wooley had the photographs, he would have seen the broken glass on the Oriental rug in one of them, and he would have seen the big contradiction between the witness testimony and what those photographs show, but sharing such information was not part of the agenda.

He would also have had the poem transcription. He wouldn't even have had to go to the trouble that we did to find a hand-written memo-

---

138 David Martin, "Seventeen Techniques for Truth Suppression," http://dcdave.com/article3/991228.html.

randum for comparison purposes. One look at Forrestal's signature is sufficient to see that Forrestal didn't do that transcription. Walter Millis begins his 1951 book, *The Forrestal Diaries*, with 12 pages of photographs. The final page is a full-page formal portrait photograph of Forrestal with his signature beneath it.

We might be inclined to give *The Post* the benefit of the doubt on whether it had access to the Willcutts Report, but for its abysmal record in this case and other such high-level cases. Recall from the previous chapter that they loved those last lines of the poem so much that they wrote that they stood out in "firm and legible handwriting" in Forrestal's transcription, when those words actually come several lines later than what they and the other newspapers say Forrestal copied. *The Post* was also in the very forefront in selling the story that Deputy White House Counsel Vincent W. Foster, Jr., of the Bill Clinton administration killed himself.[139]

The Pentagon Book

Any such benefit of the doubt for *The Post* on the Forrestal case should have been gone by 2007, three years after the Willcutts Report had been released to the public. I had publicized its revelations on my web site, including the fact that the poem transcription was clearly not in Forrestal's hand, the Seeley Mudd Manuscript Library of Princeton University put the long-suppressed report on its web site, and even the Wikipedia page on Forrestal made mention of it. That was the year that *Washington Post* Pentagon correspondent, Steve Vogel, came out with *The Pentagon: A History.*

Since Forrestal was the first secretary of defense to preside over the Pentagon, Vogel had to write about him, and writing about him meant also writing about his untimely demise. It also meant, predictably enough, that he would write the same tired old, now provable, lies. Vogel happened to have a book presentation at a bookstore near me shortly

[139] See David Martin, "America's Dreyfus: The Case of the Death of Vincent Foster," http://www.dcdave.com/article1/961127.htm.

after the book's release, and I used the occasion in the question and answer period to point out his inaccuracies. Noting that in his presentation he had talked of tracking down a couple of people who worked on the Pentagon and interviewing them, I suggested that in the process of correcting his errors he might perform a real service by tracking down possible surviving witnesses on the 16th floor of the Bethesda Naval Hospital the night that Forrestal went out the window, particularly Hospital Apprentice Robert Wayne Harrison.

Vogel showed not the slightest interest and demonstrated an almost Bill Murray sort of boredom at having his errors about Forrestal's last hours pointed out to him and the gathered audience. "That was not what the book was mainly about," was how he dismissed the whole matter.

To make sure that he understood the full gravity of his falsehoods about Forrestal's death, I was moved to write him a letter as a follow-up. At this point we must request the reader's indulgence in reading things that already have appeared in the book. It is repeated, as it will be done several times throughout the work so readers can see precisely what facts have been given to various influential people, facts that they have all scrupulously kept to themselves:

> Dear Mr. Vogel,
>
> Since you managed to brush me off rather effectively at your book presentation at the Bailey's Crossroads Borders last Wednesday night (June 13), I would like to take this opportunity to state, in detail, what is not true in your account of the death of our first Defense Secretary, James Forrestal. Here is what you wrote in your recently published book, *The Pentagon: A History*:
>
>> On the night of May 21, Forrestal stayed up late reading. A Navy corpsman stationed outside his room looked in on Forrestal around 1:45 A.M. and found him writing on sheets of hospital paper, copying a poem from a red leather-bound anthology of world poetry. About 3 A.M., while the corpsman was on an errand--possibly sent by Forrestal himself--the former defense secretary left his room and slipped across the corridor to a kitchen. Forrestal removed the unsecured screen from the window and tied one end of his bathrobe sash around a radiator below the window and the

other end around his neck. He climbed out the window and was perhaps suspended for a few moments before the sash slipped off the radiator. The soaring granite tower conceived by Franklin Roosevelt and built by John McShain nearly a decade earlier proved to be more than an adequate platform for Forrestal to end his life. His broken body was discovered on the roof of a third-floor passageway connecting to another wing of the hospital.

On the bedside table in Forrestal's room, his book was found open to the poem he had been copying, "The Chorus from Ajax" by Sophocles. It included these lines:

When Reason's day
Sets rayless—joyless—quenched in cold decay,
Better to die, and sleep
The never-waking sleep, than linger on
And dare to live, when the soul's life is gone.[140]

Your account is almost completely consistent with the very first news accounts of Forrestal's death, even down to the quoting of the lines of poetry that were not part of the hand-written transcription that was said to have been found in Forrestal's room along with the book. However, none of the newspapers reported that Forrestal's Navy guard, hospital apprentice Robert Wayne Harrison, actually saw him copying the poem. That was reported for the first time by the author Arnold Rogow, whom you give as one of your two sources, in his 1963 book, *James Forrestal, A Study of Personality, Politics, and Policy*. Your other source, *Driven Patriot, the Life and Times of James Forrestal*, by Townsend Hoopes and Douglas Brinkley, also says that the guard witnessed Forrestal copying the poem, but their source is Rogow. Rogow, however, has no source, and he could not have a source, because we now know that what he wrote is simply not true. I should think that it would bother you that you have repeated Rogow's fabrication. (You also must have more sources than the two you supplied, because neither of them quotes the lines of the poem that you do.)

Mr. Rogow probably thought that his lie would never be discovered because at the time of his writing the report of the official investigation of Forrestal's death had remained secret for over a decade and would remain secret for more than four more decades until I was able to obtain a copy through the Freedom of Information Act in the spring of 2004. I provided a copy to the Seeley Mudd Manuscript Library of Princeton University, which houses Forrestal's papers, and they put the entire document on their web site in the fall of 2004, where it has been ever since. They also sent out a press release announcing that they had put up this important document that had not seen daylight for 55 years.

---

[140] Steve Vogel, *The Pentagon: A History*, Random House, 2007, p. 350.

Unfortunately—though not surprisingly—this important news was not reported by any mainstream press organs. Its significance was recognized, however, by the History News Network of George Mason University, which did announce the availability, at long last, of the official report on Forrestal's death and by the web site, Secrecy News. Since you cover the Pentagon for *The Washington Post*, I would say that there is a very high likelihood that the Princeton press release passed across your desk.

Here is the exchange between members of the panel of the review board convened by Admiral Morton D. Willcutts, the head of the National Naval Medical Center, and Hospital Apprentice Robert Wayne Harrison, who came on duty at 11:45 on the night of May 21, 1949:

Q. At what time did you last see Mister Forrestal?
A. It was one forty-five, sir.

Q. Where was he then?
A. He was in his bed, apparently sleeping.

Q. Where were you at that time?
A. I was in the room when I saw him.

Q. Did you leave the room at that time?
A. Yes, sir, I did.

Q. Where did you go?
A. I went out to the nurse's desk to write in the chart, Mister Forrestal's chart.

Q. Were the lights on in Mister Forrestal's room when you took over the watch - the overhead lights?
A. No, sir, not the overhead lights; just the night light.

Q. Did Mister Forrestal do any reading?
A. Not while I was on watch, sir.

So much for your assertion that the hospital attendant saw Forrestal transcribing a poem from a book shortly before he went out the window (That would be 2 A.M., not 3 A.M. as you mistakenly have it.). So much, as well, for your speculation that the attendant might have been sent on an errand by Forrestal.

Why is this important? Those who want to convince us that Forrestal took his own life would have us believe that he was so suddenly moved by the rationale for suicide in the poem that he rushed out and killed himself—though he was not in such a rush as to just jump out the 16th floor window, but, curiously, in the little time he had before the attendant would return, went to the trouble to hang himself out of the window by a belt that might not have been long enough for the job.

But don't we have the book open to the page and the transcription of the poem? Maybe he copied the poem earlier in the evening and the suicide was just a delayed reaction, you might argue.

First, there's a problem with the book. In the Willcuts review board's investigation, the book never enters into evidence. Since it is absent entirely, no one is identified who might have found it. One can look at the "crime scene" photographs taken of Forrestal's room, and there's no book, either on the table beside his bed, as you have it, or on the nearby radiator, as some other accounts have it. There is, however, broken glass on the carpet at the foot of Forrestal's bed, and the nurse who first saw Forrestal's fully lighted empty room testified that she saw broken glass on the bed.[141] These apparent signs of a struggle are hard facts that have been reported only on my web site, as opposed to the gossamer about Forrestal copying a morbid poem that you in the mainstream press have woven.

Gossamer? But we have the transcription in Forrestal's very own handwriting, I can hear you protest.

There's a big problem with the transcription, though. It was never examined by anyone for handwriting authenticity, and if you have a look at it, along with a number of examples of Forrestal's writing_obtained from the Truman Library you can see why it was not authenticated.[142] It's clearly not authentic. It wouldn't be right to call it a forgery, because no effort was made even to attempt to copy Forrestal's distinctive writing style.

So where does that leave you as an author who has written something about a matter of great importance that is patently untrue—that you should have known was untrue? Fortunately, you're not just an author, but a reporter for one of the world's most powerful newspapers, and the Forrestal story is on your beat. It's not too late for you to set the record straight.

I'm sure you will understand why I am not at all optimistic, however, that your employer will permit you to redeem yourself, whatever your personal inclination might be. What is far more likely, I'm sure you will agree, is that they will continue in this as in other important matters

---

141 At this point I linked to http://www.dcdave.com/article4/040916.htm, which has the photographs we see in the frontispiece.

142 A link was given to http://www.dcdave.com/article4/040916.htm, where the photographs seen in the frontispiece can be found.

> with what author Rodric Braithwaite, in describing Soviet movies of the late Stalin era, calls "their breathtaking disdain for historical truth, [making] them feel almost greasy to the touch."[143]

My prediction was, of course, accurate. I heard nothing from Vogel, and the publisher came out with a paperback edition the next year with the same old untruths in it. In the meantime, I have ended my *Washington Post* subscription; the newspaper was beginning to give me the same feeling that those Soviet movies gave to Braithwaite.

---

143 Rodric Braithwaite, *Moscow 1941: A City and its People at War*, Alfred A. Knopf, 2006, p. 284.

CHAPTER 6

Britain's Forrestal

Irgun Murder Plots

Re: Forrestal and Bevin,
I can tell you this:
For Menachem Begin,
It was hit and miss.

Imagine this scenario: A powerful, radical Middle Eastern movement, with a record of terrorism, decides to embark upon a program of bombings and assassinations of high government officials in the home territory of a major Western power. The plot is to be carried out by five teams infiltrated into the Western country, and the primary target is the leading government minister opposing the actions and the aspirations of the radical group.

As luck would have it, the secret service of the Western country discovers the plot, and the terrorist movement has to fall back to a plan of sending 20 letter bombs to various government officers, including the aforementioned leading opponent of the terrorists as well as his predecessor. The letter bombs also fail to reach their intended targets.

What would the Western power do in response to these bombing and assassination attempts? You would be right if you answered that it would keep quiet about them for sixty years. In the meantime, it would be a party to giving the terrorist group everything it hoped to get, and more, from the failed assassination. It would even help the terrorists to develop their own nuclear weapons.

The scenario is not fanciful. According to British intelligence documents declassified in 2006, it actually happened. The targeted official was British Foreign Minister, Ernest Bevin. His targeted predecessor was Anthony Eden. The terrorists were the Zionist gang *Irgun Tsvai Leumi*, or *Irgun*, for short. Its leader at the time of the assassination attempts in 1946, before the state of Israel had been carved out of Palestine, was Menachem Begin. Begin would later become Israel's Prime Minister and would be awarded the Nobel Prize for peace in 1978 for the agreement that he would reach with Egypt's president, Anwar Sadat, known as the Camp David peace accords.

The intelligence documents were declassified in early March of 2006. The assassination attempts occurred in 1946 and 1947; the supplying of plutonium to Israel by Britain first occurred in 1966, but it had supplied heavy water, another nuclear weapons ingredient, in the 1950s. *The Times* of London reported on the failed assassinations on March 5, and the BBC reported on the illegal nuclear assistance on March 9.[144]

These shocking, extraordinarily important new revelations shed a lot of light upon what we have virtually proved to be the assassination of America's first Secretary of Defense, James Forrestal. The parallels in

---

[144] Curiously, *The Times* took the article down from its web site after only one week. It is preserved on the Internet, though, by Information Clearing House at http://www.informationclearinghouse.info/article12205.htm.
The BBC still has its article up at
http://www.bbc.co.uk/pressoffice/pressreleases/stories/2006/03_march/09/israel.shtml. The story was not completely new in 2006. The *Sydney Morning Herald* in Australia had a short, sketchy article about the letter bomb part of the plot in 1947, attributing it to the Stern Gang. See
https://trove.nla.gov.au/newspaper/article/18029698.

the government careers of Bevin and Forrestal are great. Although Bevin came up through the labor movement and was a member of the opposition Labor Party, Tory Prime Minister Winston Churchill had made him his Labor Secretary during World War II. In that capacity, he played a key role in mobilizing Britain's economy for the war.

As noted previously, Forrestal was a Wall Street investment banker whom Franklin Roosevelt made Under Secretary of the Navy. A tireless worker, Forrestal was the key liaison person between the Roosevelt administration and the private industrial sector, and he was largely responsible for the transformation of the economy from production for consumption to production for the war effort.

When the Labor Party won a majority after the war, Bevin was appointed foreign secretary in the new government. Forrestal had been elevated to Secretary of the Navy when the previous Secretary died near the end of the war. He continued in that position when Harry Truman replaced Roosevelt upon the latter's death in 1945. When the National Security Act of 1947 consolidated the armed services, Truman made Forrestal the first Secretary of Defense.

Though both men were very popular and both were very successful in their government careers, each suffered major setbacks over the issue of the creation of a state for Jews in the territory of Palestine. The Labor Party, heavily influenced by its Jewish members, when out of power during the war actually favored expulsion of the Arab population of Palestine to clear the way for a Jewish state. As Foreign Minister of the new Labor government, Bevin, repulsed by Zionist terrorist actions directed at British military and government officials in Palestine, steered the British government toward a position more heavily favoring the rights of the Arab residents of the region. In doing so, he made himself British public enemy number one of the Zionists.

Also, as we have previously noted, Forrestal was enemy number one of the Zionists in the United States. Near the end of Chapter One we told of the December 4, 1948, letter to *The New York Times* signed by a number of prominent Jews, including Albert Einstein, warning the American public about Menachem Begin and his terrorist organization upon Begin's visit to the United States. At the conclusion of the letter recounting the Begin organization's murderous activities, we asked this question, "Would men like Menachem Begin and his followers have hesitated at assassinating the most popular, outspoken, and powerful critic of the nascent state of Israel in the United States if given the opportunity?"

How apt that question was has now been made manifest! Since 2006, we now know that they had no compunction against assassinating Forrestal's precursor and counterpart in Britain. The main difference seems to be that the powers that be in Britain did not give them the opportunity, while those in the United States did. Maybe that is a measure of the relative power of the Zionists in the two countries. The federal government and the organs for molding public opinion were penetrated at the very top in the United States by the most extreme and violent elements of the Zionist movement, and they continue to be so, or, at least, effectively so.[145]

That is not to say that the Zionists are exactly weak in Britain. Official Britain hardly reacted with appropriate fury at the outrage. Rather, the country sat on information about the attempted assassination, and soon fell into line behind the United States in its pro-Israel policies. It even got a bit ahead of the United States over the nuclear weapons issue, as we have noted, and also during the Eisenhower administration when the British, the French, and the Israelis attempted a power grab known as the Suez Crisis.

The release of the news of the outrage of the attempted Bevin assassination was, in fact, extremely timid. A search of the Internet some three weeks after the initial revelation showed only one other major newspaper in the world picking up on the story, the *Sydney Morning*

---

[145] See John Mearsheimer and Stephen Walt, "The Israel Lobby," *London Review of Books,* March 23, 2006, pp. 3-12. https://www.lrb.co.uk/v28/n06/john-mearsheimer/the-israel-lobby.

Herald in Australia.[146] It had a slightly different version of events, though, claiming that it was the Stern gang, rather than Irgun, that planned the assassinations, though both stories are ostensibly based upon the same release of British intelligence documents. *The Times*, itself, has barely squeaked out the news. When I telephoned the newspaper, attempting to locate the reporter of the story, Peter Day, the person I talked to was unable to find Day in their directory, nor could he find the article in the hard copy of the March 5 *Times*. The online version of the story lists no page number. The folks at *The Times* foreign desk, with whom I was then connected, were familiar with the story, which the first contact person was not, but they did not know Mr. Day. They were able to confirm only that he was not one of their own regular reporters. Later I would learn that, curiously enough, his regular place of employment was with the *Telegraph*. Maybe the publishers of *The Times* had some second thoughts about what they did in letting this news out. It seems that the article never appeared in the newspaper's hard copy, and as of April 5, 2006, the article could no longer be found on its web site., either.

The veritable radioactivity of the subject would explain, as well, the complete blackout of this news by the mainstream news organs of the United States. The news suppression is of a piece with the complete failure of the U.S. press to report that the long secret report on the investigation of Forrestal's death was finally made public in 2004. The Seeley Mudd Manuscript Library of Princeton University even sent out a press release, and the online History News Network of George Mason University made mention of it, but the mainstream press made certain that this very important news, like the news of the attempted assassination of Britain's foreign minister, never reached the attention of the general public.

---

146 "Telegram told of plot to kill MPs," *Sydney Morning Herald*, March 7, 2006. https://www.smh.com.au/world/telegram-told-of-plot-to-kill-mps-20060307-gdn3mr.html.

That the American press should vigorously suppress this news should hardly surprise us. As we see throughout the book, they were a very active party in selling the story that the far-sighted statesman, Forrestal, the man who saw better than anyone where America's Middle East policy was leading it, ended his own life. The last thing such a press would want would be for the public to learn of the existence of powerful evidence that undermines the suicide thesis, and worse, points the finger of blame at Zionist terrorists.

The complete suppression of the news of Irgun's assassination attempt on Foreign Minister Bevin for all these many years is almost as important as the attempt, itself. Imagine how much stronger that 1948 *New York Times* warning letter by Albert Einstein and a number of other prominent American Jews about the murderous proclivities of Menachem Begin and company could have been had they known about Begin's previous attempt on the life of Bevin. In all likelihood, no such warning letter would have even been needed. If Begin had been known to have attempted to kill Britain's most powerful opponent when Britain was the power over Palestine, he and his organization would certainly have been regarded as a similar threat to Forrestal when the United States had become the main controller of Palestine's destiny.

Actually, three years prior to the shocking story in the *Times*, Peter Day had co-authored a piece in London's *Telegraph* with essentially the same revelations, and a bit more, that got even less attention than the *Times* article did. Probably by coincidence, it came out 54 years to the day after James Forrestal's death, May 22, 2003. The article is about an ambitious bombing campaign involving both Irgun and the Stern Gang that MI5 got wind of. Bevin was to be a primary target:

> Security Service files also contain details of an outlandish plan by the followers of an American Zionist rabbi to bomb London from the air. Details of that plot have been heavily censored.
>
> The warnings came in 1946 from James Robertson, head of the Security Service's Middle East Section.

> He wrote:" The Stern group has been steadily recruiting in recent months and may now number 600 followers, most of whom are desperate men and women who count their own lives cheap.
>
> "In recent months it has been reported that they have been training selected members for the purpose of assassinating a prominent British personality. Special reference has been several times made to Mr Bevin."
>
> The plot to bomb the capital from the air was said to be the product of followers of one Rabbi Korff...
>
> Robertson identified Menachem Begin, the future Israeli prime minister, as leader of the 5,000-strong Irgun.
>
> Bevin was a hated figure among all the Jewish groups trying to establish a homeland, arguing that Jews needed to be re-assimilated into the nations of Europe in the aftermath of the Holocaust. He accused the United States of encouraging illegal migration to Palestine in contravention of British quotas.[147]

But what's this about a Jewish terrorist plot to bomb London from the air? Could this have been real? Yes, it was. "Plot to bomb London was thwarted by heroic pilot," reads the headline in an article in the July 13, 2014, edition of Britain's *Birmingham Post,* another newspaper story that seems not to have gotten around at all. It was of interest to the people of Birmingham, because the man whom Rabbi Korff enlisted for the bombing job—who also promptly turned him in—was a native of that city. His family had emigrated to the United States and he had become a decorated pilot in World War II in the U.S. Army Air Force:

> A new book has revealed the astonishing story of how an ex-Spitfire pilot from Birmingham foiled an international plot to firebomb London.
>
> The year was 1947 – and in war-weary Britain the rubble from years of Nazi air raids and rocket attacks was still being cleared away.

---

[147] *The Telegraph*, unlike *The Times*, has not taken its article down from the Internet, at least, as of this writing. See https://www.telegraph.co.uk/news/1430766/Jewish-groups-plotted-to-kill-Bevin.html.

But across the English Channel a group of fanatical terrorists were planning a new aerial blitz on the capital.

Members of the radical Zionist terror group the Stern Gang had decided to drop improvised bombs on the Foreign Office in Whitehall as part of their fight for a homeland.

The full details of the extraordinary plot and the heroic Spitfire pilot from Birmingham who helped foil it have now been revealed by American Middle East expert Alison Weir in her new book about the tangled history of US-Israeli political relations, *Against Our Better Judgment*.

"When Britain failed to accede to Zionist demands, an American rabbi named Baruch Korff fomented a plan to drop incendiary bombs on London," she revealed.

In the summer of 1947 Ukrainian-born Korff, a passionate supporter of the creation of a Jewish State, travelled from his home in Boston and made contact with members of the Stern Gang in Paris.

The Jewish militant group was at the time waging a brutal terrorist campaign against British forces which were in control in Palestine, in an attempt to force the Government to pull out of the territory.

Korff proposed hiring a civil aircraft in France and using it to scatter propaganda leaflets over London, following this up by dropping six home-made bombs on the city.

MI5 documents released in 2003 confirmed there was "A project for an air raid on London, in the course of which leaflets were to be dropped in the name of the Stern Gang, together with high-explosive bombs".

But the full details of the planned aerial attack have only now emerged in Weir's book.

In late August 1947, Korff approached Reginald Gilbert, a decorated 25-year-old World War II veteran, who flew Spitfires in the US Army Air Force (USAAF) during the war. At the time was studying at the University of Paris, and offered him a large cash sum to fly the plane on its bombing mission over London...

Gilbert pretended to accept Korff's offer but immediately after their meeting went to the French police, who warned the British Embassy of the Stern Gang's plot. MI5 then became involved, persuading Gilbert to play along with their plan.

On the evening of September 6, as Gilbert, Korff and a female Stern Gang member, Hungarian Judith Rosenberger, climbed aboard the aircraft at Toussus-le-Noble airfield near Versailles – which, ironically, had

> been used by the Luftwaffe to bomb England during the Blitz – French police officers disguised as ground crew drew their pistols and arrested Korff and Rosenberger.
>
> In two suitcases carried by Korff were found thousands of propaganda leaflets demanding that the British Government withdraw its forces from Palestine.
>
> Gilbert was secretly flown to an RAF base in England and placed in protective custody by Special Branch.
>
> Days later, he gave an interview to a US newspaper in which he shed more light on the Stern Gang plot, revealing that Korff had changed the target from the House of Commons to the Foreign Office building "because Korff held a grudge against that Office for refusing him a visa to Palestine".
>
> The young pilot also disclosed that, when he pointed out to Korff fog could prevent him finding the target, the rabbi told him to drop the bombs anywhere over London, brushing aside Gilbert's concerns that innocent civilians would be killed.
>
> "They are British," Gilbert recalled Korff telling him, "so they are our enemy."
>
> In the days following Korff's arrest 10 other members of the gang were rounded up by the French police and the explosive devices to be used in the raid – contained in six fire extinguishers – were discovered in a Parisian apartment...[148]

Notice that the writer of the *Birmingham Post* article, which carries no byline, seemed to be unaware that at least the bare essentials of the story had been reported by the *Telegraph* eleven years before, another indicator that the *Telegraph* story had no legs.[149]

---

148 https://www.birminghampost.co.uk/news/local-news/plot-bomb-london-thwarted-heroic-7411721.

149 The story has now made it onto Rabbi Korff's Wikipedia page. One will even find some expression of outrage toward the good rabbi: "Korff became an active supporter of Richard Nixon, despite Nixon's known anti-Semitism." His attempted mass murder in London, on the other hand, has been treated with a good deal more solicitude. https://en.m.wikipedia.org/wiki/Baruch_Korff.

Who Knew?

Although it is apparent that those signers of the warning letter to *The New York Times* had no knowledge of the previous attempt on the life of Ernest Bevin or the London air raid attempt, one must wonder who, outside the ranks of British intelligence, did know about it. In particular, we have to wonder if one so connected to the higher reaches of power in the world as Bernard Baruch, when he warned his friend Forrestal in February of 1949 that he had already become too identified with opposition to Israel for his own good, knew more than he was telling about the danger that Forrestal faced. And when Forrestal complained about being followed and bugged, did he know that the Irgun crowd had come pretty close to snuffing out the life of his British counterpart? Could such knowledge have been behind his resistance to commitment to Bethesda Naval Hospital and his reported claim that he would never leave the hospital alive when he attempted to get out of the car taking him there? Might that have been the revelation from Secretary of the Air Force Symington on the day of Forrestal's departure from office that drove him into his sudden funk?

And after Forrestal's death, could there have been any doubt in the minds of those aware of the attempt on Bevin who had ultimately been behind the later crime? Might these have included those powerful friends such as Ferdinand Eberstadt and Robert Lovett, who had failed to visit him in the hospital and then, when the results of the investigation of his death were never made public, failed to register any public complaint? At the very least, those in the know included the contemporary and future leaders of Great Britain, and the knowledge that the leaders of the United States government had conspired with Zionist thugs in the assassination of the one courageous voice of reason in their midst would very likely have animated their own future Middle East policy.

One must also wonder if Forrestal and other key people in the Truman government knew about the still little-known fact that the Jewish Stern Gang actually made an assassination attempt on President Truman in 1947. They did it by sending a letter bomb to the White House, but the mail room was on alert because they knew of the previous attempt against the British officials, and they intercepted it. It seems not to have been reported by any news media at the time and biographers of Truman and other historians have kept the matter a secret even though it was reported in a book by the former head of the White House mail room in 1949 and again by Margaret Truman in her book about her father in 1972. [150]

Zionists and Communists

The Times article on the Bevin assassination attempt has one particularly intriguing passage, which might fill in some more pieces of the puzzle. That is that Britain's foreign intelligence service, MI6, believed that Menachem Begin was backed in his terrorist activities by the Soviet Union. One might wonder whether their belief was founded on solid evidence and, if so, how far this backing went. Did they just generally encourage him in his murderous endeavors, or were they actually calling the shots? If MI6 was right, then those like author Cornell Simpson who argue that the Communists killed Forrestal and those who suggest that the Zionists did it are probably both right.

The Soviets, as Simpson explains quite well, certainly had ample reasons to want to be rid of Forrestal. Not only was he the leading anti-Zionist in the Truman administration, but he was also the leading anti-Communist. Interestingly enough, the same can probably be said for Ernest Bevin in Britain's Clement Atlee administration. Bevin's anti-Communism carried a particular potency because he came from a British

---

[150] Ira R.T. Smith with Joe Alex Morris, *"Dear Mr. President..." The Story of Fifty Years in the White House Mail Room,* Julian Messner, Inc., 1949, pp. 229-230; Margaret Truman, *Harry S. Truman*, Morrow, 1973, pp. 489-490. See David Martin, "'Jews' Tried to Kill Truman in 1947, http://www.dcdave.com/article5/120510.htm.

labor movement that was heavily influenced and infiltrated by the Communists.

In many instances in the United States in the 1930s and 1940s pro-Communism and pro-Zionism could be found in the same individuals, who were also almost invariably Jewish. As we noted in the Chapter One, that appears to have been the case for the very powerful and secretive adviser to both Franklin Roosevelt and Harry Truman, David Niles.

The following passage from Alfred Lilienthal's 1953 classic *What Price Israel?* is very revealing of the person described by Alfred Steinberg in the December 24, 1949, *Saturday Evening Post* as "Truman's Mystery Man":

> There were many ways in which Niles served the State of Israel after partition, too. Early in 1950, when the United States first awoke to the Soviet danger in the Middle East, our Government requested the various Arab countries for information regarding troops, equipment, and other confidential military data. These statistics were necessary in order to plan possible assistance under the Mutual Security Act. The Arab nations were naturally assured that the figures, supplied for the Chief of Staff, would be kept secret.
>
> Late that year, military representatives of the Middle East countries and of Israel were meeting with General [W.E.] Riley, who headed the United Nations Truce Organization. Trouble had broken out over the Huleh Marshes, and charges and countercharges of military aggression were exchanged between Israel and the Arab countries. The Israeli military representative claimed that the Syrian troops were employed in a certain manner, and General Riley remarked: "That's not possible. The Syrians have no such number of troops." Whereupon the Israeli representative said, "You are wrong. Here are the actual figures of Syrian military strength and the description of troops." And he produced the confidential figures, top-secret Pentagon information. General Riley himself had not been shown the new figures given by the Syrian War Ministry to his superiors.
>
> When the question of Egyptian military strength was raised, a similar security leak appeared. It was obvious that top-secret figures had been passed on to the Israeli Government. Both the Central Intelligence Agency and the Army G-2 investigated the security breach but discovered only that these figures had been made available to the White House. How and through whom they leaked out of the White House remained forever obscure. However, the Chairman of the Joint Chiefs, General Omar Bradley, reportedly went to the President and told the Chief Executive that he would have to choose between him (Bradley)

> and Niles. Not too long after this reported intervention, David Niles resigned from his post as Executive Assistant to the President and went on a visit to Israel.[151]

And David was not alone in the Niles family when it came to serving the interests of Israel over those of the United States. An investigation in 1948 determined that his brother, Lieutenant Colonel Elliot Niles, a former high official of B'Nai B'rith, while working in the Pentagon, had turned over to the Zionist Army, Haganah, Adjutant General's Office records of the names of former officers in the U.S. Army that met Haganah's recruitment needs.[152]

With these new revelations, David Niles is due even greater scrutiny than before as the most likely coordinator of the Forrestal assassination. Some measure of Niles's power can be gained from the following passage in the oral history interview of Truman aide, Stephen J. Spingarn:

> David Niles worked with nobody. He was *sui generis*. David Niles was the oldest senior staff man in point of service. He came over from the Roosevelt administration. His titular jurisdiction was minorities. But, actually, his main job, I suppose you could say, was Jewish problems on the one hand, and the intricate politics of New York City, those two things; maintaining liaison with Dave Dubinsky and Alex Rose and the Liberal Party there, you know, and keeping the White House abreast of that. But David Niles seemed to me to pay very little attention to Negro and other minority matters, so it seemed to me. Philleo Nash was his assistant and Philleo paid a lot of attention, but it didn't seem to me that Dave paid much. And there was another interesting thing, Dave Niles did not attend the President's morning staff conferences—ever.
>
> [JERRY] HESS: Can you tell me about those morning staff conferences?
>
> SPINGARN: Yes. The President held a morning staff conference every morning at 9:30 -- I think it was 9:30. It was indispensable to a staff

---

151 Alfred Lilienthal, *What Price Israel?,* Henry Regnery Company, 1953, pp. 72-73.

152 Stephen Green, *Taking Sides: America's Secret Relations with a Militant Israel,* William Morrow and Company, Inc., p. 54.

> man -- a senior staff man -- to attend that thing, but it was a very delicate matter as to who attended. [153]

Elsewhere Spingarn makes it clear that Niles was very much a part of Truman's inner circle, so it would have been natural for him to attend these daily meetings. The impression one gets is that he was so powerful, and confident of his power, that the staff meetings were actually beneath him. He didn't have to go in order to stay on top of the issues that really mattered, and to continue to have the ear of the putative boss, President Truman. Or perhaps he realized that it wasn't all that important to have influence with Truman, when he had influence with the people who really mattered.

At this point, the observations of the son-in-law of President Franklin Roosevelt, Colonel Curtis Dall, as relayed by Henry Makow, are apropos:

> Dall maintained a family loyalty but could not avoid several disheartening conclusions in his book [*FDR: My Exploited Father-in-Law,* 1970]. He portrays the legendary president not as a leader but as a "quarterback" with little actual power. The "coaching staff" consisted of a coterie of handlers ("advisers" like Louis Howe, Bernard Baruch and Harry Hopkins) who represented the international banking cartel. For Dall, FDR ultimately was a traitor manipulated by "World Money" and motivated by conceit and personal ambition.[154]

If such a commanding politician as Franklin Roosevelt, a man widely believed to be the most powerful president the United States has ever had, was really little more than a quarterback executing plays called in by the coaching staff, what would that have made the former haberdasher and protégé of the Kansas City machine of boss Tom Pendergast? Certainly, it was not Truman's idea to have James Forrestal assassinated and very little was required of him for the assassination to be carried out and covered up. In matters such as this, the President would not have been calling the shots.

---

[153] Truman Library, Oral History Interview of Stephen J. Spingarn. https://www.trumanlibrary.org/oralhist/sping1.htm.

[154] http://www.savethemales.ca/310702.html.

Consider, finally, this entry on the "Talk" page on Wikipedia on the September 17, 1948, assassination in the new state of Israel of United Nations mediator, Count Folke Bernadotte of Sweden, by the Stern Gang (Lehi), an entry that seems no longer to be there:

> Contrary to what you say, Lehi being a terror organization is very much disputed. Most (or at least many) Israelis (myself included) do not consider Lehi to be a terrorist organization. Lehi never targeted innocent civillians [sic] in attempt to terrorize them. All of Lehi's attacks were against military or government targets (including high-ranked officials such as Bernadotte). This is very different than what "proper" terrorist organizations do - attacking random civilian targets such as busses or airplanes.
>
> Avraham Stern's memorial day is attended every year by Israeli political and government officials. Given Israel's effort to gain international support for its ongoing war against terrorism of all kinds, you wouldn't expect Israeli leaders to associate themselves with the memory of someone who led a terrorist organization. Indeed they don't - like me they believe that Lehi, while sometimes using extreme measures, was not a terrorist organization.
>
> I'm not really trying to convince you that Lehi was not a terrorist organization (you are entitled to your own opinion on that) - only that the issue is disputed. Since it is indeed so, the proper place to discuss it is on the Lehi page - rather than have it stated on every page which mentions Lehi.

This is a perfect example of the attitude toward the attempted Bevin assassination described in the aforementioned *London Times* article:

> Lord Bethell, author of The Palestine Triangle and an expert on Soviet intelligence, said Bevin was detested by Zionist groups. He added, however: "Zionists would be very angry if you compared these people with terrorists now. You have to remember that Irgun were the grandfathers of today's ruling politicians.
>
> "They would say they were at war with the British and behaved well, fighting under Marquess of Queensberry rules. They would say that they didn't target civilians."

James Forrestal, as the leading opponent in the United States government of the new state of Israel would have been regarded as anything but an "innocent civilian," and that would have made this great American patriot fair game for assassination in Zionist eyes. Hardly anything could be more incriminating of them than their own words, unless it is their known deeds.[155]

---

155 "Who used terrorism first?" Qumsiyeh: A Human Rights Web, http://qumsiyeh.org/whousedterrorismfirst/.

CHAPTER 7

James Carroll on Forrestal

Guilty Accusers

How can our press pretend to condemn
The peddlers of products illicit,
When they cover up the largest of crimes,
Making themselves complicit?

Throughout House of War, *Carroll hammers home his heavy-handed theory that Forrestal's suicide is a metaphor for the Pentagon.*
Dierdre Donahue, *USA Today*[156]

In our letter to Steve Vogel, the *Washington Post* author of the 2007 book on the Pentagon, we alluded to the press release sent out by the Princeton library announcing the availability of the Willcutts Report. Here is that document:

---

[156] May 10, 2006, https://usatoday30.usatoday.com/life/books/reviews/2006-05-10-house-of-war_x.htm.

For immediate release: November 29, 2004

Contact: Daniel J. Linke, (609) 258-6345, mudd@princeton.edu

Princeton obtains long-secret report on Forrestal's death

Willcutts Report details investigation around death of first secretary of defense

PRINCETON, N.J. – The investigation into the death of the nation's first secretary of defense, James V. Forrestal, resulted in a lengthy report long kept from the public. Admiral M. D. Willcutts, the commanding officer of the National Naval Medical Center, convened the review board that looked into James Forrestal's death in 1949. Now, more than 55 years later, the Navy has released the report, which is available electronically through Princeton University's Seeley G. Mudd Manuscript Library Web site at: http://www.princeton.edu/~mudd/.

The documents were procured by David Martin of Virginia via a Freedom of Information Act request in April 2004. Martin scanned the report and gave the files to the Mudd Library, which also included five photographs obtained through the request.

The Willcutts Report, issued in July 1949, investigated the circumstances around Forrestal's death. Forrestal, a member of Princeton's class of 1915, was a Wall Street investment banker who, on the eve of World War II, became undersecretary of the Navy. He became secretary of the Navy in 1944 and, with the passage of the National Security Act of 1947, President Harry S. Truman appointed him the first secretary of defense. He resigned in March 1949 and entered the Bethesda Naval Medical Center suffering from exhaustion similar to battle fatigue, and soon after fell to his death from a window.

The Willcutts Report supplements documents included in the James V. Forrestal Papers held at the Mudd Library, which include Forrestal's diaries. The report, along with a guide to the holdings of Forrestal's papers, may be viewed at the Mudd Library's Web site. For more information about this collection, contact the Mudd Library at (609) 258-6345 or mudd@princeton.edu.

Also, as we mentioned in our letter to Steve Vogel of *The Washington Post*, The History News Network of George Mason University, picked up on the press release and further spread the news of the belated availability of the investigation with its September-December, 2004, report.[157]

---

[157] https://historynewsnetwork.org/article/8613.

Then it was ignored. It is as though the Warren Report on the death of President John Kennedy had been withheld from the public for more than half a century and then was made public, and the entire American press and history community found the matter completely unworthy of their notice. Furthermore, historians, journalists, and other authors have continued to write about Forrestal's death as if there were no public Willcutts Report, repeating important "facts" from now-discredited secondary sources.

The first person to do so was the excommunicated leftist Catholic priest and Boston journalist, James Carroll, and he doled out the misinformation in a spectacular fashion in his tendentious 2006 book, *House of War: The Pentagon and the Disastrous Rise of U.S. Power*, in which he assigns virtually all blame for the Cold War upon warmongers in the U.S. government. Who knows if the findings of the Willcutts Report had come to his attention, because it was in his interests to ignore it. Like Loftus and Aarons, who would want us to believe that anti-Zionism is crazy, it was convenient for them to further the myth that the leading anti-Zionist in the country went crazy and killed himself, so it Is convenient for Carroll to have us believe the same thing about the government's leading anti-Communist, who was the same man, James Forrestal.

There is certainly no evidence in his book that Carroll knew anything about the fruits of our research, which included by that time most of the analysis of the Willcutts Report that we now see in Chapter Four. His sources are almost exclusively the three superseded and largely discredited books, primarily Rogow and Hoopes and Brinkley. Worse than that, he gives great prominence to the story clearly invented by prominent Leftist columnist Drew Pearson that in the throes of his breakdown Forrestal, hearing sirens late at night, had run out of his house exclaiming, "The Russians are coming." Carroll knows that that is not true, indicating in an endnote that Pearson had made a number of unverifiable and scandalous charges against Forrestal that call his credibility into question. Nevertheless, the anecdote is just too good for his malign purposes for Carroll to let go of it. A central thesis of his book is that the Cold War was a product of the paranoia centered in the Pentagon and that we never had anything to fear from the Communist menace. That the loudest voice warning of the Communist threat—which would soon manifest itself in North Korea's attempt to take over the entire country by force of arms—should be that of an insane man driven to suicide by his paranoia fits his thesis too well for him to concern himself too much with mere truth. Do I exaggerate? Here he is promoting his book on WAMU's Diane Rehm show. WAMU is a National Public Radio affiliate in Washington, DC.[158]

> **Interviewer Susan Page:** You talk about the apostolic succession. What does that mean?
>
> **Carroll:** I'm a Catholic. The apostolic succession is a phrase that refers to handing on of the power of the Church from St. Peter forward through the bishops. I use the analogy with the handing on of powers of nuclear assumptions and strategic air war and the entire dynamic toward war that's generated in the Pentagon, a succession that begins with James Forrestal who was the first Secretary of Defense. Forrestal was a man who embraced a paranoid notion of Soviet threats. He put in place... He was the single most important architect, I argue, with early American Cold War mentality. He was the sponsor of George Kennan's important "long telegram" and "Mr. X" article. He embraced a kind of quasi-religious notion of the threat from Soviet communism. He saw the world in radical good and evil terms. He was, in that sense, a Manichean. Every threat loomed so large in his imagination that he argued we had to be doubly, triply quadrupally prepared to meet it. It was under Forrestal that this terrible mindset really took hold in the Pentagon and in America. He had protégés. His first protégé was George Kennan. The equal to Kennan in those years was a young man named Paul Nitze who had come down to Washington with Forrestal from Wall Street. Nitze and Kennan became competing protégés. When Kennan, seeing what happened to Forrestal, was appalled and frightened by it, Forrestal's political paranoia had a personal aspect and he wound up committing suicide having been reported only a few days before he was institutionalized and found in the streets in his pajamas screaming, "The Russians are coming! The Russians are coming!" It seems like something out of a film but it happened. Or is reported to have happened. That's the defining moment at the beginning of a particularly

[158] The Scribe, May 1, 2006, http://prairieweather.typepad.com/the_scribe/2006/05/5106_npr_james_.html.

> paranoid mindset in American. It was carried forward by a succession of figures...

Is it possible to imagine a more dishonest human being than James Carroll? With his sentence fragment, "Or is reported to have happened," he shows that he knows that this story is not true, as he must know almost everything he passed on about Forrestal's "suicide" from those books is not true. By the year 2006, almost all serious research began with a search of the Internet, and anyone researching Forrestal's death could hardly have failed to discover the report of the Willcutts Review Board. Actually, Carroll was even more dishonest than we initially thought. Sometime after our first reading, we took another look at his endnote on "The Russians are coming" episode reported by Pearson. His basic source is page 739 of David McCullough's *Truman,* but the full McCullough quote is, "Drew Pearson reported that Forrestal was 'out of his mind' and *claimed incorrectly* that in Florida Forrestal had rushed out into the street screaming, 'The Russians are coming'." (emphasis added). Could he really have failed to notice the words that I have emphasized?

Consider, as well, how he begins his answer of the interviewer's question: "I'm a Catholic," he says. Here's what C. Joseph Doyle had to say about that in the March 2000 issue of the *Catholic World Report:*

> After abandoning his orders and his vocation, Carroll would marry outside the Church before he was laicized; he mentions in his autobiography that he thus incurred the penalty of excommunication—a fact which has not deterred him from regularly identifying himself as a member of the Catholic Church.
>
> Carroll would claim he left the priesthood because of Pope Paul VI's encyclical reaffirming traditional Catholic opposition to artificial birth control, saying the Pope was "in the grip of a savage Catholic neurosis about sex." Yet Humanae Vitae was issued in 1968, a year before Carroll was ordained. An April 1997 Boston Globe article on Carroll offered a different explanation for his decision to leave the priesthood, saying that he was unwilling to give up social activism—although he was deeply involved in social activism throughout his brief priestly career. Whatever actually motivated him to leave the priesthood, the decision evidently brought upward social mobility, in the form of a home on Boston's exclusive Beacon Hill, a summer cottage on Cape Cod, positions at

> the Boston Globe and Harvard's Kennedy School of Government, and an education for his children at the elite, historically Protestant Milton Academy. [159]

That a liar like Carroll should exhibit an affinity for the malicious utterances of a liar like Drew Pearson is only natural, one must suppose. In their testimony before the Willcutts review board, Forrestal's doctors are unanimous that he had never attempted suicide before his fatal fall, but shortly after that fall, Pearson wrote that Forrestal had made four previous suicide attempts, the latest of which had occurred right there at Bethesda Naval Hospital.

The Encounter

As luck would have it, Carroll, while in Washington on his book promotion tour, spoke at the Politics and Prose bookstore on the night of May 25. This came only a couple of days after his interview on the local Diane Rehm Show. He didn't come down quite as hard on Forrestal in his talk as he did in his interview or he does in his book, but he did allude to him as one of his "villains." He also gave us a good lead-in to our comments and question by his response to the questioner ahead of me, which had to do with nuclear proliferation. Carroll expressed his dismay at the build-up of nuclear weapons in the world and, predictably, laid the full blame on a procession of Pentagon warmongers.

I began by saying that as an opponent of the use of nuclear weapons, he was way off base to make James Forrestal a bad guy in his book. If Forrestal had been listened to when he was Secretary of the Navy, I said, we would never have committed the greatest war crime in human histo-

---

159

https://www.catholicculture.org/culture/library/view.cfm?recnum=2873. Doyle also tells us of Carroll's likely Deep State connection: "James Carroll, 57, is the son of the late Air Force Lieutenant General Joseph F. Carroll, who was the Director of the Defense Intelligence Agency, a top advisor to former Defense Secretary Robert McNamara, and a key figure in the US Air Force bombing campaign in Vietnam. Before entering the service, Joseph Carroll had been an agent in the Federal Bureau of Investigation, and a confidant of legendary FBI chief J. Edgar Hoover."

ry, the dropping of the atomic bombs on Hiroshima and Nagasaki, because a negotiated surrender would have already taken place. Furthermore, there would have been no Korean War, because the surrender would have taken place before the Russians entered the war against the Japanese and they wouldn't have had the chance to grab half of Korea. That was Forrestal's primary interest in hastening the surrender of the Japanese, who knew that they were thoroughly defeated by the end of 1944.

Knowing from experience that moderator Barbara Meade was poised to cut me off by demanding that I ask a question or sit down, I then asked this: "On the matter of Forrestal's death, why would you rely exclusively on three books, one of which was published by the John Birch Society over a pseudonym and none of which has any direct evidence from anyone who was on Forrestal's floor of the hospital around about the time he went out the window? Why would you do that when the long-secret official report on his death, which *does* have the testimony of the witnesses, has been on the web site of the Seeley Mudd Manuscript Library of Princeton University since the fall of 2004?"

At that point Carroll, not challenging my initial statement in support of Forrestal's peace role with respect to Japan, offered to give some background to my question. I interjected with the background that Forrestal had been committed to the Bethesda Naval Hospital for some sort of breakdown and had been kept there involuntarily for seven weeks before going out a 16th floor window in the wee hours of May 22, 1949.

The background he had in mind, responded Carroll, was that the fatal fall of a prominent Czech anti-Communist leader not too long before Forrestal's fall was thought by many people to be an assassination, so this could easily lead people to be suspicious of Forrestal's death. "But does the report say anything different from what is in the books?" he asked (He gave the impression that he was hearing about the Willcutts Report for the very first time and asked me to come up and tell him more after the questions and book signing were over.).

"Indeed, it does," I responded. "For one thing it has among its exhibits the handwritten transcription of a morbid poem that served as Forrestal's 'suicide note,' and it was clearly written in a hand other than Forrestal's. You and the books also say that Forrestal was paranoid, but none of the Bethesda doctors who testified ever described him as paranoid, or even used the words "paranoid" or "paranoia."

"So, if he was killed, who do you think killed him?" asked Carroll.

"You want me to solve the crime?" I asked, knowing that there would be no opportunity to build any kind of a case in that venue.

At that point, Carroll addressed himself to the audience, saying that the general view of everyone who has studied the matter is that Forrestal committed suicide, and that was his own opinion as well. As for the doctors not saying that Forrestal was paranoid, it was because military doctors were loath to suggest that the Secretary of Defense might have been mentally ill while on the job.

"That's a lie," I could not restrain myself from saying, knowing, as Carroll also surely knows, that virtually the whole case for Forrestal's mental illness was publicly put forward by Captain Raines in the wake of the death, and that it was upon Raines's statements that Arnold Rogow and everyone who followed him had painted the picture of Forrestal as a very sick and suicidal man.

Before I could explain my charge, the moderator, Meade, jumped in and said, "Let's give some of these other people a chance to ask a question," and that was the end of our exchange.

I did approach Mr. Carroll just as he was signing his last book and quickly presented him with another question, "Did you know that there was an official Navy report on Forrestal's death?"

Now, with the audience gone and few people near to hear him, his manner turned brusque. "I'll have to go check with my sources," he responded. "I'll look at what you have written," he continued, and then he looked away, indicating that he was through with me for the night and indicating as well that, though he may look at what I have written—and probably already has—he would reserve the right to ignore it.

The Lesson

If you search the Internet for "James Carroll" and "Forrestal" together, you will find a great number of review articles about Carroll's book. The reviews are decidedly mixed, although you certainly won't find a one of them faulting Carroll, as I have, for his indefensibly shoddy scholarship on Forrestal's death. The most salient fact about the reviews is that the book was given a lot of attention. In the quantity of publicity it received, both good and bad, it is very much like Arnold Rogow's book. As noted in the first chapter, Rogow's book was the most heavily publicized of the books that deal with Forrestal's death and, at the same time, had the most distorted and deceptive treatment of the subject. Both dubious distinctions probably now belong to Carroll's *House of War.*

As those of us who care about truth and justice in this country have discovered more about the alarming facts surrounding Forrestal's death, the molders of public opinion are working overtime to see that what the American public thinks it knows about the death is, in fact, false. The opinion molders certainly chose the right man to spread the falsehoods.

How long will we have to wait for a recognized scholar, who is also honest, to take up the subject?

CHAPTER 8

Earliest Letters to Historians

Apathy in Academia?

What does their loathing for
The facts I give them show?
They'd rather not know more
Than it's safe to know.

Sitting back and waiting for America's historians to seize upon our discoveries concerning Forrestal's death, we expected from the beginning, would not prove to be very fruitful, considering how little real interest they had shown from the time that it happened. We knew all along that we would have to lead this particular horse to water, but as we have seen so far and will see in the coming chapters, up to now it has been impossible to make him drink.

The first and most natural target for our attention was the young co-author of *Driven Patriot*, Douglas Brinkley. He churns out books with some regularity, and his book promotion tours often bring him to Washington, DC. I encountered him on two such occasions, the first of which, discussed later, was at the Politics and Prose bookstore. The second time was in 2007 when he came to Catholic University promoting his book *Parish Priest: Father Michael McGivney and American Catholicism*. I don't recall what I asked him from the audience at the close of his presentation, but it concerned what he had erroneously written about James Forrestal's death and it was designed to make him uncomfortable, which it clearly did. It might have been about my letter to him that he never answered. There was a very nice reception afterward with lots of tasty goodies, including shrimp, as I recall. Brinkley, as the speaker, was the guest of honor, but at the close of the question and answer period he informed the host that he had a tight flight schedule and would not be able to make it to the reception.

David Roll co-authored the 2005 biography of Forrestal's successor, *Louis Johnson and the Arming of America: The Roosevelt and Truman Years*.[160] He is a lawyer employed in Washington by the law firm that Johnson co-founded, Steptoe and Johnson, and I have encountered him three times. After the first encounter I wrote him a letter. He responded and requested that we meet for lunch. Although the lunch meeting did not take place until several weeks had passed, Mr. Roll appeared to know no more about the case than he had shown when I talked to him previously. He simply used our brief time together to ask me a number of simple questions that are answered in great detail in "Who Killed James Forrestal?" I tried to give some short, simple responses to his questions, but the best thing I could tell him was to go read what I had written and then ask questions. He was not at all prepared to challenge anything I had written, and no progress was made toward getting at the truth at the meeting. I was left wondering why he wanted to meet in the first place.

Now here are my letters:

August 18, 2005

Professor Douglas Brinkley
Director

---

[160] Keith D. McFarland and David L. Roll, *Louis Johnson and the Arming of America: The Roosevelt and Truman Years*, Indiana University Press, 2005.

Theodore Roosevelt Center for American Civilization
Tulane University
New Orleans, LA 70118

Dear Professor Brinkley:

When Truth or Virtue an Affront endures, Th'Affront is mine, my Friend, and should be yours. -- Alexander Pope

More than two months have now passed since that night at the Politics and Prose bookstore in Washington, DC, when you asked me for my home telephone number and promised to call me to talk about the serious inconsistencies I have found between your account of the death of our first Defense Secretary, James Forrestal, and what I have discovered through the use of the Freedom of Information Act (FOIA). Your account, you will recall, is in Chapter 32 of the book you co-wrote with the late Townsend Hoopes and published in 1992 entitled *Driven Patriot, the Life and Times of James Forrestal.* What I have found is in the Navy's official report on the death, that of the review board convened by Rear Admiral Morton D. Willcutts, the head of the National Naval Medical Center, which supervises the Bethesda Naval Hospital where Forrestal fell to his death from a 16th floor window in the wee hours of May 22, 1949. The Willcutts Report had been kept secret for some 55 years, and it is now, unredacted [sic, "Mark Hunter" discovered that there is a small part missing, which he has noted at his web site[161]] and with almost all the exhibits, on the web site of the Seeley Mudd Manuscript Library of Princeton University. [162]

Perhaps you need a brief reminder of the occasion for your asking for my telephone number. You had given a talk on your new book, *The Boys of Pointe du Hoc.* In the questions period following, I reminded you that I had called you more than a year before on C-Span and praised *Driven Patriot* generally, but had faulted you for your use of sources on the details surrounding Forrestal's death. The best sources, I observed, would have been the Navy personnel on duty that night on the 16th floor of the hospital and, short of tracking down those among them who are still living and interviewing them, the best evidence as to what those people saw and heard would be found in the official report, that is, the Willcutts Report. You neglected to tell the readers that there was any such thing as an official report and that it remained withheld from public scrutiny. Further, the sources you used for the most important details, I said, were hard-to-trace third-hand sources. In my examination of Forrestal's death, on the other hand, I told you that I had

[161] http://ariwatch.com/VS/JamesForrestal/WillcuttsReport.htm.

[162] https://findingaids.princeton.edu/collections/MC051/c04531.

made two FOIA attempts to get the report and that I had been quite illegally ignored both times. In your response on C-Span you did not dispute my characterization of your sources but said that you had tried to get the Willcutts Report yourself, and had failed as I had. If there were to be a new edition, you said, you would correct your omission and would talk about the Willcutts Report. In the meantime, you said, I should keep trying to get it.

I did, and, wonder of wonders, on the third try I got it, no questions asked. That was what I announced to you and the audience at Politics and Prose. Your reaction was one of surprise at my success and you asked me what was in the report. I said that it generally contradicted what you had written in your chapter and suggested that we might co-write an article to set the record straight. At that, you asked me for my opinion as to what had happened. My response was to hold up the transcription of the morbid poem by Sophocles that was characterized as Forrestal's suicide note and to observe that the handwriting was clearly not that of James Forrestal. "What conclusion would you draw from that," I asked you and the audience.

I don't recall your exact answer to that. I think that it was something along the lines of, "I'd have to see it." My main recollection is that at that point you moved on to the next questioner.

At the end of the evening, after you had signed a number of books and I had talked to some members of the audience about my important discoveries, I gave you a chance to see for yourself, presenting you with a copy of the poem transcription and some known samples of Forrestal's handwriting, all of which look very much like one another and nothing like the transcription. You demonstrated considerable interest, with several other attendees looking on, and at that point requested my home telephone number for what you said would definitely be follow-up in the none-too-distant future.

I realize that with the large new responsibilities that you have assumed, directing the new Theodore Roosevelt Center at Tulane University, promoting your book, working on a new book, and preparing for classes, your time has been limited. At the same time, I should think that you would want to do everything possible, as soon as possible, to set the historical record straight, now that we know that a number of things that you wrote in your influential book about Forrestal's death are inconsistent with the facts, as they are now known.

Your misrepresentation of the poem transcription as Forrestal's work—like everyone else who has written on the subject—may be the most glaring inconsistency, but there are a number of others that you should be aware of. They center on the words and actions of the two Navy corpsmen who, in sequence, were responsible for observing Forrestal on the 16th floor, Edward William Prise, who was on duty until 11:45 pm, and Robert Wayne Harrison, who was on duty thereafter.

Hoopes and Brinkley (H & B):

Prise had observed that Forrestal, though more energetic than usual, was also more restless, and this worried him. He tried to alert the young doctor who had night duty and slept in a room next to Forrestal's. But the doctor was accustomed to restless patients and not readily open to advice on the subject from an enlisted corpsman.

Willcutts Report (WR):

Q. These occurrences that you have just related in regard to Mister Forrestal's behavior on that night, did you consider them sufficiently unusual to report them to the doctor?

A. No, sir, I reported his walking the room to Doctor Deen and I put it in the chart and then Doctor Deen asked me how come the door was locked back there and I told him I thought I better lock it being as he raised the blind.

Q. Did you attach any particular significance to this type of behavior?
A. No, sir, I didn't at the time.

H & B:

Midnight arrived and with it the substitute corpsman, but Prise nevertheless lingered on for perhaps half an hour, held by some nameless, instinctive anxiety. But he could not stay forever. Regulations, custom, and his own ingrained discipline forbade it...

The corpsman Prise had returned to his barracks room, but could not sleep. After tossing restlessly for an hour, he got dressed and was walking across the hospital yard for a cup of coffee at the canteen when he was suddenly aware of a great commotion all around him. Instantly, instinctively, he knew what had happened. Racing to the hospital lobby, he arrived just as the young doctor whom he had tried unsuccessfully to warn emerged from an elevator. The doctor's face was a mask of anguish and agony. As Prise watched, he grasped the left sleeve of his white jacket with his right hand and, in a moment of blind madness, tore it from his arm.

WR:

Q. Other than the conversation you have given with Mister Forrestal did he say anything else to you on that night?

A. No, sir, he asked me if I thought it was stuffy in the room and he asked that several times since I have been on watch; he liked fresh air. When I was on night watch, twelve to eight in the morning he always got a blanket out for us to wrap around us because he had the windows wide open.

Neither the recorder nor the members of the board desired further to examine the witness.

The board informed the witness that he was privileged to make any further statement covering anything relating to the subject matter of the investigation which he thought should be a matter of record in connection therewith, which had not been fully brought out by the previous questioning.

The witness made the following statement:

He started reading a book at about twenty hundred and whenever the corpsman would come in the room he would turn the bed lamp off and sit down in the chair and so far as the writing I don't know. It appeared that he was but I couldn't say for sure.

Neither the recorder nor the members of the board desired further to examine this witness.

The witness said he had nothing further to state.

The witness was duly warned and withdrew.

In short, the fevered sense of dread is utterly missing from the testimony of corpsman Prise to the Willcutts review board. He sounds hardly alarmed at anything that had transpired.

Next, we have the observations of the man who relieved corpsman Prise, corpsman Harrison, whom neither you nor a previous Forrestal biographer, Arnold Rogow, identify by name.

H & B:

At one-forty-five on Sunday morning, May 22, the new corpsman looked in on Forrestal, who was busy copying onto several sheets of paper the brooding classical poem "The Chorus from Ajax" by Sophocles, in which Ajax, forlorn and far from home, contemplates suicide. (As translated by William Mackworth Praed in Mark Van Doren's *Anthology of World Poetry*.) The book was bound in red leather and decorated with gold.

WR:

Q. At what time did you last see Mister Forrestal?
A. It was one forty-five, sir.

Q. Where was he then?
A. He was in his bed, apparently sleeping.

Q. Where were you at that time?
A. I was in the room when I saw him.

H & B:

In most accounts of what happened next, it is said that the inexperienced corpsman "went on a brief errand." However, Dr. Robert Nenno, the young psychiatrist who later worked for Dr. Raines, quotes Raines as telling him that Forrestal "pulled rank" and ordered the nervous young corpsman to go on some errand that was designed to remove him from the premises.

WR:

(Following immediately after the Q & A above)

Q. Did you leave the room at that time?
A. Yes, sir, I did.

Q. Where did you go?
A. I went out to the nurse's desk to write in the chart, Mister Forrestal's chart.

Dr. George Raines, the head psychiatrist in charge of Forrestal's care, was, as you know, in Montreal at a conference at the time of Forrestal's death. Some other exchanges with Harrison are also pertinent to what you and Townsend Hoopes have written:

Q. Were the lights on in Mister Forrestal's room when you took over the watch - the overhead lights?
A. No, sir, not the overhead lights; just the night light.

Q. Did Mister Forrestal appear cheerful or depressed in the time that you observed him?
A. He appeared neither, sir.

Q. Did Mister Forrestal do any reading?
A. Not while I was on watch, sir.

You might also be interested to know that the thick, elaborately bound *Anthology of World Poetry* never makes a single appearance in the Willcutts Report. It is not among the exhibits and no witness is produced who saw it in Forrestal's vacated room. The nurse who got the first good look at the room reported broken glass on the bed, with the bed clothes half turned back and the forensic photographer captured broken glass on the carpet at the foot of the bed, but the nurse said nothing about a book—or a transcription, for that matter—and it shows up in none of the photographer's pictures of the room.

The transcription, itself, is included among the exhibits, but no one is identified who might have discovered it. It is mentioned only once, in this exchange with Captain Raines:

Q. Captain Raines, I show you a clinical record, can you identify it?
A. This is the nursing record of Mister Forrestal. The only portion I don't recognize is this poem copied on brown paper. Is that the one he copied? It looks like his handwriting. This is the record of Mister Forrestal, the clinical record.

We have seen previously that Dr. Raines was probably misleading in his explanation for the corpsman leaving Forrestal's room. Now he volunteers that the copied poem appears to be done in Forrestal's handwriting, when, in fact, the handwriting looks nothing like Forrestal's (See enclosures.). You and other commentators have also made much of the "fact" that the transcription cuts off in the middle of the word "nightingale." The one included in the exhibits sent to me, however, ends 11 lines before the line with the word "nightingale" in it is reached. I wrote the Navy's Judge Advocate General's office, the people who supplied me with the Willcutts Report, and asked them if they were sure that they had sent me the entire transcription, noting that all published accounts had said that more of the poem was copied. I received no reply.

In addition to the handwriting enclosures, I have enclosed some of the forensic photographs of Forrestal's room. The proper time to take them would have been between 2 and 3 am, while everything was as Forrestal had left it. You will notice from the angle of the light entering the room that the photographs were taken some 8 hours or more later, and that all bedclothes have been stripped from the bed. The elapsed time has clearly been used for tampering with the "crime scene."

In announcements that I have seen about your new Theodore Roosevelt Center, you say that one of the things you'd like to do would be to organize symposia around important topics in American history. Might I suggest that this would be a very good way to get a lot of important facts cleared up with respect to Forrestal's death? It could also be an opportunity for the public to get insights into how professional historians and biographers go about their work.

I would be particularly interested to hear about your use of the undated, unpublished outline of a manuscript by John Osborne to describe the goings on before and after midnight on the 16th floor of the Bethesda Naval Hospital on the night of Forrestal's death. As you know, in the contemporary newspaper accounts and in previous books about Forrestal, there was only one naval corpsman with primary responsibility for Forrestal on duty through all of those key hours. The newspapers and the author Cornell Simpson say that this person's shift began at 9:00 pm. For the author Arnold Rogow, the corpsman who earlier reported that Forrestal had declined his sleeping pill and the corpsman on duty when Forrestal went out the window were the same person, consistent with Simpson and the newspaper accounts. Osborne says, on the other hand, that there were three shifts for Forrestal's primary attendant, and he concentrates on the account of the one whose shift, he says, ended at midnight.

I would very much like to know how you came across this Osborne material and why you chose to believe that he was correct and the other accounts were not with respect to the guard shifts. As it happens, Osborne was right about that, as verified by the Willcutts Report. He even has the corpsman's name spelled correctly, Edward *Prise,* while the Willcutts Report spells it *Price* incorrectly throughout. Osborne is also consistent with the Review Board testimony of Captain Stephen Smith, read somewhat between the lines, when he reports that the doctor "second in rank and authority to the psychiatrist in charge of the case believed throughout its course that Forrestal was wrongly diagnosed and treated. But he also thought that Forrestal was recovering despite the treatment..." This is quite a revelation, by the way, though it went unreported in your book.

On the other hand, Osborne says that he has interviewed "every person known to have been with Forrestal after his collapse and now alive and available..." and the only person he cites to lend credence to the suicide thesis is the corpsman Prise, whose evidence is based on nothing more than his worries, noted above, over Forrestal's restlessness, and his presumed clairvoyance: "In his barracks room, two hours after he left Forrestal, Prise cannot go to sleep. He dresses; he is walking across the hospital yard to a canteen for a cup of coffee when he becomes aware of commotion all about him. Instantly, he knows."

This, I trust that you recognize, is really no evidence at all. Perhaps Osborne, his editor, or his potential publisher recognized it as well, which might explain why his work was never published. One must also wonder what all those witnesses who were actually on duty at the time of Forrestal's death had to say to Mr. Osborne and why he chose to cite none of them, and why he had nothing to say about the celebrated poem transcription.

Would you not agree that it is much better to live in a country whose history is based upon openness and truth rather than on secrecy and lies? I look forward to hearing what plans you might have to correct the historical record, now that so much more evidence is available than when you and Townsend Hoopes wrote your Forrestal biography.

Sincerely,
David Martin

Professor Brinkley never responded to the letter, just as he did not call me after he promised to do so after our encounter at the Politics and Prose bookstore. It is hard to escape the conclusion that his later skipping out of the reception at Catholic University had something to do with these two previous failures.

Letter to David Roll

November 1, 2005

Mr. David Roll
Steptoe & Johnson
1330 Connecticut Avenue, NW
Washington, DC 20036

Dear Mr. Roll,

As you will recall, during the question and answer period following your October 18 Eisenhower Institute presentation on your new book, *Louis Johnson and the Arming of America*, co-written with Keith McFarland, I noted that new research had shown that an observation of yours on page 153 is entirely incorrect. The passage, which follows, was written to support the popular conclusion, which your book endorses, that Johnson's predecessor as Secretary of Defense, James Forrestal, had committed suicide:

"But everyone knew [Forrestal] was deeply disturbed. Moments before his death, he was copying Sophocles' poem 'The Chorus from Ajax,' in which Ajax, forlorn and 'worn by the waste of time,' contemplates suicide."

With respect to the first sentence, I noted that those who worked most closely with Forrestal certainly did not "know" that he was "deeply disturbed." Most notable among them was his top assistant, Marx

Leva. This comes from the oral history interview of Leva by Stephen Hess found on the web site of the Truman Library:

HESS: What do you recall about the unfortunate mental breakdown that overtook Mr. Forrestal?

LEVA: Well, I may have been in the position of not being able to see the forest for the trees because I was seeing him six, eight, ten, twelve times a day and both in and out of the office. A lot of his friends have said since his death, "Oh, we saw it coming," and, "We knew this and we knew that." The only thing that I knew was that he was terribly tired, terribly overworked, spending frequently literally sixteen hours and eighteen hours a day trying to administer an impossible mechanism, worrying about the fact that a lot of it was of his own creation. I knew that he was tired, I begged him to take time off. I'm sure that others begged him to take time off.
http://www.trumanlibrary.org/oralhist/leva.htm.

In your defense, you said that you had relied completely upon *Driven Patriot, the Life and Times of James Forrestal*, by Townsend Hoopes and Douglas Brinkley for information concerning Forrestal's death. However, Leva's observations are reinforced by this quote from page 426 of their book:

"Given the extent and pace of his decline, it is astonishing that colleagues at the Pentagon, including members of his inner staff, failed to recognize it. In retrospect they attribute their failure to Forrestal's formidable self-control, his brusque, impersonal method of dealing with staff, and the simple fact that they saw him too frequently to note much change in his condition or demeanor. "

Though Hoopes and Brinkley do not support your claim concerning what everyone *knew* about Forrestal, they are clearly the source for the account of Forrestal transcribing a specific morbid poem "moments before his death." They are proved to be wrong on this point, however, by recently uncovered evidence. Their sole source for the claim that Forrestal was actually seen copying the poem shortly before he plunged from a 16th floor window was Arnold Rogow, in his book, *James Forrestal, a Study of Personality, Politics, and Policy.* Rogow, though, has no source at all, and it is no wonder, because it is now clear that he made the story up. The naval corpsman who was in charge of Forrestal's security and who was the witness, according to Rogow, of the transcribing incident, testified that Forrestal did no reading while he was on duty and that the last time he looked in, Forrestal was apparently sleeping in the darkened room. That is precisely the time, 1:45 a.m., that Rogow says that the corpsman saw Forrestal busy copying the poem.

The following passage comes from testimony of Apprentice Robert Wayne Harrison, who came on duty at 11:45 p.m. the night of Forrestal's death. It has only been available since its release through a Freedom of Information Act request in 2004:

Q. At what time did you last see Mister Forrestal?
A. It was one forty-five, sir.

Q. Where was he then?
A. He was in his bed, apparently sleeping.

Q. Where were you at that time?
A. I was in the room when I saw him.

And this comes a little later in Apprentice Harrison's testimony:

Q. Did Mister Forrestal appear cheerful or depressed in the time that you observed him?
A. He appeared neither, sir.

Q. Did Mister Forrestal do any reading?
A. Not while I was on watch, sir.

It goes without saying that if he did no reading, he did no copying from any books. So much for the statement as to what Forrestal was doing "moments before his death."

Actually, what we now know amounts to far more than a mere quibble over the timing of Forrestal's actions. On October 18, 2005, I gave you a copy of the handwritten transcription that appears among the exhibits accompanying the official investigation, along with a couple of samples of Forrestal's handwriting that I obtained separately from the Truman Library. These can be found at http://www.dcdave.com/article4/041103.htm. From a mere glance one can easily see that the lines of the poem were copied by someone other than Forrestal.

Nevertheless, with this evidence in hand, at a presentation at the Politics and Prose bookstore in Washington, DC, on October 29 you made the statement that internecine squabbling within the newly-created Defense Department contributed to Forrestal's demise and ultimate "suicide." Afterward, you will recall, I told you that you could not possibly still be maintaining that Forrestal committed suicide if you had examined the evidence that I had given you more than a week before. You replied that you had not yet looked at the evidence.

I'm sure that your clients would expect you to be a good deal better prepared to defend them than you were to defend what you have written in your book and repeated in your book-promoting presentation. At the very least, I should think you would have exhibited just a little bit of natural, human curiosity. Perhaps it is that old saying about feline curiosity that has prevented you from wanting to know the truth, even when you are on record with a demonstrably untrue statement.

Fortunately, your co-author, Keith McFarland, whom you seem to have protected from the evidence I gave you, participated with you in that Politics and Prose presentation. He told me that he was "open-minded" and that he has told his students in the past that history writing is an ongoing process and that we should always be prepared to revise our views as we learn more. Let us hope that he is as good as his word in this case and that you and he will soon take steps to correct your error.

Might I remind you that James Forrestal was the leading government official warning against pursuit of the foreign policy that has us in our current mess in the Middle East? I realize that, to many, that is ample reason why the news that he did not commit suicide, but was actually assassinated, should be suppressed. But to anyone interested in truth and justice and concerned about the fate of this country and the world, it is even greater reason why this unpleasant news should be spread widely and quickly. Anyone who, at this late date, has perpetuated the false story of Forrestal's suicide has a special obligation to set the record straight.

Sincerely,
David Martin

cc: Dr. Keith McFarland

As noted at the beginning, this letter led to an unproductive lunch meeting with Roll, but I never heard anything further from Professor McFarland, who was at the time president of Texas A & M University Commerce.

CHAPTER 9

Academic Ostriches

Academic Ostriches

Bring up the death of Forrestal
Historians run and hide.
They'd like to believe Count Bernadotte
Committed suicide.

David E. Kaiser, with both a bachelors and a Ph. D. from Harvard University, was a professor in the strategy and policy department of the United States Naval War College in Newport, Rhode Island, from 1990 to 2012. He has a blog entitled "History Unfolding" with the subtitle, "A historian's comments on current events, foreign and domestic." We discovered that on December 18, 2005, he had written favorably there on Drew Pearson and his attacks on Forrestal. This was more than a year after the release of the Willcutts Report, yet Kaiser routinely described Forrestal's death as a "suicide" in the process of praising the execrable Pearson. Hoping that his intentions might not be all that bad and that he had simply been misguided, perhaps by his ideology or by lack of information, we wrote him as follows on December 13, 2007:

Dear Professor Kaiser,

I thought you would like to know that a couple of days ago I left a comment on your December 18, 2005 "History Unfolding" blog at http://historyunfolding.blogspot.com/2005/12/they-were-giants-in-those-days.html. _ The title of your article is "They were giants in those days," and you are referring primarily, and most appallingly as I see it, to the journalist, Drew Pearson. Here is my comment:

> Your admiration for the smear specialist, Drew Pearson, is, in my opinion, completely misplaced. Nowhere are you more off the mark than in the following quote:
>
> "During early 1949 Pearson had been writing that James Forrestal, the first Secretary of Defense, was mentally unstable, and eventually he reported correctly that Forrestal had tried to commit suicide."
>
> Pearson did, indeed, write scurrilous things about Forrestal, including that he consciously cowered in his New York apartment while his wife was assaulted outside it, which was not true. It is also not true that Forrestal had attempted suicide. The day after Forrestal's death from a fall from the 16th floor of the Bethesda Naval Hospital, Pearson reported that Forrestal had made four previous suicide attempts. That claim, according to the doctors who treated Forrestal at Bethesda, was also false.
>
> Looking at Pearson's record, I tend to agree with what President Franklin Roosevelt wrote about him in a letter to General Patrick Hurley on August 30, 1943, "His ill-considered falsehoods have come to the point where he is doing much harm to his own Government and to other nations. It is a pity that anyone anywhere believes anything that he writes."

You might regard my words as a bit harsh, but, all things considered, I think that I have been quite forbearing. You went on to say, after all, that Forrestal did commit suicide shortly after the purported attempt, and you wrote those words near the end of 2005. Here's what I had to say about the author, James Carroll, on my web site: "Anyone who would write about Forrestal's death in 2006 and ignore completely the evidence contained in the Willcutts Report would have to be very irresponsible, indeed." See "James Carroll on James Forresatal."[163] The Willcutts Report is the long suppressed official investigation of Forrestal's death, made public with a press release by the Seeley Mudd Library of Princeton University in the late summer of 2004 [Sic. Writing from memory, I forgot that the library did not send out its press release until a couple of months after posting the report on its web site.]. One

[163] http://www.dcdave.com/article5/060609.htm.

can readily see why the report had been kept secret.[164] The information it contains thoroughly undermines the case for Forrestal's suicide.

Although you were writing at about the same time as Carroll, you are perhaps less at fault for getting your facts wrong. You were writing only a short article whose subject was mainly Drew Pearson. Carroll, in his book about the Pentagon, on the other hand, writes about Forrestal at considerable length. Your scholarly reputation is also a good deal higher than his, so I am proceeding upon the assumption that you have simply made an honest mistake. Carroll, on the other hand, is well beyond such consideration. I conclude in my article that Carroll is clearly a conscious spreader of lies:

"As those of us who care about truth and justice in this country have discovered more about the alarming facts surrounding Forrestal's death, the molders of public opinion are working overtime to see that what the American public thinks it knows about the death is, in fact, false. The opinion molders have chosen the right man to spread the falsehoods."

With my following sentence, which concludes the essay, I might well have been writing about someone like you:

"How long will we have to wait for a recognized scholar, who is also honest, to take up the subject?"

When I was able to get through on C-Span to Forrestal biographer Douglas Brinkley and fault him for failing to mention that there was even such a thing as an official investigation of Forrestal's death, much less that it had been kept secret, he responded that he would consider correcting his omission if there were a paperback edition. See "Letters Concerning James Forrestal."[165] That is the advantage of having a blog. You don't have to wait for such an opportunity.

Sincerely,

David Martin

Sadly, exactly one week later, Professor Kaiser revealed that he was not at all the sort of person I was looking for by responding peremptorily

164 https://findingaids.princeton.edu/collections/MC051/c04531.
165 http://www.dcdave.com/article4/060102.htm.

and dismissively—not to say insultingly. Perhaps he considered it his prerogative as a Harvard man.

He began loftily, saying that he couldn't see much purpose in discussing the matter of Forrestal's death with me because my interpretation of events was "a bit too creative" for him. He allowed as how, from his quick look at the Willcutts Report that it was clear from the doctors' views that Forrestal "was depressed and very suicidal." The main question at issue in the report, it seemed to him, was whether the victim had attempted to hang himself from the window or had merely jumped. The number of times Forrestal had actually attempted to kill himself before he regarded as little more than a quibble, which could only be ascertained by examining Drew Pearson's notes on his Hobe Sound sources, something for which he lacked the time. He also volunteered that the report confirmed that Forrestal would have had no way of knowing what Pearson was writing or saying about him during his hospitalization, absolving Pearson of blame, I suppose, for driving Forrestal to suicide, as others such as Westbrook Pegler had suggested.

He then concluded in the same tone with which he began, and with finality: "It's a free country and a free internet. I don't see any reason to alter what I wrote."

As one might imagine, his response got my juices flowing. It was evident that either he had spent very little time with the Willcutts Report and even less with my "creative interpretations," or he had shown himself to be quite lacking in critical faculties. I responded on the same day, immediately upon receiving the email:

> Dear Professor Kaiser,
>
> May I take it, then, that with regard to whether or not Forrestal committed suicide, you consider of no consequence the revelations that:
>
> 1. the handwriting of the transcribed poem, which, for the press, served as his suicide note, does not resemble Forrestal's at all
>
> 2. that broken glass was on his bed and on the carpet at the foot of the bed

3. that Forrestal's room was not photographed until many hours after he was found dead and that when it was it did not resemble the room that the nurse who first got a good look at the vacated room described. The photos show a bed with nothing but a bare mattress and pillow on them, whereas Nurse Turner testified that, as one might expect, "The bed clothes were turned back and towards the middle of the bed and I looked down and [the slippers] were right there as you get out of bed." No slippers or any other sign that the room had been occupied are evident in the photographs, either.

4. that the influential biographer, Arnold Rogow, apparently fabricated the story that the guard saw Forrestal transcribing the morbid poem when he last looked in on him, because the guard testified that when he last looked in the room Forrestal was apparently sleeping and the lights had been off and Forrestal apparently did no reading or writing during the guard's time of duty which began at midnight

5. that the influential newspapers reporting on the death apparently fabricated the story that the transcription ended in the middle of the word "nightingale" or, depending on which article in *The Washington Post* you read, the transcription included the lines, "When Reason's day sets rayless–joyless–quenched in cold decay, better to die, and sleep the never-ending sleep than linger on, and dare to live, when the soul's life is gone."

6. that the findings of the Willcutts Report were not issued until several months had passed and then, the findings did not include the conclusion that Forrestal had committed suicide

7. that photographs of Forrestal's body were first withheld from the FOIAed material on the grounds that they might disturb Forrestal's surviving loved ones, and when told that there were no surviving loved ones the Navy changed its story and claimed that they were lost

8. that the book from which Forrestal supposedly copied the damning poem does not appear in official evidence nor is the supposed discoverer of either the book or the transcription ever officially identified

9. that the Willcutts Report was kept secret for 55 years, when its whole purpose was to clear the air and establish the facts publicly concerning the nature of Forrestal's death?

Surely, with respect to Drew Pearson's credibility, you don't believe, as you imply, that it is immaterial that Pearson wrote that Forrestal had made four suicide attempts, the last of which such attempts had occurred right there at Bethesda Naval Hospital, when those claims are contradicted by the Bethesda doctors and Pearson had no details or named sources for his claims?

I must say that I am amazed that it is I, in contrast to Pearson, that you regard as the "creative" one when it comes to interpreting the evidence surrounding Forrestal's death. What I have done is to analyze the evidence carefully, with a skeptical eye. Doing so, I certainly do not conclude as you do (see Part 2), that, "The doctors explain in great detail that he was depressed and very suicidal."[166] Only Captain Raines, whose credibility is called into question by many other things he said, claimed that he was suicidal, and the second in command of the doctors, Captain Stephen Smith, appears to contradict him. That he does contradict him, even apparently with respect to the "depressed" diagnosis, is reinforced by the unpublished manuscript of the *Time* magazine writer, John Osborne, as I mention in my previously-referenced letter to Douglas Brinkley. Furthermore, there seems to be virtual unanimity among those who saw Forrestal near to the time of his death that he seemed to be quite normal by that time. That was the reason given for relaxing the guard and allowing access to belts, razor blades, etc., after all.[167]

Finally, I am puzzled by your assertion, for what it is worth, "that there is no way that Forrestal could have read or heard about what Pearson had broadcast and written during his hospitalization." Could he not have heard about it from any number of visitors, particularly his wife, or from letters? This is from testimony by Captain Raines that I quote in Part 2:

"From the very first Mister Forrestal's mail and other communications were handed to him unopened. He was allowed to see all of them on the theory no one can live in a vacuum and might just as well be exposed to whatever came along; that is the method of dealing with it; it would depend on how well he was or how sick he was. It was as simple as that. Actually he dealt quite well with almost everything."

In sum, based upon how you have handled the evidence up to now, it's possible that you may not actually see any reason to alter anything that you have written, but I surely do. As at least your figure of speech would have it, though, it's a free country.

---

166 "Who Killed James Forrestal?" Part 2, http://dcdave.com/article4/040922.html.

167 My "Part 2" reference is to the second installment of "Who Killed James Forrestal?" http://dcdave.com/article4/040922.html.

Sincerely,
David Martin, Ph.D.

Several years have now gone by and it has become pretty clear that Professor Kaiser has taken refuge in the tall grass and will not be further heard from, content, apparently, in the belief that power effectively trumps truth.

With the floor now all to myself, may I note a further error in Kaiser's admittedly incomplete reading of the Willcutts Report? With respect to the question of what caused Forrestal's death, he says, "...the only doubt seemed to be about whether he purposely jumped out the window or was trying to hang himself."

In fact, the question was never addressed in those terms. How could it have been? Surely no one suggested that Forrestal went to the trouble to tie a bathrobe belt tightly around his neck before jumping, freestyle and untethered, out the 16th floor window. What purpose, then, could the belt tied to his neck have possibly served?

One must wonder if this is the sort of critical thinking that Professor Kaiser is teaching America's leading Naval officers to apply to important historical events. What must he tell them, for instance, about the 1967 Israeli attack on the *USS Liberty*?[168]

In our exchanges I also failed to mention one of the worst of Drew Pearson's slanders of Forrestal. Here is the account from *Driven Patriot: The Life and Times of James Forrestal*:

> Pearson had, in fact, decided to fire his heaviest ammunition in a radio broadcast on April 9 [1949]. He charged that Forrestal, awakened by the sound of a fire siren (on the night of April 1 at Hobe Sound), had rushed out of his cottage screaming, "The Russians are attacking." He defined Forrestal's condition as "temporary insanity." In subsequent newspaper columns he asserted that Forrestal made three suicide attempts while in Florida—by drug overdose, by hanging, and by slashing

168 See "*Remember the Liberty*" http://dcdave.com/article5/170608.htm.

> his wrists. According to a later statement by [Navy psychiatrist Captain George] Raines, all of these assertions were lies.[169]

Since Raines was the one doctor at Bethesda Naval Hospital who maintained in his testimony to the Willcutts Review Board that Forrestal was suicidal and would therefore be more likely to embrace any story that buttressed his case, his debunking of Pearson's unsupported claims carries particular weight.

So much for Professor Kaiser's journalistic "giant."

Christopher Sharrett

In early February of 2008 I discovered another article (which I cannot now locate) that said that James Forrestal committed suicide. Since the article by tenured professor of communications at Seton Hall University, Christopher Sharrett, boldly challenged the official line in the John F. Kennedy assassination, the prospects seemed bright that we might have found someone who would actually be excited over my Forrestal discoveries and would publicly embrace my conclusion that Forrestal was assassinated. On February 3 I sent the following email to his Seton Hall address:

> Dear Professor Sharrett,
>
> I just ran across your 1999 article on the Net in which you characterize the John Kennedy assassination as a coup d'état. You are quite right, of course. I drew the same conclusion in a poem called "Barren Summit" on the 40th anniversary of the killing.[170] It was a coup that involved the active participation of our press, as you can see here, and other important opinion molders.[171] See "Chomsky, the Fraud" and "Martin Lies about Kennedy Assassination" for samples of the latter.[172] As Gregory Treverton has written, "Propaganda is the bread and butter of covert action."

---

[169] Hoopes and Brinkley, pp. 455-456.

[170] http://www.dcdave.com/poet12/031122.html.

[171] "Fake Media Critic?" http://www.dcdave.com/article3/990808.html.

[172] http://www.dcdave.com/article4/010318a.html; http://www.dcdave.com/article3/010122.html.

Unfortunately, and I hope inadvertently, you have perpetuated some of that pernicious propaganda with one statement that you make in the article, and I quote:

"The national security state's lapdogs in the press, including Walter Winchell and Drew Pearson, ridiculed Forrestal, terming him a 'liar and a coward.' Forrestal suffered a nervous breakdown and eventually committed suicide."

The first sentence is true; the second sentence is false. Writing as you were in 1999, you certainly had a good excuse for making such a mistake. At that time, the only thing written that seriously questioned the conventional wisdom of suicide in James Forrestal's case was a very obscure book published by the John Birch Society, *The Death of James Forrestal*, by someone taking the *nom de plume* of "Cornell Simpson."

Fortunately, with the ready availability of the Internet, you can easily set the record straight and sever the connection between your professional reputation and a gigantic historical lie. To be sure, there has been a degree of stubbornness in which other residents of the groves of academe have clung to the lie, as I document in Part 5 of "Who Killed James Forrestal?"[173]

Your article on the Kennedy assassination suggests to me that you might be different. I hope that I am right.

Sincerely,
David Martin

My email was greeted with silence from Professor Sharrett, so I wrote him on February 14 as follows:

Dear Professor Sharrett,

Almost two weeks have now gone by, and I have had no response to my email to you notifying you of the serious historical error you have in your article of the Kennedy assassination, and I have had no response. Perhaps I should ask you what, if anything, you plan to do to correct the error. I await your response.

Sincerely,
David Martin

---

173 http://www.dcdave.com/article5/080113.htm.

The chance that Professor Sharrett will take up the cause of justice for James Forrestal now appears remote. It is not only his failure to respond to my emails that leads me to that conclusion. Perhaps he never received them for some reason. The full paragraph of his article in which the quote about Forrestal's "suicide" appears is telling:

> Cold War propaganda gave legitimacy to the national security state, although debate raged on within state and private power against the backdrop of the sleepy fifties. Many felt that the creation of the "garrison state" would bring about an enormous deficit and weaken us in relation to our Western capitalist rivals. Kennedy was not the first victim of the fierce internecine battles that began almost immediately with the creation of the national security state. Secretary of Defense James V. Forrestal became a victim in 1949 of what was referred to as "the revolt of the admirals." As each sector of the military fought over their share of public revenues, with the Joint Chiefs "at each other's throat" in a climate of unbridled avarice, Forrestal attempted at least to inject a note of civility as the military sensed its unprecedented authority. Forrestal was eventually "ground down by the bickering and backstabbing in the Pentagon." He was "under constant attack from the admirals and generals he supposedly commanded." The national security state's lapdogs in the press, including Walter Winchell and Drew Pearson, ridiculed Forrestal, terming him a "liar and a coward." Forrestal suffered a nervous breakdown and eventually committed suicide.

If Forrestal was under fire from the press, led by Winchell and Pearson, it was not because of his earnest efforts to bring order to the Pentagon, but because of his principled position against the creation of the state of Israel. Winchell was a cold warrior, but Pearson was not; he came a lot closer to being pro-Communist. The big thing that the two had in common, as we have seen, was that they were strong Zionist partisans.

Although he goes a step further than either of them when it comes to pursuit of the truth in the JFK assassination, Sharrett's "national security state" boilerplate—so reminiscent of *The Washington Post* in its 50th anniversary article—and his studied avoidance of the outsized role of the Zionists in Forrestal's demise suggest that he is in the same *faux* leftist league as the aforementioned Noam Chomsky and the notorious James Carroll.

A blurb from Sharrett's employer, Seton Hall University, is also revealing. "Sharrett frequently works with media," it says, "and has been interviewed by such widely known national news media as The History Channel, USA Today, Dallas Morning News and FOXNews.com."

These organizations are not exactly known for their pursuit of the truth in the Kennedy assassination or in any other major scandal, for that matter. When these propagandists publicly consult Professor Sharrett, they must know that the expertise that he brings to bear is not in unvarnished truth-seeking.

Forrestal Killing More Sensitive than JFK's?

Scores of books have been written challenging the conclusions of the Warren Report on the assassination of President Kennedy. As of this date, the only people doing any serious original research into the preposterous "suicide" story in Forrestal's case are the present writer and two people choosing to remain anonymous, "Cornell Simpson" and "Mark Hunter," the proprietor of the Ariwatch.com web site.[174] Had I kept those facts in mind, I probably would have not been so disappointed in the brush-off I received from Professor Sharrett.

We jump ahead to 2015 and across the Atlantic to Great Britain for another example of a writer who would freely take issue with the authorities over the JFK murder while parroting the popular propaganda line with respect to Forrestal. We are talking about John Simkin.

Perhaps it's just too ambitious a project for one man to carry on. Here is how Wikipedia describes it:

> **Spartacus Educational** is a free online encyclopedia with essays and other educational material on a wide variety of historical subjects (including British History and the History of the USA, as well as other sub-

[174] We purposely exclude those writers who claim that Forrestal was killed because of what he knew about the Roswell UFO incident. All these people have contributed is a possible motive for his assassination, which is most likely a distraction from the much more obvious real one. They have broken no new ground at all as to the particulars of Forrestal's death. I detest the expression, "conspiracy theorist," but there are instances where it might just be fitting. See Richard Dolan's September 18, 2018, YouTube presentation: https://www.youtube.com/watch?v=mDKPtUc4MJQ.

> jects including the First World War, Second World War, Russian Revolution, Slavery, Women's Suffrage, Nazi Germany, Spanish Civil War, and The Cold War). It is used by history teachers and students.
>
> Based in the UK, Spartacus Educational was established as a book publisher in 1984 by former history teacher, John Simkin, and Judith Harris. It became an online publisher in September 1997.
>
> A survey carried out by the Fischer Family Trust showed that the Spartacus Educational website was used by more history students in the UK than any other website, including that of the BBC. The Spartacus Educational website is recommended by a number of online educational resources, such as Manchester Metropolitan University, SchoolHistory.co.uk, Science and You, and St Mary's College, Hull.

At some point Judith Harris seems to have fallen by the wayside because Simkin's is the only name currently appearing on the site. I have not spent enough time at the site to profess to be any sort of an authority on its overall probity. Simkin's willingness to look with seriousness at alternative explanations to the Warren Report for President John F. Kennedy's assassination certainly marks him as a cut above anything one is likely to find associated with the establishment press in the United States. On the other hand, those school endorsements and what Simkin has to say about himself on his home page make him look very much like a member of the British establishment:

> As well as running the Spartacus Educational website John Simkin has also produced material for the Electronic Telegraph, the European Virtual School and the Guardian's educational website, Learn. He was also a member of the European History E-Learning Project (E-Help), a project to encourage and improve use of ICT and the internet in classrooms across the continent.

It is rather obvious that he toes the U.S. establishment line on Secretary of Defense James Forrestal's apparent assassination—calling it a suicide—is because it is a lot hotter political potato than JFK's assassination.

The "hot potato" factor, then, is probably the best explanation for the fact that what Simkin has to say about Forrestal's death is little different from what one would find in the U.S. mainstream. It is not consistent with the evidence that I have discovered, though. On his biography page

Simkin writes, "If you find any mistakes on any of my webpages please send details to: john@spartacus-educational.com." I accepted his invitation and sent him the following email:

> Hi John,
>
> I think that it is about time that you corrected your conclusion on your James Forrestal page that Forrestal "committed suicide by throwing himself out of a 16th floor hospital window."[175] I see that you updated the page in August of last year, but when you did so you must have overlooked virtually everything that I have discovered in recent years, particularly the official transcript of the Navy's inquiry into his death.[176] I was able to obtain that inquiry through a Freedom of Information Act request in 2004. The fact that it had been kept secret for 55 years should be enough to raise anyone's suspicion as to the veracity of the conclusion of suicide.
>
> Please note that I do not say *official* conclusion of suicide. That inquiry, which we may call the Willcutts Report after the convening officer of the board of inquiry, Admiral Morton C. Willcutts, may be considered the government's last word on Forrestal's death, and it did not conclude that Forrestal committed suicide. It concluded only that the cause of his death was the fall from the window and that no member of the Navy had any responsibility for that fall.
>
> Your statement that he "threw himself" from the window is not even consistent with the conclusion reached by the press in the matter. A bathrobe belt was tied around Forrestal's neck. The newspapers attempted to account for it by saying that he must have been attempting to hang himself from the 16th floor window by tying one end to the radiator beneath the window and then climbing out the window to hang himself--as if the long plummet would not do the job. Various writers on the subject have said that the belt either broke, came untied, or unexplainably just "gave way." The Willcutts Report in its conclusion—like anyone who says simply that Forrestal jumped or threw himself out the window—makes no attempt to account for the presence of the belt. They address the belt only by implication, concluding that the fall rather than the belt had killed him. And, oh yes, they do conclude that the belt was intact and had not broken.

---

175 https://spartacus-educational.com/USAforrestal.htm.

176 http://dcdave.com/article4/040927.html.

> The list of what you call "primary sources" is really nothing of the sort. They are secondary sources. The best primary source on Forrestal's death at this point is the Willcutts Report. You will also find there a copy of the morbid poem that Forrestal was said to have been transcribing shortly before his plunge from the window. I have found copies of Forrestal's handwriting and it is evident that someone else did that transcription. Your "primary source," biographer Arnold Rogow, wrote that the navy corpsman guarding Forrestal's room had witnessed him doing the transcribing, but in his testimony to the Willcutts review board, the corpsman said that the room had been dark the entire time he was on duty and he had seen no reading or writing going on. Rogow had no source for his clearly fabricated assertion.
>
> You also cite the scandalous columnist Drew Pearson as an authority for several of his negative assertions about Forrestal. No source could be less reliable. Pearson also claimed that Forrestal had made four previous suicide attempts, an obvious falsehood with no source for the claim. For more about Pearson's spurious assertions see my article "Oliver Stone on James Forrestal."[177]
>
> If you will examine only the short articles to which I have referred you, I am sure you will conclude that the claim that Forrestal threw himself from that hospital window is not the truth; rather, it is what one would expect from the Ministry of Truth.
>
> Dave[178]

As you might expect, in spite of his public invitation to anyone who would offer corrections to any mistakes he might have made, Simkin gave me the Professor Sharrett treatment and ignored me. His Forrestal page remains completely unchanged. Maybe the late Don Bohning was right when he wrote in 2008, "In the guise of education, John Simkin's website delivers agitprop."[179] Says Bohning, "It takes a little digging to figure out Simkin is much more interested in indoctrination than education, in keeping with his unreconstructed left-wing views. Simkin exemplifies the kind of militant socialists, once peculiar to the Labour Party, who were all but run out of that party by former Prime Minister Tony Blair."

---

177 www.dcdave.com/article5/151016.htm.

178 http://ariwatch.com/Links/DCDave.htm#JamesForrestal.

179 Don Bohning, "Indoctrination U," June 11, 2008, http://www.washingtondecoded.com/site/2008/06/simkin.html.

If Simkin is an ideologically blinded left-winger as Bohning describes him, maybe that would explain his different treatment of the Forrestal and Kennedy deaths. The Kennedy assassination is generally regarded to be more of a left-wing issue, certainly more than the suspicious death of the dedicated anti-Communist Forrestal, about which only the Birch Society has published a critical book.

Though Simkin did nothing to refute the specific charges that Bohning leveled at him, Bohning did not get out of the exchange unscathed. Simkin revealed that Bohning had been an informant for the CIA while working as a reporter for the *Miami Herald.*[180]

I can assure you that Simkin will be unable to find any such dirty linen in this writer's closet, and that he will likely simply remain silent and leave his Forrestal page unchanged. The best bet, in other words, is that his reaction will be no different from what one would expect from an employee of the Ministry of Truth in George Orwell's *1984*.

We also had unsatisfactory exchanges with Donald A. Ritchie, U.S. Senate Historian; Nickolas Roth of the Nuclear Files Peace Foundation; and Loren Ghiglione, the Richard Schwarzlose Professor of Media Ethics at Northwestern University's Medill School of Journalism concerning errors in their writing about Drew Pearson and Forrestal's death. Those exchanges can be found at "Who Killed James Forrestal, Part 5."[181] Further letters of complaint to the Arlington Cemetery and Find a Grave web sites, producing no results, are at "Persistent Lies about James Forrestal."[182]

---

180 https://spartacus-educational.com/JFKbohning.htm.
181 http://www.dcdave.com/article5/080113.htm.
182 http://www.dcdave.com/article5/150108.htm.

CHAPTER 10

Oliver Stone on Forrestal

Orwell Lives

I never thought that I'd learn how it feels
To experience dystopia in action,
But it's day after day of spinning your wheels:
The truth can't get any traction.

One need not spend the time slogging through all 784 pages of Oliver Stone and Peter Kuznick's *The Untold History of the United States* to realize that what you are going to get is what one might call "approved establishment-left history."[183] It might as well have been co-written by Noam Chomsky and Amy Goodman or a team of writers from *Z Magazine*. (Who knows? Maybe it was, or by a team at Langley, Virginia.) In fact, Goodman has already given the co-authors a softball promotional interview on her program.[184]

---

183 Simon and Schuster, 2012.

184 https://www.democracynow.org/2012/11/16/oliver_stone_on_the_untold_us.

To an awful lot of people these days, by far the biggest untold story in American history concerns what really happened on September 11, 2001. By that litmus test, at a book presentation in California, in the view of one of the attendees, the authors are complete failures, if not phonies.[185] But they do pass the establishment-left test with flying colors.

That they have the ruling establishment's stamp of approval is shown by the fact that the book was piped into lots of homes by the Showtime cable-TV network in the form of a 10-part mini-series. Showtime is owned by CBS, which is really all that we need to know.[186] Superficially, there would appear to be a bit of a contradiction here in that CBS has been a leader in attacking any challenge to the official lone-nut and magic-bullet story of the John Kennedy assassination, when Stone's movie *JFK* is still probably the best known such challenge. Stone, though, in this instance, along with American University history professor Kuznick, is primarily wearing his left-liberal, virtually pro-Communist hat. Recall that it was CBS and their newsman Edward R. Murrow who did the big hatchet job on anti-Communist crusader Senator Joe McCarthy, as celebrated by the movie, *Good Night and Good Luck.*[187] If anti-anti-Communism is primarily what you're hawking, Showtime is the natural platform from which to hawk it.

And if you're gunning primarily at American anti-Communism in the mid-20th century, the godfather of the movement, James Forrestal, must also be in the crosshairs.[188] Forrestal, as we have seen, was a formidable man, one of the most talented, hard-working, farsighted public servants this country has ever had. They say he killed himself, but we have demonstrated beyond any serious doubt that he was assassinated. In spite of all the falsehoods that we have revealed in the mainstream press's story of Forrestal's demise, Stone and Kuznick show us that focus upon this supposed "suicide" remains the primary means by which his persistent enemies attack

---

185 https://www.youtube.com/watch?v=LW3jRvFEV84&feature=youtu.be.

186 David Martin, "Clinton and Cronkite, Odd Couple?" http://www.dcdave.com/article2/082798.html.

187 David Martin, "M. Stanton Evans on *Good Night and Good Luck.*" http://www.dcdave.com/article5/110614.htm.

188 David Martin, "James Forrestal and Joe McCarthy," http://www.dcdave.com/article5/110928.htm.

his message. Nothing sums up the approach better than the caption under their photograph of Forrestal on page 225:

> The first secretary of defense, James Forrestal, suffered a nervous breakdown and, tormented by his own anti-Communist paranoia, committed suicide, jumping from his sixteenth floor room at Bethesda Naval Hospital.

The core supporting text is as follows:

> Drew Pearson informed his radio audience that Forrestal was "out of his mind" after Forrestal was discovered in the street and shouting, "The Russians are coming!" He believed that the Russians had invaded the United States. Pearson later reported that during his brief stay in Florida, Forrestal had attempted suicide four times by hanging, slashing his wrists, and taking sleeping pills. (pp. 224-225)
>
> Alone in his room, he suffered constant nightmares. He thought he would suffer the same fate as Czechoslovakian Foreign Minister Jan Masaryk—to be pushed out of a window. But his condition began to improve, and on the night of May 22, 1949, he stayed up late copying Sophocles' "The Chorus from Ajax," in which the hero ponders his fate far from home. At the word "nightingale" he put his pen down and jumped. (p. 226)

Their references are a newspaper article by the scurrilous Pearson and *Boston Globe* establishment-left journalist, James Carroll's 2006 book, *House of War: The Pentagon and the Disastrous Rise of Pentagon Power*. How's that for scholarship? They would have done a lot better with Wikipedia.

The reference to Carroll is page 151 of his book, which is in Chapter 3 entitled "The Cold War Begins" with section heading titles like "Forrestal Agonistes," "Foundational Paranoia," and "The Russians are Coming," which encompasses page 151. Sure enough, referring to Forrestal's brief stay in Hobe Sound, Florida, at the estate of Under Secretary of State Robert Lovett, Carroll has this passage:

> Rumors flew around Washington. One radio report had it that Forrestal was found in his pajamas a few blocks from Lovett's house, and he was calling out, "The Russians are coming!"

At that point Carroll has an endnote, which Stone and Kuznick have apparently chosen not to have noticed. Carroll's reference is to page 739 of David McCullough's *Truman,* but he adds the following:

> Drew Pearson was the source of this report. His previous vilifications of Forrestal make the report unreliable, but Forrestal's mental illness definitely included delusions that the Soviets had invaded the United States. See also Hoopes and Brinkley, *Driven Patriot,* 451, 455.

Unreliable indeed! Furthermore, Carroll's assertion that Forrestal definitely believed the Soviets had invaded the United States is a flat-out lie...if not a "delusion" reflecting, perhaps, his own "mental illness." Turning to those pages in Hoopes and Brinkley, we find nothing resembling a belief by anyone that the Soviets had invaded the United States. What we get is a rehash of Arnold Rogow's attempt to paint Forrestal as paranoid because of his very legitimate concern that two groups with proven homicidal track records were out to get him, the Communists and the Zionists, and that they were monitoring his conversations. As he put it upon arriving in Florida, "Bob, they're after me." They were, and they still are. (See Chapter One, especially the "On the Beach" and "Forrestal *Was* Bugged" sections.)

Just as Stone and Kuznick should have checked out Carroll's endnote before relaying Drew Pearson's fanciful Forrestal vilification as gospel truth, Carroll should not have stopped his Hoopes and Brinkley reading at the end of page 455. As it happens, the key passage is quoted on the Wikipedia page for "The Russians are coming," and it has been there since 2006:

> The allegation originated with Forrestal's bitter political enemy, columnist Drew Pearson, and has been verified by no other person. This is what Townsend Hoopes and Douglas Brinkley have to say about the episode in their 1992 book, *Driven Patriot, the Life and Times of James Forrestal*:
>
>> Pearson had, in fact, decided to fire his heaviest ammunition in a radio broadcast on April 9. He charged that Forrestal, awakened by the sound of a fire siren (on the night of April 1 at Hobe Sound), had rushed out of his cottage screaming, "The Russians are attacking." He defined Forrestal's condition as "temporary insanity." In subsequent newspaper columns he asserted that Forrestal made

> three suicide attempts while in Florida — by drug overdose, by hanging, and by slashing his wrists. According to a later statement by [Navy psychiatrist Captain George] Raines, all of these assertions were lies. — pp. 455-456.

New York Times reporter Arthur Krock is too kind to Pearson in his speculation about the origins of the "Russians are coming" story. This is from his 1968 *Memoirs* (The "Z" to whom he refers is clearly Ferdinand Eberstadt, as we are able to deduce from other sources.):

> After dinner Forrestal went to bed and slept soundly, and Z and Forrestal's former aide, Rear Admiral John Gingrich, watched him through the night. He slept so soundly, with the aid of a sedative, that he did not hear a siren blow at about six o'clock in the morning. After noting that this had not awakened Forrestal, Z went down to the beach for a swim. He thinks that whoever was reporting to Drew Pearson saw Z come out of the house at that point, and that this gave rise to Pearson's statement that Forrestal had rushed out of the house when the siren blew, thinking the Russians had attacked the United States.[189]

What he means is that this at-best mistaken identity episode "gave rise" to a complete fabrication for malign purposes. But it gets even worse for Pearson and Carroll, and, by extension, for Stone and Kuznick. Carroll's basic reference for his "Russians are coming" assertion, page 739 of McCullough's *Truman,* has this passage, "Drew Pearson reported that Forrestal was 'out of his mind' and claimed *incorrectly* that in Florida Forrestal had rushed out into the street screaming, "The Russians are coming." (Emphasis added)

So, as we pointed out previously, Carroll knew that the information didn't just come from an unreliable source but that it was revealed as untrue by the Truman biographer whom he references for it. Nevertheless, he goes forward with his Forrestal slander, making it the title of a section heading and the centerpiece of his case against the former defense secretary. Stone and Kuznick then proceed to state it as fact because it was reported by Drew Pearson

---

189 Arthur Krock, *Memoirs: Sixty Years on the Firing Line*, Funk and Wagnalls, 1968, p. 256.

and repeated by James Carroll. Is this scholarship, dear readers, or is it out-and-out propaganda of the Big Lie variety?

Now let's look at the rest of what Stone and Kuznick have written about Forrestal's demise, starting with the photo caption. Did Forrestal really suffer a nervous breakdown and was he tormented by paranoia? What did the doctors who treated him at Bethesda Naval Hospital have to say? Until 2004, when this writer was able to shake the official investigation free from the government with repeated Freedom of Information Act requests, we didn't know what that was, except for sketchy statements to the press by lead psychiatrist Captain George Raines and various hospital spokesmen. Now we not only have the Willcutts review board interviews of all the doctors online, but since February of 2010 we have it in a searchable htm format.[190]

Give it a try. You'll see that the word "nervous" comes up only once when a testifying doctor describes his qualifications. "Nervous breakdown" does not appear. "Paranoia" shows up only in this sentence by the editor, the host of the ARIWatch web site, "Mark Hunter": "Forrestal has been called crazy, yet you will search the report in vain for such words as delusion, persecution, anxiety, paranoia." You won't find "paranoid" either, except again in the words of the editor telling us that Forrestal's Navy driver said that he was neither depressed nor paranoid.

Not that it matters a great deal, but the word "nightmare" doesn't turn up either nor can it be found as anything that Forrestal experienced at the hospital in Arnold Rogow's exercise in quack psychoanalysis. That Forrestal might have feared that he would suffer the same fate as the anti-Communist Jan Masaryk appears more as a manifestation of common sense rather than paranoia, not unlike his belief that he was being bugged and followed by Zionist operatives or that U.S. support for the creation of the state of Israel would in due time cause us to be dragged militarily into the Middle East and would alienate the Arab world.

Not only is virtually everything that Stone and Kuznick say about Forrestal's demise provably false, but they don't even do a very good job of par-

---

[190] https://findingaids.princeton.edu/collections/MC051/c04531; http://ariwatch.com/VS/JamesForrestal/WillcuttsReport.htm.

roting their flawed sources. Drew Pearson didn't say that Forrestal tried to kill himself four times during his brief stay in Florida. The fourth unsuccessful attempt supposedly occurred at Bethesda Naval Hospital, according to Pearson. We have seen that Captain Raines denied that any such attempts took place, and it's really very hard to imagine that anyone as capable as Forrestal could have been so incompetent at the suicide act. Raines, as we have seen, by the way, was alone among the doctors in even suggesting that Forrestal might have had any suicidal tendencies. One can tell that he was trying his very best to uphold the suicide story without resorting to outright whoppers.

Forrestal did not go out the window of his hospital room; he went out the window of the kitchen across the hall from his room. Also, in saying twice that Forrestal "jumped" Stone and Kuznick fail to address the question of what that bathrobe belt was doing tied around his neck. The newspapers and the establishment authors, as we have seen, have solved that conundrum by speculating that he must have been trying to hang himself out the 16th floor window, as improbable as that sounds. It's not quite the same thing as free-style jumping, as suggested by Stone and Kuznick.

We also know that Forrestal was not seen writing from any book just before he went out the window. The Naval corpsman on duty, testifying before the Willcutts review board, said that when he looked in at that time the room was dark and Forrestal appeared to be sleeping and that he had witnessed no reading or writing by Forrestal the whole time that he had been on duty.

Finally, Forrestal didn't copy "Chorus from Ajax" by Sophocles that night or at any other time, even though Dr. Raines, trying his best to help the suicide case, volunteered in his testimony that the handwriting looked like Forrestal's. The reader can see for himself that it looks nothing of the sort.

Drew Pearson

We first encountered Pearson, from a historical chronology standpoint, acting as a shill against Franklin Roosevelt's anti-Communist, anti-Zionist emissary General Patrick Hurley. The story is told in "The Old

Zionist Smear Machine."[191] Hurley's letter of complaint to Roosevelt elicited the following response:

> PERSONAL AND CONFIDENTIAL August 30, 1943
>
> Dear Pat:
>
> Thanks for yours of August nineteenth referring to a printed story in Drew Pearson's column. You are quite right in answering none of the letters from Jews or others who believe Drew Pearson's columns.
>
> His ill-considered falsehoods have come to the point where he is doing much harm to his own Government and to other nations. It is a pity that anyone anywhere believes anything that he writes.
>
> So much for Mr. Drew Pearson.
>
> Always sincerely,
>
> (s) FRANKLIN D. ROOSEVELT

The following passage from Arthur Krock's *Memoirs* speaks volumes about the character of Drew Pearson and of the American press generally:

> But not until the succession of radio broadcasts by Drew Pearson of which Forrestal was the target did I get an impression of irrationality and indecisiveness that was so completely at variance with the man I had known so well. After each of these Sunday broadcasts Forrestal would telephone me to discuss, but never decide, what to do about them.
>
> Then came a broadcast that upset him more than any—a report that when Mrs. Forrestal was being held up in front of their Beekman Place home in New York City, her husband "hid" in his quarters. It happened by chance that I was in a position to refute the charge, having spent that evening in Forrestal's company and having slept in his guest room that fronted on the East River, a location where we could not—and did not—know of the holdup until the following morning. It was typical of Mrs. Forrestal that she did not awaken her husband to inform him of what, after all, was a *fait accompli.*
>
> To Forrestal's fervently expressed relief, I volunteered to acquaint Pearson with the facts, offering the opinion that he would undoubtedly

---

[191] David Martin, http://www.dcdave.com/article5/061108.htm.

> withdraw the charge. But though Pearson, on receipt of a written and detailed account, wired me "THANKS. WILL DO," the retraction was never forthcoming. From that time forward I did observe a deterioration of spirit in Forrestal, though, in fairness, it should be noted that the broadcast was only one of the causes. [192]

Indeed, I should think a bigger cause for despondency on Forrestal's part would have been that his friend Krock, who wrote for the most influential newspaper in the country, would treat something like this as primarily Forrestal's problem and a reflection upon Forrestal because he was unable to solve it. *The New York Times* by itself had the power to expose Pearson, even to drum him out of the profession. No one of his character should have been permitted the national megaphone that he had, both with a widely circulated syndicated column and a Sunday night broadcast. His standards of probity were demonstrably so low that he should not have been allowed into the company of decent people, much less to practice journalism. And to think, it is the likes of a Drew Pearson that Oliver Stone and Peter Kuznick exalt as an authority and whose allegations form the very centerpiece of their book, and it is the likes of the deeply patriotic and dedicated James Forrestal that they disparage.

Stone and Kuznick and James Carroll are not alone in coming down on Forrestal, the reason for which was obviously his anti-Communism and, much more importantly, his anti-Zionism. It started early when his "friends" in the journalistic community like Krock and Walter Trohan lay low while Pearson and Winchell poured out their calumnies.[193] It continued when he was confined to Bethesda Naval Hospital for almost two months and not one of his powerful friends and admirers bothered to pay him a visit. These included Robert Lovett, Artemus Gates, Ferdinand Eberstadt, and Bernard Baruch. Not even the man closest to him at the

---

[192] Krock, pp. 250-251.

[193] On the conservative *Chicago Tribune*'s Walter Trohan, see David Martin, "The Pearl Harbor Betrayal and James Forrestal's Death, http://www.dcdave.com/article5/121004.htm.

Pentagon, top aide Marx Leva, bothered to come see him. It is likely that they could all see which way the wind was blowing.

Forrestal could no doubt see it himself. He knew all about how Communist infiltration of the executive branch had resulted in making Joseph Stalin the biggest winner of World War II. He must have known about the letter bombs that the Stern Gang had sent in an attempt on the life of President Truman in 1947. What must he have thought when he saw the whole episode hushed up? He must have felt like Deputy White House Counsel Vincent Foster's sons when they read the unanimous opinion of the press that their father had committed suicide and further, that the police had been turned away from the Foster house the night of his death and that they, the sons, had never come back to the house that night when they knew none of it was true.[194]

The abandonment of Forrestal continued when Pearson's preposterously false claim of four previous suicide attempts went unchallenged at the time and when the delay in issuing the report of the investigation of his death dragged on and on. It continued when only the sketchy conclusions of the report were released some four and a half months late and no one seemed to notice that the report did not conclude that Forrestal had committed suicide. Then, they all held their tongues—including those great press "friends" of his, Krock and Trohan—as the report of the investigation itself was held back and kept secret. The American molders of public opinion continued to hold their tongues when Princeton's Seeley Mudd Manuscript Library put out a press release announcing that after 55 years the report on Forrestal's death was finally available to the public.

Down with Forrestal, Up with Wallace

It is hardly a surprise that authors who would make the anti-Communist, anti-Zionist Forrestal a major villain of their book should make FDR's vice-president before Truman, Henry Wallace, a hero. Consider this excerpt from a predictably glowing review by *The Nation:*

---

[194] See David Martin, "Seth Rich Equals Vince Foster" http://www.dcdave.com/article5/170525.htm.

> At many pivotal moments, Stone argues, history could have taken a radically different course. The missed opportunities, the roads not taken—these are Stone's central themes, which he argues with energy, passion and a mountain of evidence (the companion volume has eighty-nine pages of footnotes).
>
> Case number one: if Henry Wallace had won the vice presidential nomination in 1944, he would have become president when Roosevelt died in 1945, and we probably would not have bombed Hiroshima and Nagasaki, and could have avoided the cold war as well. It's a startling and intriguing argument. Usually we teach about Wallace as the hopeless, left wing third-party candidate of 1948, when he split from the Democrats and ran on the Progressive Party ticket. McCarthyism had already taken hold of American politics, and Wallace was redbaited into a crushing defeat.
>
> Four years earlier, however, the situation was very different: Wallace was Roosevelt's incumbent vice president, and the Soviets were our allies. A Gallup poll in July 1944 asked likely Democratic voters whom they wanted on the ticket as veep. Sixty-five percent said Wallace, while Truman came in eighth, with just 2 percent. Roosevelt announced that, were he a delegate, he would vote for Wallace. Claude Pepper, a Democratic senator from Florida, tried to nominate Wallace at the convention, but the conservative party bosses, who opposed him, adjourned the proceedings. "Had Pepper made it five more feet [to the microphone] and nominated Wallace," Stone argues, "Wallace would have become president in 1945 and...there might have been no atomic bombings, no nuclear arms race, and no Cold War."[195]

We have had a brief look at the quality of those "eighty-nine pages of footnotes," and it is not encouraging. But if Forrestal had been listened to, not only would we not have dropped atom bombs on Japan or anyone, but it is very likely neither China nor North Korea would have been captured by the Communists.[196] Furthermore, you can take it to the bank that if Wallace had succeeded Roosevelt, all of the Korean peninsula would now be under the Red boot of the latest ruler from the Kim family

---

[195] John Wiener, "Oliver Stone's 'Untold History'," *The Nation*, November 14, 2012, https://www.thenation.com/article/oliver-stones-untold-history/.

[196] David Martin, "Forrestal Ignored: Korean War Fought, China Lost to Reds," http://www.dcdave.com/article5/110530.htm.

dynasty. Communist sympathizer Owen Lattimore might well have been his Secretary of State.[197]

Here is some more pertinent information about Wallace. It comes from an undated article in the *Jewish Post* online:

> [Henry] Wallace attracted many Jews: around 30% of his followers were Jews. Among them his fund-raiser, William Gailmore, was an ex-rabbi. He controlled the Bronx thanks to Leo Isaacson who was elected to the congress as a member of the progressive party. Many communists and Jewish communists supported Wallace who always was blamed as a front for Moscow. But Wallace did something else, he never forgot to declare his support of Zionism and a Jewish state. On Dec. 1947, he visited Palestine as a guest of the Labor movement. Wallace also believed in the Judeo-Christian idea and a project to develop the Middle-East for Jews and Arabs alike. Furthermore, he helped the 'Friends of Lehi in the U.S." (the so-called 'Stern Gang.') And Karabell wrote that on July 23, 1948 the Progressive Party's convention hosted "the Stern Gang, the Israeli underground paramilitary organization that had blown up buildings and assassinated British officials in Palestine..." He wrote that the Lehi (Freedom Fighters of Israel) were close to the Irgun's Menachem Begin, but Yitzhak Shamir was the Lehi's commander together with Natan Yellin-Mor and Israel Eldad. Truman was pushed by his pro-Zionist advisors (Mark Cliford) [sic] to support Israel in 1948 in order to attract the Jewish vote away from Wallace's camp. Also, Dewey was pro-Zionist.[198]

Consider also the following passage from an article "Former VP Henry Wallace, Forgotten Zionist, Stars in Oliver Stone's New TV Series" in *The Algemeiner*, which fashions itself "the fastest growing Jewish newspaper in America":

> Annoyed by Wallace's pressure for a more conciliatory U.S. position toward the Soviet Union, Truman ousted him in 1946.
>
> Wallace then became editor of *The New Republic*. In its pages he strongly defended the Zionist cause, at one point going so far as to suggest that the Jewish underground's guerrilla war against the British was "in some respects like the fight the American colonies carried on in 1776..."

---

[197] David Martin, "Truman Administration Adviser Counseled Surrender of Korea to Reds," http://www.dcdave.com/article5/110602.htm.

[198] Gad Nashon, "The Last Campaign: How Truman Won in 1948," *Jewish Post,* http://www.jewishpost.com/archives/news/the-last-campaign-how-truman-won-in-1948.html.

> In October 1947, Wallace spent 10 days in the Holy Land, surveying Jewish settlements and industries and meeting with leaders such as Jewish Agency chairman David Ben-Gurion. Wallace's glowing prediction that the Zionists would turn the Negev desert into "a veritable garden" received widespread attention. He also met with Irgun Zvai Leumi underground chief Menachem Begin.[199]

Where to start? First, Wallace did not just become editor of *The New Republic,* he was chosen for the job by a spy for the Soviet Union affiliated with the Cambridge Five, publisher Michael Whitney Straight.[200] Second, this Lehi organization that he was said to have helped, and which supported him, is the Stern Gang, the terrorists who tried to kill Truman and perpetrated numerous other outrages. And not long after Wallace saw fit to cozy up to Irgun leader Menachem Begin in Israel, as we noted in Chapter One, a group of prominent Jewish American intellectuals led by Albert Einstein and Hannah Arendt wrote a letter to *The New York Times* detailing the Irgun's numerous crimes and outrages. Wallace was ousted from the Democratic ticket in 1944 in the nick of time and we slowly began to resist the Communist takeover, but the warning by Einstein *et al.* was not heeded, and the capitulation to the worst elements of Zionism continues apace. That it is a complete certainty that no one in the mainstream press will point out Oliver Stone's lies about the death of James Forrestal is but one measure of the degree of our capitulation.

---

199 Rafael Medoff, "Former VP Henry Wallace, Forgotten Zionist, Stars in Oliver Stone's New TV Series," The Algemeiner, November 18, 2012, http://www.algemeiner.com/2012/11/18/former-vp-henry-wallace-forgotten-zionist-stars-in-oliver-stone%E2%80%99s-new-tv-series/.

200 See Roland Perry, *Last of the Cold War Spies: The Life of Michael Straight, the Only American in Britain's Cambridge Spy Ring,* Da Capo Press, 2005; *Washington Post* review at http://www.washingtonpost.com/wp-dyn/content/article/2005/08/07/AR2005080700970.html?noredirect=on.

CHAPTER 11

Spook Shrink Flubs Script

Respected Spook?

They say that the writer's "respected,"
But his C.V. suggests he's connected
To the CIA.
If so, there's no way
That with deceit he would not be infected.

Readers will notice that in the following letter to George Washington professor, Jerrold M. Post, M.D., I adopt a somewhat different tone than I have in previous letters to members of the academic community with respect to the death of Secretary of Defense James Forrestal. In those instances, I held out at least the faint hope that I was communicating with honest men who might actually overcome the strong herd instinct of the species and embrace the truth once it had been pointed out to them. One need not linger long over Professor Post's pedigree to see that such assumptions have no place in his case. One might as well write a hopeful letter on this matter to a representative of the American news media or to a Congressman.

Here is the email I sent to Dr. Jerrold M. Post, who at the time was Professor of Psychiatry, Political Psychology and International Affairs and Director of the Political Psychology Program at The George Washington University, and who also founded and directed the Center for the Analysis of Personality and Political Behavior at the Central Intelligence Agency :

March 8, 2008

Dear Professor Post,

I realize that truth is not exactly a CIA long suit, but you really ought to be a bit more careful in your writing. It would help your credibility if you would at least make your "facts" consistent with the popular fiction produced by others writing for a similarly deceptive purpose. I refer in particular to the conclusion of your section on the death of James Forrestal on page 64 of *Leaders and their Followers in a Dangerous World*:[201]

"Before he leaped to his death, Forrestal copied in a notebook the melancholic chorus from Sophocles' play Ajax:

Thy son in a foreign clime
Worn by the waste of time
Comfortless, nameless, hopeless
Save in the dark prospect of the yawning grave.

Oh, when the pride of Grecia's noble race
Wanders, as now in darkness and disgrace,
Better to die and sleep
The never waking sleep than linger on
And dare to live when the soul's life is gone.

"A psychiatrically trained medical corpsman would have recognized this as a literary suicide note, but the corpsman assigned to Forrestal paid no attention to the poignant despair conveyed by this selection."

I dare say that no psychiatric training at all is necessary to recognize the fairly obvious suggestions of suicide in the passage, and the press, from day one, has certainly energetically sold it as a "literary suicide note," but belaboring the obvious is not your biggest offense

[201] Cornell University Press, 2004.

here. Dramatic though those last three lines may be, they were never transcribed by Forrestal, even according to the approved script. Although one *Washington Post* reporter on the day after the death wrote that those lines stood out "in a firm and legible hand" in the transcription, a longer article in the same newspaper reproduced the whole poem, with the part he was said to have transcribed in italics. The italics stop in the middle of the word "nightingale," many lines before those last three lines are reached. That story is the one that has been repeated by authors of books on Forrestal, from Walter Millis, to Arnold Rogow, to Townsend Hoopes and Douglas Brinkley, and it is the one to which a proper professional in your trade should conform.

Furthermore, Hospital Apprentice Robert Wayne Harrison, Forrestal's guard that night, was hardly remiss in not recognizing the ominous nature of the words. According to biographer Rogow, Harrison (whom Rogow does not name) last looked in on Forrestal at 1:45 am and saw him transcribing something from a book. By the time anyone got a look at what had been written, Forrestal had gone out the window. The transcription was reportedly found later (not in a notebook as you have it, but on a loose sheet of paper from a hospital notepad). Interestingly, no contemporary newspaper accounts said that Harrison witnessed Forrestal copying from the book. They only reported that the transcription and book had been found, but never by whom. Some accounts say the book was found open on the radiator near the bed, others that it was found open on the table next to the bed.

When I wrote about the matter somewhat more carefully and less credulously than you, two years before your book was published, I speculated that Rogow had probably made up the story that Forrestal was witnessed transcribing the poem. He had cited no source for his claim, and he was alone in making it. It turns out that I was right.

In 2004, when you were busy sloppily parroting the fable about a depressed man copying a morbid poem and then plunging out a high window, I was submitting Freedom of Information Act requests for the long suppressed official investigation of Forrestal's death. On my third attempt, I got it.

In his testimony to the review board convened by the head of the National Navy Medical Center, Admiral Morton Willcutts, Apprentice Harrison said he last looked in on Forrestal at 1:45 am, exactly the time that Rogow had Harrison witnessing Forrestal copying the poem. He testified that the room was dark and Forrestal was apparently sleeping. He related further that the room was, in fact, dark the whole time that he was on duty, starting at midnight, and he did not see Forrestal do any reading.

It gets worse, much worse, for your nice, neat suicide-from-depression thesis. The book of poems that the newspapers described so precisely was never entered into evidence, nor was anyone produced who claimed to have found either it or the transcription. A transcription of the first few lines of the Sophocles poem was among the exhibits, and Captain George Raines, the lone doctor who claimed that Forrestal made suicidal statements, volunteered that the handwriting looked like Forrestal's. That one very brief mention, virtually in passing, is the only appearance that the "literary suicide note" makes in the entire report. Nothing, whatsoever, is said about its text.

It's little wonder that the review board steered so far clear of it. Have a look at the note along with known Forrestal handwriting samples. What do you think? It's not even close to Forrestal's handwriting, is it? And not that it matters much compared to the patent fraudulence of the note, but the transcription also cuts off several lines short of the line with the "nightingale" in it, which was supposed to be the stopping place.

Wrong on Foster, Too

Backing up to page 63, I see that you also colored outside the accepted lines in your account of the aftermath of the death of Deputy White House Counsel, Vincent Foster. In your over-eagerness to sell the ever-popular suicide-from-depression story in this case, too, you write, "When his body was found, he had with him an unfilled prescription for an antidepressant from his doctor in Little Rock and the names of three Washington area physicians, whom he never consulted."

The official story, as contained in the report by Kenneth Starr and reported in the newspapers, is that the prescription was conveyed by telephone to the Morgan Pharmacy in Georgetown the night before Foster's death and that Foster had taken the medicine. There was no written prescription for Foster to have had on his person when his body was found, and, certainly, no one has been reported to have found such a prescription. Furthermore, the doctor said that at the small level of dosage prescribed, the medication was only for the treatment of insomnia, not depression.

The likelihood is high that none of these stories about medicine prescribed from Arkansas is true. No telephone records of the call from Foster to the doctor or from the doctor to the pharmacy, nor the prescription, nor the pills themselves were ever entered into evidence. In the toxicology report accompanying the autopsy, it was reported that there were no drugs in Foster's system, and antidepressants were among the drugs being searched for. In the early days after the death when the official word was that no one had any idea why Foster might have killed himself, the doctor in Little Rock held his tongue, as did everyone close to Foster. On July 24, four days after the death, White House spokesperson Dee Dee Myers is quoted as saying that, "His family says with certainty that he'd never been treated [for depression]." Nothing was said about any prescription for it.

There are problems with that list of Washington-area doctors, as well. It first appeared on the official record in an article on page A8 of *The Washington Post* of July 28 with these lines, "White House officials searching the office of Vincent Foster, Jr. last week found a note indicating the 48 year-old deputy White House counsel may have considered psychiatric help shortly before he died July 20 in what investigators have concluded was a suicide, federal officials said yesterday."

The note, as it turned out, was that list of physicians, who, in an article two days later, *The Post* said were two in number, and it named them. In that article, the discovery site was said to be Foster's car at the park where the body was found, although the Park Police, too, had held their collective tongues when the word had been that no one had any idea why Foster might have killed himself. The "three psychiatrists" number that you report is consistent with the Park Police report released almost a year later. The names of the doctors in that report are redacted. They later appear unredacted in released Senate documents. The first name, that of the doctor not previously identified by *The Post*, is written in block letters; the latter two in cursive style. Strange!

Scruples aside, I can almost sympathize with you and your journalistic cohorts sometimes. It's not easy to sell a story that keeps changing. I gather, though, noting the nine members of your profession who weighed in back in 1998 on behalf of admitted would-be double murderer, Ruthann Aron, that this is the sort of thing that you are paid to do as an expert witness from time to time.[202] With that experience, you should have done a slicker job than you have done in your recent volume.

Finally, if I might dare to poach on your dubious turf a bit, I must take issue with your postmortem personality profiles.[203] I know that you are doing only brief, thumbnail sketches, but I find it most unfortunate that you should seize upon the word "ambitious" to sum up both Foster and Forrestal. It conjures up in the mind the power-hungry careerist type, who, like Richard Rich in *A Man for All Seasons,* would jettison

---

[202] David Martin, "Expert Witnesses," http://www.dcdave.com/article1/040198.html.

[203] David Martin, "Mencken on Psychology." http://www.dcdave.com/article3/000910.html.

everything that is good and noble for his own personal advancement. From everyone who knew Forrestal, in particular, it is hard to imagine anyone who was more completely opposite from that kind of person. Hoopes and Brinkley chose well when they titled their biography of Forrestal, *Driven Patriot.*

To cite just two of many possible examples, a personally ambitious person would hardly have risked being sacked for insubordination for the efforts he made to bring about Japanese surrender on terms different from those desired by the White House, as Forrestal did as Secretary of the Navy in 1944, and he would not have brushed off his friend Bernard Baruch's warning that he had become too closely identified with opposition to the creation of the state of Israel for his own good, as he did as Secretary of Defense in 1948.[204] I think that even the historical psychoanalyst, Rogow, would have found your suggestion novel in the extreme that Forrestal became "depressed" because he had seen his "political future destroyed."

Foster, for his part, was a man of broad interests and great accomplishment in the legal field. He was known for the style and clarity of his legal briefs, so different from the text of the peevish, sophomoric note, torn into 27 pieces (but without residual fingerprints) said to have been found in a briefcase that had previously been emptied in the presence of a number of people. He shunned the limelight and was trying to quit his job and go back to his practice in Little Rock. To me, that doesn't sound like much of a Richard Rich type, either. Rather, the personality type seems to fit much better the husband and wife couple for whom he worked.

I'm not much into pop psychology myself, but your manner of describing these two men looks to me like a classic case of projection.[205]

Sincerely,

David Martin

Hardly surprisingly, Professor Post did not respond, nor did anyone respond on his behalf, and I am still alive to record the experience here.

---

[204] Under "terms different from those desired," we embedded a link to the June 6, 1950, *Look* magazine article, "How We Bungled the Japanese Surrender," by Rear Admiral Ellis M. Zacharias. http://ussslcca25.com/zach12.htm.

[205] https://en.wikipedia.org/wiki/Psychological_projection.

CHAPTER 12

The Mendocracy Versus the Citizenry

Drop the Subject

Was James Forrestal thrown from that window?
Was he murdered for reasons of state?
Well, didn't Frank Olson of the CIA
Suffer a similar fate?

Speaking of Deep State operatives, consider the first man in the national mainstream silence to mention the Willcutts Report. After having ignored the long-delayed publication of the official proceedings of the Navy board of investigation into the violent death of the first U.S. Secretary of Defense James Forrestal, the national opinion-molding apparatus (NOMA) finally broke its five-year-long silence. Some of the discredited "facts" are still there, but in his book published in 2009, Nicholas Thompson in *The Hawk and the Dove: Paul Nitze, George Kennan, and the History of the Cold War* perpetuates the myth of Forrestal's suicide and explicitly acknowledges the Willcutts Report as one of his sources.[206]

One could hardly have found a more representative member of the American establishment opinion-molding club to do the silence breaking than Thompson. Here's what they had to say about him on the now taken-down web site for his book:

> Nicholas Thompson is a senior editor at *The New Yorker*, a contributing editor at Bloomberg Television, and the author of *The Hawk and the Dove: Paul Nitze, George Kennan, and the History of the Cold War.*
>
> Prior to *The New Yorker*, Mr. Thompson was a senior editor at *Wired*, a senior editor at *Legal Affairs* and an editor at the *Washington Monthly*. He has written about politics, technology, and the law for numerous publications, and he currently writes regularly for the *New York Times* Book Review. He is a frequent guest on CNN's American Morning, NBC's Today Show, and Live with Regis and Kelly. He has also appeared multiple times on every other major cable and broadcast news network. He is also currently a senior fellow at the New America Foundation and an official panelist on CNN International's "Connect the World" with Becky Anderson.

Updating Thompson's résumé, he is now editor-in-chief of *Wired*, a contributor to CBS News, and a fellow at the Council on Foreign Relations. He also happens to be Paul Nitze's grandson.

Not surprisingly, his book was heavily publicized and widely distributed. Working across the street at the Bureau of Labor Statistics at the time, I discovered the paperback version prominently displayed at the Union Station branch of the national chain of the now defunct B. Dalton bookstores. The book's web site listed favorable quotes from reviews in *The Washington Times, The Washington Post, The Washington Post Book Review, The New York Times, The New York Times Book Review, The New York Review of Books, Newsweek, Time Magazine, The New Republic, The Washington Monthly, The National Review, Booklist, Library Journal, The Daily Beast, Talking Points Memo Café,* and the major British weekly, *The Economist.*

---

[206] Nicholas Thompson, *The Hawk and the Dove: George Kennan, Paul Nitze, and the History of the Cold War, Henry Holt and Co., 2008.*

Even Stephen Colbert gave him a book-promoting softball interview on his popular Comedy Channel show, The Colbert Report. Not since James Carroll, with his 2006 book on the Pentagon, had an author been given so great an opportunity to spread untruths about the violent death of the leading U.S. opponent of the creation of the state of Israel (Oliver Stone's book came four years later in 2012.). The following is from pp. 88-89 (He has endnotes in which the source is given for particular passages. We show them in parentheses.):

> Forrestal lasted six weeks [sic] in the hospital, until the night of Saturday, May 21, 1949. According to a report long kept secret, he spent most of the evening pacing. At 12:20, he got a cup of orange juice and said he was going to bed; at 12:35, he got up to grab a cup of coffee; ten minutes later, he was apparently asleep. At 1:30, he popped out of bed and the corpsman on duty asked if he wanted a sleeping pill. Forrestal said no, but the corpsman went to ask the doctor whether he could have one anyway. When he returned, Forrestal was gone. (Admiral M.D. Willcutts, "Report on the Death of James Forrestal," part 2, p. 176.)
>
> Lower in the building, people heard a thud. Forrestal's body, dressed in pajamas, was found facedown on the asphalt and cinderblock ledge outside room 384. He had plummeted thirteen floors, bouncing off other ledges as he fell. His bathrobe sash was tied tight around his neck (ibid. part 1, p. 62); upstairs, a razor blade (ibid. p. 81) was found near his slippers. He had tried to hang himself and then either jumped or fallen out the window. At some point that evening he had copied out lines from a translation of Sophocles' *Ajax,* where the Chorus laments, "Better to die, and sleep/The never-waking sleep, than linger on/And dare to live when the soul's life is gone."

In the first paragraph, the part about Forrestal pacing the floor does come from the Willcutts Report. To this writer's knowledge, it had not been reported elsewhere in the mainstream press or books. It can be found in the testimony of the orderly on duty before midnight, Edward Price/Prise. The coffee and orange juice drinking after midnight are also reported for the first time in the Willcutts Report, but the exact times given here can only be described as spurious. Navy nurse Regina M. L. Harty/Margie Hardy and hospital apprentice Edwin Utz agree that Forrestal had coffee at around 1:00 am. He apparently had orange juice twice, once when Price/Prise was on duty and again shortly before he had the coffee, but the orderly at that time, Robert Wayne Harrison, could not recall the time. The news that Forrestal popped out of bed at 1:30 can't be found in anyone's testimony, nor can the revelation that Harrison was absent from Forrestal's room because he had gone to inquire about a sleeping pill. Harrison testified that at 1:45 he looked in on Forrestal, and he was apparently sleeping in a darkened room. He said he was absent when Forrestal disappeared from the room because he had gone down the hall to write in the nurse's log.

Thompson is most disingenuous in the beginning of that second sentence, "According to a report long kept secret...." Kept secret? Why would the government want to keep such a report secret? He doesn't even speculate. And how was the secrecy ended, why was it ended, and when, exactly, was it ended? The reader must guess about all of that.

It's pretty clear that he does not want people to know that the report was held back for 55 years and would most likely still be secret but for the efforts of this writer. We first announced the fact that the report was available to the public in Part 2 of our series, "Who Killed James Forrestal?" published in September of 2004. Simultaneously, as we have noted, the Seeley Mudd Manuscript Library of Princeton University, which houses Forrestal's papers, posted a copy of the report that we had sent them on their web site.[207]

And why did the Navy keep the report secret? In 2003 we drew the common-sense conclusion that it was because they had something to hide.[208] As it turned out, with the release of the report some months later, we were quite right, in spades. That's apparently something that Thompson doesn't want you to know, either.[209]

---

[207] https://findingaids.princeton.edu/collections/MC051/c04531.

[208] David Martin, "Secret Forrestal Investigation," http://www.dcdave.com/poet12/031026a.html.

[209] The release of the report might have been a fluke. We twice filed Freedom of Information Act requests for the report with the National Naval Medical Center, following their procedures to the letter. Our request was, quite illegally, ignored both times. The law requires a response of some kind within 20 busi-

In his second paragraph, quoted above, the description of the surface upon which Forrestal landed clearly comes from the Willcutts Report, except that Thompson has not read very carefully. It is from the testimony of the autopsy doctor, Captain William M. Silliphant, who once describes the surface as "asphalt and cinder rock" and again as "asphalt and cinder-rocks," not "cinderblock," as Thompson has it. The bouncing off several ledges is original with Thompson, and it is preposterous on its face if you think about it. The review board, without any testimony to support it, says at one point that he first struck a ledge of the fourth floor. That is probably accurate, though. Nurse Dorothy Turner speaks of hearing a "double thud." What the board describes as a ledge was more than likely the sloping roof of a bay window, seen in the photograph of the tower. (See frontispiece)

Thompson's mention of the discovered razor blade—also from Willcutts Report testimony—is obviously strategic, meant to convey the impression that Forrestal was accumulating a veritable arsenal of self-killing devices. Also strategic is Thompson's tired old account of the supposed morbid poem transcription by Forrestal. From the first day that Forrestal's death was reported, that poem has been placed on center stage as evidence of Forrestal's suicidal intentions. In spite of the manifest evidence of its lack of authenticity, Thompson keeps it there.

---

ness days, with the possibility of a 10-day extension. We were on the verge of filing a FOIA lawsuit when we happened upon a Navy web site that allowed for online FOIA requests, which we made in a matter of minutes. Within a couple of weeks we received a letter from the Navy's Judge Advocate General's Office promising me the report, and, indeed, it did arrive forthwith. The rest is history, except that it's not yet history to the historians and other major opinion molders, the Thompson work notwithstanding.

Nurse Turner's Crucial Testimony

As with his first paragraph, what's really important is what Thompson leaves out. To know about the razor blade, he had to be familiar with the testimony to the Willcutts review board of the nurse, Lieutenant Turner. Her name had appeared in contemporary newspapers only as the person who heard Forrestal land on the third-floor roof. What the press did not tell us is that she had rushed upstairs and was the first person to get a good look at Forrestal's lighted vacated room. Here is part of what she said:

> So I went up to tower sixteen and told Miss Harty there was a man's body outside the galley window and he wasn't mine. We both went into his room and he wasn't there and we noticed the broken glass on the bed and looked down and noticed the razor blade and told him he was missing (sic) and she said it was one forty-eight.

Broken glass on the bed!!?? How could anyone ignore that fact as if it were insignificant? But Thompson is not alone; the review board, as we have seen, ignored it as well. They completely pass over the mention of the broken glass, asking only about the razor blade that she had mentioned (and slippers that she had not) in the recorded transcript:

> Q. You said you saw his slippers and a razor blade beside them; where did you see them?
> A. The bed clothes were turned back and towards the middle of the bed and I looked down and they were right there as you get out of bed.

In her answer, Lt. Turner drops another bomb in light of what the review board had been shown up to that point. She is testifying on the third day of the proceedings. On the first day, the board had gone to see Forrestal's hospital room. On the second day, it had heard the testimony and examined the photographs of the vacated room. One can see from the photographs of the room that there are no bedclothes on the bed, turned back or otherwise. (see frontispiece)

No one on the board had a thing to say about the inconsistency, nor does Thompson. Surely it must have dawned upon at least one of the Navy doctors—all employees of the National Naval Medical Center with no qualifications as criminal investigators—the moment they laid eyes on that room that something was seriously amiss. It bears no resemblance whatever to a room that has been lived in for over six weeks and hastily abandoned in the middle of the night, that is, to the room that Lt. Turner saw.

As we observed in Chapter Four, the board must have had their marching orders because, not only did they know what not to ask Lt. Turner, they knew what not to ask the photographer, as well. In contrast to their questioning of the first photographer, the one who photographed the body, they didn't ask when the room photographs were taken. Had they done so, they would have had to have asked him why there was a delay of several hours, as is evident by the bright sun streaming in the windows. They also didn't ask the first photographer, who showed up promptly, if he had also taken room photos, and if not, why not, and if so, what they showed.

After Thompson makes a complete muddle of an attempt to explain why there was a bathrobe sash tied around Forrestal's neck, he shows that he must have marching orders as well with his reference to the famous poem transcription. From the Willcutts Report, he must know that the account by Forrestal biographers Arnold Rogow and Townsend Hoopes and Douglas Brinkley that the corpsman (Harrison) looked in on Forrestal at 1:45 and saw him transcribing the poem is a complete fabrication. Harrison testified that at that time the room was dark, and Forrestal was apparently sleeping. Furthermore, he said, the room was dark the whole time that he was on duty and Forrestal did no reading or writing. Thompson knows now that he can't just parrot what the "definitive" biographies have said, so he has the unseen writing occurring at some time earlier in the evening. As others have done, he then quotes from the particularly morbid last lines of the poem that occur well past the purported transcribed lines.

The big problem with this continued invocation of the transcription as though it amounted to some sort of a suicide note is that, as we show in Chapter Five, Forrestal didn't do any transcribing of a Sophocles poem that evening or any evening. The handwriting of the transcription is clearly that of someone other than Forrestal.

Now one might argue that since no one in the "mainstream" has picked up on it, Thompson might simply be ignorant of the fact that the transcription is bogus, because he is unaware of my web site. That is not very likely because the Wikipedia site for Forrestal up to that time had linked to my handwriting samples for several years, and one would think that simple curiosity alone would have made him check out Forrestal's Wikipedia page. It might not have the last word on a subject, but for most serious writers of non-fiction these days, Wikipedia is one of the first stops to make.

Bad Psychology and Bad References

There is further evidence that Thompson has marching orders, that he is not his own man, and the evidence involves that Forrestal Wikipedia page. To get to it we must quote Thompson some more, going back to the bottom of page 87 when he first broaches the subject of Forrestal's supposed breakdown. Note that he makes it entirely the result of the strains of fighting the Cold War:

> In Kennan's view, at least, Forrestal ultimately went too far. He helped Kennan considerably in setting up the Office of Policy Coordination. But reflecting back decades later, Kennan would lament OPC's growth and blame the Pentagon for it. He wanted it small and elite; Forrestal and the Pentagon wanted black propaganda offices franchised in embassies worldwide. "There is no method, there is no way except the method of worry, of constant concern, and of unceasing energy that will give us our security," (Jeffery Dorwart, *Eberstadt and Forrestal*, p. 149) the defense secretary said in 1947.
>
> The constant concern eventually devoured Forrestal: by the late 1940s, he had begun a slow-motion nervous breakdown. Isolated and profoundly alarmed, he saw demons everywhere. Nitze's sister once found him in the bushes near the Plaza Hotel in New York. She asked what he was doing. Watching people, he said. I am just watching people going about their business. (Paul Henry Nitze, *Tension between Opposites*, p. 97)
>
> In March 1949, the president replaced Forrestal as secretary of defense. Soon, he had become completely paranoid. Zionists were trailing him and the Soviets had bugged beach umbrellas all over Miami. Early that spring, he was committed to the U.S. Naval Hospital in Bethesda,

> Maryland, where the doctors began treating him with psychotherapy and insulin injections. (Willcutts Report, part 1, p. 35) They considered, but rejected, using electroconvulsive therapy. (ibid. p. 41)

In contemporary newspaper accounts, through the 1992 book, *Driven Patriot, The Life and Times of James Forrestal,* those making the suicide argument gave prominent place to the pressures and press attacks that Forrestal had suffered on account of his opposition to the creation of the state of Israel. With its 1999 article, written upon the 50th anniversary of Forrestal's death, noted in Chapter Five, *The Washington Post* began a trend of Soviet-style airbrushing of that out of history. We saw the same thing in the online article the same year by the Seton Hall professor with the numerous mainstream media connections, Christopher Sharrett. Thompson continues the trend; there's no trace of the big Israel dust-up in his account, making Forrestal's legitimate concern that he was being trailed and bugged by Zionist agents look all the loonier.

Concerning Forrestal's supposed imaginary demons and paranoia, one may contrast Thompson's spin on the story showing Forrestal's quite normal penchant for people-watching with the observations in *Driven Patriot* that his staff had noticed no change in his condition or demeanor at all.[210] His closest aide, Marx Leva, we noted in Chapter One, echoed those observations.

Note, furthermore that Thompson has no reference for the fantastic claim that Forrestal said that, "Soviets had bugged beach umbrellas all over Miami." Doubtless, he has taken liberties with an account in *Driven Patriot* and elsewhere of Forrestal's conversation with Robert Lovett at Hobe Sound, Florida. The *Driven Patriot* reference is Arnold Rogow's biography of Forrestal, but Rogow has no reference. Also, as noted in Chapter One, a Department of Defense oral history interview of Lovett has nothing about bugged beach umbrellas, only Forrestal telling Lovett that "they're really after me." All the indications are that he was right.

---

210 Hoopes and Brinkley, p. 426.

Thompson's final quoted sentence about the medical treatment at Bethesda is meant to suggest that Forrestal badly needed it. It comes from the testimony to the Willcutts board of the lead doctor, Captain George Raines. Bear in mind that this is the same man, as we see in Chapter Four, who volunteered that the handwriting of the transcribed poem looked like Forrestal's. We have also seen from John Osborne's unpublished manuscript that Captain Stephen Smith, "second in rank and authority to the psychiatrist in charge of the case believed throughout its course that Forrestal was wrongly diagnosed and treated. But he also thought that Forrestal was recovering despite the treatment...."

Another Version of the Willcutts Report?

Now let's look a little more closely at Thompson's Willcutts Report references. The first one in the first paragraph cited above is "part 2, p. 176." The only public copy of the Willcutts Report available when Thompson's book came out in September of 2008 was the one online at the site of the Seeley G. Mudd Manuscript Library. It does not have a "part 1" and "part 2." Rather, it displays the report as "First Half" and "Second Half." The second half is simply a collection of unnumbered nurses' records and various exhibits. The body of the report itself is all in the library's first half. Scrolling to the bottom, one can see that it is only 61 pages in length and that it does not have a "part 1" and a "part 2." No regular member of the public looking for Thompson's citation would find it.

The same thing can be said for all of his other references, that is, as of the time that the Thompson book was published. The page numbers are not right for the Willcutts Report, proper, as one sees it at the Seeley Mudd site. They do work, however, if one converts the entire file to html from the pdf file that one sees at the Seeley Mudd site. Then the computer program generates its own page numbers, starting with the various solicited endorsements included before the review board's actual work begins. Thus, when the Willcutts Report is telling us on its page 1 what happened on the first day, Thompson's copy is already up to page 28. He apparently does not realize that he is using a sort of insiders' copy that has been generated for him by someone else. (Heaven only knows how that first page reference came about.) Otherwise, he would have made his references in accord with the version one sees at the library site.

At this point things really begin to get interesting. On May 14, 2008, an extremely eclectic and copious contributor to Wikipedia who uses the signature "JDPhD" inserted a section to the page on James Forrestal entitled "Psychiatric Treatment."[211] The timing corresponds quite well to the period when Thompson's book would have been in preparation. The purpose is clearly the same as Thompson's, to make Forrestal look insane, and the reference is to the page numbers for Captain Raines's testimony as they would appear in an html version. This "JDPhd," like young Nicholas Thompson (assuming that he is not Thompson, himself), obviously doesn't realize that he is referring people to a version of the Willcutts Report to which he and some privileged few others might have access, but the public does not.

Recall at this point what we noted in Chapter Five about that 50th anniversary *Washington Post* article by Alexander Wooley. From the detailed description he gave of Forrestal's room and of the kitchen across the hall from his room, Wooley seems to have had access to the photographs that were only available to the general public more than five years later.

Watching their apparent bumbling, we are reminded of conversations with the late Bernard Yoh, a former intelligence operative for Nationalist Chinese leader, Chiang Kai-shek: "Yoh denied to me that he had ever worked for the CIA, saying that he thought they were too stupid for him to have anything to do with them...."[212] Also coming to mind is the young Jeff Redfern character, of "Red Rascal" fame, in Garry Trudeau's *Doones-*

---

211 https://en.wikipedia.org/w/index.php?title=James_Forrestal&diff=next&oldid=212470547.

212 David Martin, "Spook Journalist Goulden," http://www.dcdave.com/article1/081198.html.

bury comic strip. As a product of Yale University,_Trudeau should have some familiarity with the elite covert political world.

Other Voices Weigh In

We know how the page numbers work out when the entire Willcutts file is converted to htm/html, because early in February 2010, the proprietor of the web site ARI Watch put an htm up version on his page.[213] There you can see the same page numbers as they appear on the Mudd Library version as well as the computer generated page numbers, which show up in faint print bracketed by italics. The site is extremely valuable, not just because it makes things much easier to find in the report, but also, as we noted previously, because the ARI Watch proprietor, who uses the pseudonym of "Mark Hunter," has an introduction with his own analysis of the report.

To demonstrate the utility of the htm version as a research tool, we might try checking on the assertion by Thompson and a host of other journalists and historians that Forrestal suffered from paranoia by using "edit/find" on the computer's toolbar. The words "paranoia" and "paranoid" come up only in the editor's commentary, not anywhere in the Willcutts Report itself. The testifying doctors, who were questioned at much greater length than the witnesses to the actual physical evidence, never used either word or any word close to them in meaning.

Psychologist Arnold A. Rogow, in his very influential 1963 book, *James Forrestal, A Study of Personality, Politics, and Policy,* wrote "Raines diagnosed Forrestal's illness as involutional melancholia, a depressive condition sometimes seen in persons who have reached middle age." It sounds very precise and clinical. He follows it up with a long discussion explaining how that condition manifests itself. But if you try searching the rare term, "involutional," or the more common word, "melancholia," on the Willcutts Report itself, neither one comes up. He also says that Forrestal was suffering from a "severe psychosis," but "psychosis" doesn't come up, either. All one will find are the various forms of the

[213] http://ariwatch.com/VS/JamesForrestal/WillcuttsReport.htm.

poorly defined diagnosis, "depressed." Dr. Raines never used those impressive sounding mumbo jumbo expressions when testifying before his fellow doctors on the Willcutts review board. One has to wonder where Rogow got them. He has no reference. As we have discovered with respect to his claim that the corpsman saw Forrestal copying from a book when he looked in on him at 1:45, they are almost certainly Rogow fabrications.

Having communicated with him only through email, as noted before, we do not know who "Mark" is, but we are grateful to him for indexing our articles on his web site, and every serious student of history should be grateful to him for his work on the Willcutts Report.

With his introduction, Mark covers some of the same ground that we do, but even when he does, he does so with fresh insights and a slightly different perspective. His work and mine are as much complementary as repetitive. He talked by telephone with our contact, the military veteran with the former Navy nurse wife, and confirmed that "Regina M. J. Harty" was really Margie Hardy. He also reported the observation of the veteran that there were likely other patients on the floor—a point that even Cornell Simpson and I had overlooked—who could have been fake patients waiting for their moment to strike. From reading the Willcutts Report or anything else written about Forrestal's hospitalization, one gets the impression that Forrestal had the entire floor all to himself. We have previously observed that the review board did not ask Nurse Hardy, at her station just down the hall and around a corner from Forrestal's room if she had heard anything from that room at around the time the broken glass found there might have been broken, but Mark noted, as well, that they made the same omission in the case of the corpsman on duty, Robert Wayne Harrison, who was at Lt. Hardy's duty station at the same time. They do ask Harrison if he heard any unusual sounds from the *kitchen*, but not from the bedroom where an apparent struggle occurred.

We have given only a small sample of Mark's fresh insights. Mark also references the writing of a friend of ours, Hugh Turley, concerning an interview to which we alluded in a footnote in Chapter Two:

> Forrestal's chauffeur was a Navy enlisted man named John Spalding. Now living in Littlestown, Pennsylvania, in 2008 at the age of 87 he revealed in a recorded interview ("Handwriting Tells Dark Tale?" by Hugh Turley, *Hyattsville Life & Times* December 2008) how the Navy treated him right after Forrestal's death.[214] He was called into the office of Rear Admiral Monroe Kelly. "He had a big map and he said where do you want to go for duty ... You are going to leave tonight." Mr. Spalding decided on the base at Guantánamo, Cuba. (In 1949 Havana was a famous vacation spot, so this is not as strange as it would be today.) Monroe Kelly and his aide Lieutenant James A. Hooper made him sign a statement swearing that he would never speak to anyone again about Forrestal. Also in the interview Mr. Spalding said that Forrestal had never appeared depressed, paranoid or in any way abnormal in his presence.

Altogether, what Mark's work shows, along with this writer's observations, is that the Willcutts Report represents a veritable gold mine for anyone interested in the vitally important historical event of James Forrestal's death in the prime of his productive life at the age of 57. Most remarkably, for all we know, Mark's and mine represent the only two sets of eyes in the whole world who have gone over the report with anything resembling a critical eye, in spite of the fact that it has now been publicly available for more than fourteen years. One really has to wonder why that should be.

The Canary Who Could Sing but Couldn't Fly

An interested reader of our "Who Killed James Forrestal?" series—certainly not a professional historian—noting the manner of Forrestal's apparent murder, suggested that there might be a connection to Operation Underworld and the major Jewish gangster, Meyer Lansky. Operation Underworld "was the United States government's code name for the cooperation of Italian and Jewish organized crime figures from 1942 to 1945

---

[214] http://www.dcdave.com/article5/090130.htm. Spalding died in 2009. https://www.legacy.com/obituaries/name/john-spalding-obituary?pid=126202844.

to counter Axis spies and saboteurs along the U.S. northeastern seaboard ports, avoid wartime labor union strikes, and limit theft by black-marketeers of vital war supplies and equipment," as defined by Wikipedia.[215]

The reason he thought of it, he said, was the great similarity of Forrestal's death to that of the New York Jewish mobster, Abe "Kid Twist" Reles. Reles was the key informant whose testimony led to the arrest, conviction, and execution of several members of the infamous Murder Incorporated in the early 1940s.[216] But he was just getting started. New York District Attorney William O'Dwyer had hidden him away at a Coney Island hotel under constant police guard. Nevertheless, he somehow managed to fall to his death from the sixth-floor window of his room. Several sheets were found tied together hanging from the window, and the death was ruled accidental, with the conclusion that he had been trying to escape and lost his grip. Conveniently overlooked was the fact that the body was lying some twenty feet from the base of the hotel. To reveal that the police had been bribed to allow the killing of the witness would have been too great an embarrassment for all concerned.[217]

The possible organized crime connection to Forrestal's death is intriguing, and it is well known from anyone familiar with the JFK assassination that Deep State connections to the mob hardly ended with Operation Underworld. They could have easily furnished the muscle for what transpired on the 16th floor of the Bethesda Naval Hospital that night, but common criminals hardly have a monopoly on that method of killing. It's right there in the early 1950s CIA assassination manual: "The most effi-

---

[215] https://en.wikipedia.org/wiki/Operation_Underworld.

[216] https://en.wikipedia.org/wiki/Murder%2C_Inc.

[217] Joe Bruno on the Mob:
https://joebrunoonthemob.wordpress.com/2011/01/04/joe-bruno-on-the-mob-abe-%E2%80%9Ckid-twist%E2%80%9D-reles-the-canary-who-could-sing-but-couldnt-fly/.

cient accident, in simple assassination, is a fall of 75 feet or more onto a hard surface."[218]

We might also remind readers of the manner of the timely death of the anti-Communist Czech leader mentioned in our first chapter. Two witnesses in the case of accused high level Soviet spy, Alger Hiss, also died from falls, Justice Department attorney, W. Marvin Smith and former State Department official and suspected spy, Laurence Duggan. Smith was found dead at the bottom of a seven-story stairwell in the Justice Department building in Washington, DC, on October 20, 1948. Duggan, working at the time for the Institute of International Education in New York City, fell from the window of his office on the 16th floor on December 20, 1948. Cornell Simpson names the Communists as the most likely candidates in their fatal falls.[219]

The 1940s hardly has a monopoly on such suspicious deaths with political connections. On August 15, 1993, Jon Parnell Walker, Whitewater investigator for the Resolution Trust Corporation, fell to his death from his Arlington, Virginia, apartment balcony.[220] During the George W. Bush administration there was State Department official John J. Kokal on November 7, 2003, and former Reagan administration Cold Warrior, Gus W. Weiss, on November 25, 2003. Kokal fell from the roof of the State Department building in Foggy Bottom.[221] Weiss fell from the Watergate Building where he had an apartment, also in Foggy Bottom not far away. Like Walker's death and Forrestal's, both deaths were ruled suicides.

---

[218] Vikram Murthi, "*Wormwood* digs up Frank Olson's body and looks through the CIA's assassination manual," https://www.avclub.com/wormwood-digs-up-frank-olsons-body-and-looks-through-th-1821521874.

[219] Simpson, pp. 126-128.

[220] https://100percentfedup.com/just-close-friend-hillary-clinton-planned-step-away-politics-found-dead-apparent-suicide/. See #19 on the list.

[221] Wayne Madsen, "Did John Bolton 'Defenestrate' Anyone?" *Gumshoe News*, March 24, 2018, https://gumshoenews.com/2018/03/24/did-john-bolton-defenestrate-anyone/; David Martin, "Connected Iraq War Opponent a 'Suicide'" http://www.dcdave.com/article4/031207.html and "Three Important Assassinations? Joseph Stalin, Leonid Brezhnev, Gus Weiss," http://www.dcdave.com/article5/111220.htm.

Very early in the Lyndon B. Johnson administration, Edward Grant Stockdale, a man who had served as Kennedy's Ambassador to Ireland and was said to have known a lot about LBJ-crony Bobby Baker's shady business dealings and even about LBJ's connections to the JFK assassination, fell from the window of his office on the thirteenth floor of the Alfred I. Dupont Building in Miami on December 2, 1963.[222]

Most recently, Bill Gertz of the *Washington Free Beacon* reported on April 4, 2014, that a senior unnamed CIA official had died from a fall from a CIA building somewhere in Northern sometime in the previous week, also ruled a suicide.[223] That death seems to have been reported nowhere else, and the *Washington Free Beacon* had no follow-up.

One such "suicide" eventually discovered to be an almost certain unsolved homicide was the 1953 10-story fall of CIA scientist, Dr. Frank Olson, from a New York City hotel. Olson had apparently become conscience stricken over some of the dirtiest of the CIA's human experimentation programs and had to be "terminated."[224] The CIA had "admitted" to secretly giving him LSD, causing him to go temporarily out of his mind and crash through a window of the hotel. When the family had the body exhumed and re-examined, they discovered persuasive evidence of a fatal hammer blow to the head.

The manner of Forrestal's death aside, the Jewish-dominated U.S. government has been so closely tied in with organized crime for such a long time that it's hardly a stretch to characterize any Deep State murder as a mob hit. First, let's look at the following exchange with Chicago mobster Sam "Mooney" Giancana as recalled by his younger brother, Chuck on the eve of the 1948 presidential election. Chuck speaks first:

---

[222] Phillip F. Nelson, *LBJ: From Mastermind to "The Colossus,"* Skyhorse Publishing, 2014, pp. 239-245.

[223] David Martin, "Anonymous CIA Official Dies Violently," http://www.dcdave.com/article5/140410.htm.

[224] Chris Floyd, "The CIA, the Bush Gang and the Death of Frank Olson," Counterpunch, August 28, 2002, https://www.counterpunch.org/2002/08/28/the-cia-the-bush-gang-and-the-death-of-frank-olson/.

"Isn't it for sure that Truman will get in?"

"Well, let's put it this way...Dewey won't win, even if he does. Get my point?"

"Yeah." Chuck hesitated. "But really what difference does it make? ...Like you said before, they're all alike."

"Well, not this time. Luciano still hates Dewey for puttin' him in jail in the first place.... Costello's worried that the self-righteous son of a bitch has a short memory, probably doesn't even know how to conduct business. We'd have to give Dewey a few lessons and I got a feelin' he's a slow learner," Mooney said smiling. "But Truman, well, he can bullshit all he wants about bein' a common man--people eat that up--but the truth is, he grew up with our boys in Kansas City."

"Really...I didn't know that. How come nobody talks about it?"

"Christ, because it's just like Chicago out there. They had a mick mayor, Pendergast, on the take big time...loved to bet on the ponies. And they got the Italians for muscle and to make money with the rackets. So, fact is, Truman owes everything he's got to us. Pendergast made him a judge and then, with the Italian muscle behind him, got him to the Senate. When the forty-four election came up...Kelly here in Chicago got him on the ticket with Roosevelt. Shit, Chicago got Roosevelt and Truman nominated and elected. We were good to Roosevelt; he was good to us. He died and Truman's been our man in the White House ever since. It's smooth sailing with him there."

"I thought he was a schoolteacher or somethin'. He always seemed clean.... I know what you said before, but I guess I didn't know he was really connected."

Mooney sighed. "Jesus, I guess you think General MacArthur was a choirboy out there fightin' for America, too? Like I always told you, 'Give me a guy who steals a little and I'll make money.' "

He shook his head. "Well, there's connected, Chuck, and then there's connected. We pull the strings...so, shit, yeah...if they can be bought, they're connected."

Chuck took a drink and thought for a moment. "So Dewey would just fuck things up...or at least make things more'--he searched for the right word--"more uncertain?"

"Exactly. So now, think you'd like to place a bet? Truman or Dewey? Take my advice and put your money on Truman?"[225]

The following quote concerning Las Vegas developer and casino mogul Hank Greenspun reveals the U.S. mob connection with Israel:

> With support from Meyer Lansky, Greenspun had become a gunrunner for Israel in 1948 and thereafter performed as an Israeli operative. Bugsy Siegel reportedly gave $50,000 to support Irgun while "celebrity gangster" Mickey Cohen sponsored an Irgun fundraiser in 1947. *The Jerusalem Post* insisted of Greenspun, "He's like God in Israel...his contribution to the establishment of the Jewish state is widely considered to be greater than any other American." Compared to what Greenspun did for Israel, "Jonathan Pollard's act was pure innocence." In October 1961 Kennedy pardoned Greenspun who was caught smuggling U.S. military hardware to Israel and convicted of violating the Neutrality Act of 1950.[226]

In case anyone might think things have changed in any material way since the heyday of Greenspun and Giancana, see this writer's review of Sally Denton and Roger Morris's *The Money and the Power: The Making of Las Vegas and its Hold on America*, particularly the short section on the likely mob connections of current president, Donald Trump.[227]

---

225 Sam and Chuck Giancana, *Double Cross: The Explosive Inside Story of the Mobster Who Controlled America*, Warner Books, 1992, pp. 161-162. (The co-author with Chuck is not the mobster himself but his godson with the same name.)

226 Gates, p. 33.

227 David Martin, "*The Money and the Power: A Review,*" http://dcdave.com/article5/160310.htm.

CHAPTER 13

Historians Unmoved

Timorous Eunuchs

In the universities
You'll find our finest minds.
The problem isn't with their brains.
Oh no, it's with their spines.

"The Miller Center is a nonpartisan affiliate of the University of Virginia that specializes in United States presidential scholarship, public policy, and political history and strives to apply the lessons of history to the nation's most pressing contemporary governance challenges. The Miller Center is committed to work grounded in rigorous scholarship and advanced through civil discourse."[228]

In a word, the Miller Center is at the very heart of the academic establishment of writers of United States history. "Previous directors include Dr. Phillip Zelikow (1999-2005), currently White Burkett Miller Profes-

228 https://en.wikipedia.org/wiki/Miller_Center_of_Public_Affairs.

sor History at the University of Virginia and previously the Executive Director of the 9/11 Commission, in addition to numerous posts in many levels of government service."[229]

Need we say more? Under the general category of U.S. Presidents, their page for James V. Forrestal (1947-1949), under Harry S. Truman now reads, oddly enough:

> Shortly after his resignation, Forrestal was hospitalized because of severe depression. On May 22, 1949, he committed suicide when he allegedly climbed out of a window to hang himself and fell to his death from the sixteenth floor of the Bethesda Naval Hospital in Maryland.[230]

Climbing out a sixteenth-floor window for the purpose of *hanging* oneself certainly must count as one of the most bizarre ways of committing suicide ever, so the sages at the Miller Center felt it necessary to hedge themselves in a bit by describing this scenario as a mere allegation. One might think, then, that that would make the suicide claim an allegation as well, but one would reckon without the determined adherence of this clutch of scholars and experts to popular propaganda. The only alternative suicide scenario we are left with, after all, is that Forrestal went to the trouble to tie a bathrobe belt around his neck for no reason at all before taking his long plunge.

No, "suicide" it is, and suicide it will remain on the Miller Center's web site, in spite of the fact that the last official word from the government—the result of its official inquiry into the death—is only that Forrestal died from injuries caused by the fall. The report offered no

---

[229] Ibid. On September 10, 2002, Professor Zelikow spilled some beans before an audience at the University of Virginia. Our upcoming invasion of Iraq was not really motivated by any threat to us or to the Europeans by those mythical Iraqi weapons of mass destruction: "Why would Iraq attack America or use nuclear weapons against us? I'll tell you what I think the real threat [is] and actually has been since 1990—it's the threat against Israel. And this is the real threat that dare not speak its name, because the Europeans don't care deeply about that threat, I will tell you frankly. And the American government doesn't want to lean too hard on it rhetorically, because it's not a popular sell." Gates, p. 9. With equal candor these days, Zelikow might well say as much for the threat from Iran.

[230] https://millercenter.org/president/truman/essays/forrestal-1947-secretary-of-defense.

conclusion as to what caused the fall. The Miller Center's excuse for stubbornly clinging to their suicide conclusion, in spite of the availability of the official investigation report since 2004—a report that thoroughly undermines that conclusion—remains, in effect, that "established historians" still cling to it. None of those worthies, you see, has yet seen fit to weigh in on Forrestal's death in light of the latest revelations. This is a particularly disingenuous rationalization for the Miller Center to make, though, when it houses a veritable stable of such types.[231]

That statement is actually an improvement over what appeared there before we emailed them in 2008, informing them that what they had written was based upon information available before the release of the Willcutts Report, and was therefore almost four years out of date.[232] It took several emails back and forth to get to the unsatisfactory statement that has been there since 2008. One can gather how the statement read before from this last-word email to me from a Miller Center spokesperson:

> Based on your email, we have read the Willcutts report and revised some of the text on James Forrestal on American President: An Online Reference Resource. As you mentioned, the report does not use the term "nervous breakdown" but instead mentions repeatedly that Forrestal suffered from severe depression. We also changed the wording about Forrestal jumping out of a window because sources indicate that he fell out the window while allegedly trying to hang himself.
>
> But as far as whether or not Forrestal committed suicide, I think you have misunderstood the role of American President. The web site is an educational site for general users. As such, we see our responsibility as providing our users with a mainstream interpretation of history. We do not publish groundbreaking new scholarship or challenge the historical consensus that is derived from secondary sources written by established academics. If you can point us to secondary sources written by established historians that discuss the Willcutts report and cast doubt on whether Forrestal committed suicide, we would be very interested in reading them. However, until historians have analyzed and weighed

---

231 https://millercenter.org/experts.

232 David Martin, "Lies about the Kennedy and Forrestal Deaths," http://dcdave.com/article5/080429.htm.

> the report against other historical materials and written about their findings, *we will not introduce unsubstantiated theories and rumors into American President.* (emphasis added)
>
> To help us achieve our mission at American President, we enlist Consulting Editors who review our materials and add their own interpretations to various degrees. Each Consulting Editor is listed on the home page for each President. The Consulting Editor for Harry S. Truman and his administration, right on the Truman home page, is Alonzo Hamby, who is a distinguished professor of history at Ohio State University [sic. It's Ohio University] and author of *Man of the People: A Life of Harry S. Truman*. He has approved the changes to the Forrestal essay.
>
> We appreciate how strongly you feel about this subject and your determination to have the Willcutts report incorporated into the historical record. Nevertheless, American President seeks to represent the consensus of academic historians.

You'd think that they were Wikipedia with their no original research, the truth be damned, rules, but one can hardly argue with that last sentence. As of 2008 the consensus of what passes for academic historians in the country, four years after the release of the Willcutts Report, was still that Forrestal had committed suicide. As for their own reading of the Willcutts Report, it would appear that they were no more perceptive than Professor David E. Kaiser, with whom we had the exchange described in Chapter Nine. It would have been pointless to present the detailed case to the Miller Center that I presented to Kaiser, because they have already told me that their fingers are stuffed in their ears until the David Kaisers of the world speak up.

If you are wondering why they did not invoke Nicholas Thompson as someone who had read the Willcutts Report and was still calling Forrestal's death a suicide, that is because his book had not yet come out. That would be the following year. Even had he been honest and had drawn the proper inference from the evidence, that still would not have measured up by their lights because Thompson, as a mere media figure, lacks the proper credentials. He might have the right pedigree, but he is not an "academic historian."

We knew that the words would be wasted, but we could not restrain ourselves, and we responded immediately. We omit the first paragraph of pleasantries, only:

> Contrary to your speculation about my understanding of the role of American President—as opposed to the role of the history community of the University of Virginia, with whom I should expect you at least rub shoulders—I have never labored under the illusion that you would write anything that went against prevailing historical sentiment. With respect to James Forrestal's death, however, my intent was to educate you to the fact that that sentiment is apparently based entirely upon what was known prior to the release of the best evidence in the case (not "unsubstantiated theories and rumors"), which is the long-suppressed *official investigation* of Forrestal's death. Just as you have asked me to alert you to anything written by "established historians" that discusses the Willcutts report and casts doubt on the suicide conclusion, I dare say that you will not be able to point me to any historian who has had anything to say about it at all since it was made available to the public in the fall of 2004. I think you would have to agree that that fact alone does not reflect particularly well upon our established historians.
>
> And thus it has always been with this group with regard to the Willcutts report. As a prime example, in their comprehensive 1992 Forrestal biography, Townsend Hoopes and Douglas Brinkley, the main source for Hamby in his Truman biography on Forrestal's death, neglect to tell the readers that there was such a thing as the Willcutts Report, much less that it was kept secret. Furthermore, to the best of my knowledge, not one American historian since 1949 has made any public complaint or has voiced the slightest suspicion over the fact that this official investigation was kept secret, that is, that by definition a cover-up has taken place. With that sorry record before us and with the resounding silence with which the 2004 release of the Willcutts report by the Seeley Mudd Manuscript Library of Princeton University has been greeted by the history community, I must say that I am not at all optimistic that the Miller Center will have to give up its published theory that Forrestal committed suicide anytime soon.
>
> Yes, I did say "theory." You may read the 5-point conclusion of the last official word of the government on Forrestal's death, that is, the results of the Willcutts report, all you want and you will not find anywhere the conclusion that James Forrestal committed suicide. It is as though the Warren Commission had not concluded that Lee Harvey Oswald acted alone. To be sure, within hours of his death, the county coroner said that Forrestal committed suicide and the Bethesda Naval Hospital is-

sued a statement saying that he had committed suicide, and all the newspapers said that he did, but none were qualified to make such a ruling at that point. The fact of the matter is that after all the testimony was taken (though it was far from all that should have been taken) and all the evidence was gathered (again, less than there should have been), the Willcutts review board could not find it within itself to say that Forrestal committed suicide.

And as far as "unsubstantiated theories" go, I know you call it merely an allegation, but the notion that Forrestal in the fleeting time available would have gone to the trouble to attempt to hang himself out of a 16th story window is about as unsubstantiated as a theory can get. Certainly nothing in the Willcutts report comes close to supporting it. Hoopes and Brinkley write that the bathrobe cord "gave way," suggesting that it broke, but that conclusion is completely contradicted by the testimony of Hospitalman William Eliades, as close as the report gets to the subject:

"I looked to see whether he had tried to hang himself and see whether a piece of cord had broken off. It was all in one piece except it was tied around his neck."

The question of whether enough of the cord was left over for it to have been tied to the radiator under the window or whether the longest loose end appeared by its wrinkles to have been recently tied to anything was not addressed.

While in the interests of historical accuracy I would prefer that you not parade on your site the outlandish notion that Forrestal might have tried to double-kill himself by hanging from a 16th story window, as one who wouldn't mind seeing more skepticism of the insupportable suicide theory engendered in the public, I'd just as soon that you leave it alone for now.

As a final point, Professor Hamby, with whom I imagine you will share this email, is not supported at all by the doctors at Bethesda Naval Hospital in his assertion in his book that Forrestal was exhibiting classical signs of paranoia. The words "paranoia" and "paranoid" are completely lacking from the descriptions of Forrestal by the doctors. The second in command of the doctors, Captain Stephen Smith, on the other hand, was particularly impressed with Forrestal's exceptional command of reality.

I shall continue in my efforts to inform historians of the existence of the Willcutts report and of what is contained therein. Examples can be found at http://www.dcdave.com/article5/080113.htm. You could render a great public service by lending a hand. Whatever you might choose to do, I am satisfied that, in due time, the truth will out.

What we have seen that they have chosen to do now for one more decade is to leave their statement on Forrestal's death unchanged. There has been no reason for them to make any change, because the established historians have held the suicide line.

John Lewis Gaddis

As academic historians go, you don't get much more established than Gaddis. *The New York Times*, according to Wikipedia, has called him the "Dean of Cold War Historians."[233] In response to a question by this writer on the night of December 8, 2011, Gaddis claimed that he knew nothing about the release of the official investigation of the death of James Forrestal (the Willcutts Report).

According to Wikipedia, "Gaddis is best known for his critical analysis of the strategies of containment employed by United States presidents from Harry S. Truman to Ronald Reagan..."

Also according to Wikipedia, "Biographers Townsend Hoopes and Douglas Brinkley have dubbed Forrestal "godfather of containment" largely on account of his work in distributing [George F.] Kennan's writing.[234] Wikipedia calls Kennan "the father of containment."

In my question to Gaddis, I noted that he states flatly on page 354 of his later Pulitzer Prize winning biography of Kennan,_the promotion of which had brought him to the Politics and Prose bookstore in Washington, DC, that Forrestal "had a nervous breakdown and committed suicide."[235] "Could it be," I asked, "that you are unfamiliar with the official investigation of his death, kept secret for 55 years and released only in 2004? That report is on the web site of the Seeley Mudd Manuscript Library of Princeton University. No critical reader of that report could conclude that Forrestal committed suicide."

---

[233] https://en.wikipedia.org/wiki/John_Lewis_Gaddis.

[234] https://en.wikipedia.org/wiki/Containment#Origin_.281944.E2.80.931947.29.

[235] *George F. Kennan: An American Life,* Penguin Press, 2011.

Gaddis responded that, indeed, he knew nothing of this official investigation and its belated release. In stating that Forrestal had committed suicide, he said, he was simply repeating the "prevailing opinion" on the matter, sounding like the Miller Center three years earlier.

Consider what we have here. The leading opponent in the U.S. government of Joseph Stalin's Soviet Union, the one most responsible for the change of U.S. policy toward the Communists from one of accommodation to one of confrontation and containment, died violently and mysteriously. Stalin is well known for assassinating his opponents, wherever they might be. Abundant evidence has been produced that the Roosevelt and Truman administrations were laced with Stalin's agents, right up to the very top. The news that the official investigation of this violent death was suppressed for 55 years, only to be released through a Freedom of Information Act request in 2004, had been on that leading opponent of Communism's Wikipedia site for some years prior to Gaddis's book publication and his promotional presentation in Washington, DC, as had been the key evidence showing that the death was, in all probability, a murder. But America's leading scholar on the confrontation claims not to know the first thing about this and reflects as much in his book.

It is possible, we suppose. He is, after all, a professor of history at Yale. It's not very likely, though. As we said, he's a professor of history at Yale, the very cradle of the mendacious CIA. In fact, he is the Robert A. Lovett Professor of History at Yale. Lovett was the Yale Skull and Bones member to whose Florida estate, recall, Forrestal was flown after his strange, likely drug-induced, seizure in Washington.[236] That was just prior to Forrestal's eventually fatal transfer to the 16th floor of the Bethesda Naval Hospital.

As one would expect, Gaddis includes Nicholas Thompson's *The Hawk and the Dove* in his bibliography. There are therefore three possibilities with respect to Gaddis's claim of ignorance of the Willcutts Report, (1)

---

[236] For what it is worth, another party to the Hobe Sound gathering was a Yale Skull and Bones man, former Under Secretary of the Navy, Artemus Gates. (Dorwart, p. 169). Recall, as well, that biographer Townsend Hoopes was also in that secret society. It's a small world among the power elite, apparently.

Gaddis has read the book but forgot about that section, (2) he included the book in his bibliography without having read all of it, or (3) he was not telling the truth when he said that he had never heard of the Willcutts Report. None of these possibilities gives one much confidence in Gaddis as a historian.

Gregg Herken

H.L. Mencken aptly called them "the timorous eunuchs who posture as American historians."[237] That was in 1920, but little has changed. It might be a freshly minted Ph.D. from TCU, teaching at a backwater university in Texas, like Matthew A. McNiece, or the man often described as the foremost historian of the Cold War, Yale history professor John Lewis Gaddis, but the fake authoritativeness and the real pusillanimity are at least as evident today as they were in Mencken's day.[238] That is certainly the case when it comes to their writing about the very important subject of the violent death of the U.S. government's leading opponent of the creation of the state of Israel, Secretary of Defense James Forrestal.

Now comes a man who has achieved a station in the profession that, but for his inability to write coherent English, young McNiece might aspire to, University of California at Merced professor emeritus Gregg Herken. You know that Herken has made it with the ruling establishment when you see that his book on the movers and shakers who lived in the Georgetown district of Washington, DC, during the Cold War era got reviewed by *The New York Times, The Washington Post,* the *Wall Street Journal,* the *New Yorker,* the *Weekly Standard,* and numerous other publications.[239] That he has the stamp of approval as a certified court histori-

---

237 "Roosevelt, an Autopsy," http://progressingamerica.blogspot.com/2013/06/roosevelt-autopsy-by-hl-mencken-1920.html.

238 Concerning McNiece, see "Man Awarded Ph.D. for Trashing Martin, Forrestal," http://www.dcdave.com/article5/140707.htm.

239 *The Georgetown Set: Friends and Rivals in Cold War Washington*, Alfred A. Knopf, 2014.

an is further evidenced by the fact that for 15 years he was chairman of the Department of Space History at the Smithsonian Institution's National Air and Space Museum.

What strikes one in listening to his presentation about his book at Washington's Politics and Prose bookstore is his apparent lack of any sense of outrage over the very cozy relationship that existed (and still exists, we must presume) between prominent putative journalists and people at the very highest levels of America's intelligence community, that is to say, our secret government.[240] People so completely in bed with the most sinister people in the government can hardly be proper watchdogs upon them.

When it comes to ignoring everything that has been revealed about James Forrestal's death in the 21st century, Herken is comfortably in the mainstream. His offense is worse than most, though, because we know he knows better. One of his references, as I note in the March, 2015, email that I was moved to write to him (below), is to the article in which I reveal the phoniness of the transcription of the morbid poem that was sold to the public as a sort of suicide note:

> Dear Professor Herken,
>
> I was impressed by the scholarship that you demonstrated in your letter to *The New York Review of Books,* reinforcing with new evidence your already persuasive argument that Robert Oppenheimer was an active member of the Communist Party of the United States.[241] I was especially disappointed, then, to see how completely your scholarly skills seemed to have deserted you when you wrote about the death of our first secretary of defense, James Forrestal, in your most recent book, *The Georgetown Set: Friends and Rivals in Cold War Washington*:
>
>> Dismissed from his Pentagon post by Truman in March for his intransigence in the defense budget debate, Forrestal suffered a nervous breakdown weeks later and was confined to a secure wing of the navy's hospital in Bethesda, Maryland. During the early morning hours of May 22, 1949, after a restless night spent copying lines from the chorus of Sophocles's play *Ajax*, Forrestal fell to

---

[240] https://www.youtube.com/watch?v=GSYbfNmypfc.

[241] "Brotherhood of the Bomb," http://www.brotherhoodofthebomb.com/bhbsource/new_evidence_1.html.

> his death from the window of his room on the hospital's sixteenth floor.
>
> He would be the first senior-ranking American casualty of the Cold War. (pp. 94-95)

Taking your small inaccuracies first, Forrestal did not fall from "the window of his room." There were at least three windows in his room, but Forrestal, according to the official record, did not go out any of them. He went out the window of the kitchen across the hall from his room.

No diagnosis of "nervous breakdown" was made by any of the doctors examining Forrestal at Bethesda Naval Hospital. You can search the transcript of the official "investigation" of Forrestal's death and find that the word "nervous" appears only once, in the endorsing letter of Dr. James Strecker in which he states his own qualifications on the subject of nervous disorders.

It is also unwarranted to state flatly that Truman sacked Forrestal because of his "intransigence in the defense budget debate." There are any number of reasons why Truman replaced Forrestal with Louis Johnson, but by giving that sole reason you do manage to make your insupportable conclusion that Forrestal was a "casualty of the Cold War" sound somewhat plausible. Arnold Rogow's carefully hedged-in conclusion is much more supportable, which is why I lead off with it in "New Forrestal Document Exposes Cover-up."

> However history may ultimately judge his opposition to the establishment of Israel, by 1949 it was clear that Forrestal was, in a sense, one of the casualties of the diplomatic warfare that had led to the creation of the Jewish state.[242]

All these inaccuracies are relatively slight, though, compared to your statement about Forrestal's restless night spent copying those lines from Sophocles. You should have told your readers, as all the other promoters of the suicide thesis have, that the poem in question reflects a bleak and despairing state of mind. More importantly, though, you should have shared with readers the evidence that most of those other writers did not have, that is, that the handwriting of the transcription doesn't resemble Forrestal's in the least and that the corpsman on duty looking over Forrestal said that in those last two hours of Forrestal's life when the corpsman was on duty the lights were off in his room and

---

[242] http://dcdave.com/article4/040927.html.

he did no reading or writing, and that no book was entered into evidence during the official investigation.

You then proceed to compound your error in the endnote that accompanies the quoted passage:

> Internet conspiracy theorists have suggested that Forrestal was actually murdered by Soviet spies, or possibly by Mossad agents, because of his opposition to creation of the state of Israel. While some of Forrestal's "paranoia" turns out to have been justified—he was right in believing that the U.S. government had been penetrated by Russian spies—his personal papers at Princeton leave little doubt that he was deeply depressed for some time prior to his death.

Since the Mossad would not exist until a half year after Forrestal's death, not even those people you tar with the meaningless pejorative "Internet conspiracy theorists" have ever, to my knowledge, suggested that that organization had anything to do with Forrestal's death. That pro-Israel and pro-Communist partisans within the Truman government were, however, behind Forrestal's death *has* been suggested—by me in particular. You have referenced my work so you must know that I name the powerful White House aide David Niles as the most likely culprit in the plot to murder Forrestal. He was identified in the Verona intercepts as a person cooperating with Communist agents and he was eventually dismissed by Truman for passing important military secrets to Israel.

Because you specifically cite Part 3 of my "Who Killed James Forrestal?" —by web address though not by name—you know as well that I am on the firmest of ground when I say that the Sophocles transcription was not in Forrestal's handwriting. That is the article, after all, in which I revealed the dissimilarity between the handwriting in the transcription and several Forrestal handwriting samples: http://www.dcdave.com/article4/041103.htm.

Surely you must agree that nothing that might be found among Forrestal's personal papers that is suggestive of his suicide can compare in significance to the evidence that I have presented in this short email that is suggestive of his murder. The lead doctor at Bethesda, Captain George Raines, after all, said that he was suicidally depressed (although his second in command, Captain Stephen Smith, seems to have disagreed rather vigorously), but that evidence of suicide hardly compares to the physical evidence of murder: the ginned-up "suicidal transcription," and broken glass on the bed and the laundered crime scene that I discuss in Part 2 of "Who Killed James Forrestal?"

I would very much like to hear what you might have to say in defense of what you have written about Forrestal's death in light of the facts that I have presented. Should I hear nothing I shall take it as a concession that what you have written is, as it seems to me on its face, indefensible.

Sincerely,
David Martin
March 28, 2015

There was no more likelihood that he would respond than would the George Washington University psychiatrist, Jerrold Post, and he did not. No doubt he has concluded that a person with a mainstream approval rating like his need not be bothered by anything so trivial as the truth. Nobody who might threaten his aerie, in his judgment, has said anything about his errors concerning Forrestal's death, after all, so he needn't be bothered. As we have seen, he has lots of sorry company.

CHAPTER 14

Not Completely Ignored

Scarce Commodity

What with news suppression and ridicule,
The truth is not easy to find.
You need that rarest of faculties,
A thoroughly open mind.

In the Soviet Union, it was said, that if you wanted to learn anything about economics, the place to go was to work for one of the economic planning boards. What they called "economics" in college was really just Communist theology. Similarly, in the United States, college is not really the place to go if you want to learn modern history. For that, one has to rely on oneself, and we are fortunate these days to have the Internet as a good starting place to begin one's self-education.

One such autodidact is the estimable Ron Unz, the proprietor of the Unz.com web site. His ongoing "American Pravda" series is probably as good a beginning as any for one's own independent historical education. On July 2, 2018, he ventured to do what no American historian has yet dared to do by discussing our findings on Forrestal's death at some considerable length in his installment, "Our Deadly World of Post-War Politics."[243]

Next to that one, no article in the series ties in better with the themes explored in this book than his October 15, 2018, installment, "The ADL in American Society," concerning the tremendous power wielded by the Anti-Defamation League of B'nai B'rith. Reminding us that the ADL has assumed an important gatekeeping role for the powerful Internet platforms, and that the organization began in 1913, financed by the defenders of the likely guilty-as-sin Leo Frank. That now powerful organization's major accomplishment in its first big operation was to plant in the national consciousness the falsehood that Southerners are bigoted towards Jews. Unz concludes his long essay this way:

> Now suppose that all the facts of this famous case were exactly unchanged except that Frank had been a white Gentile. Surely the trial would be ranked as one of the greatest racial turning points in American history, perhaps even overshadowing *Brown v. Board* because of the extent of popular sentiment, and it would have been given a central place in all our modern textbooks. Meanwhile, Frank, his lawyers, and his heavy financial backers would probably be cast as among the vilest racial villains in all of American history for their repeated attempts to foment the lynching of various innocent blacks so that a wealthy white rapist and murderer could walk free. But because Frank was Jewish rather than Christian, this remarkable history has been completely inverted for over one hundred years by our Jewish-dominated media and historiography.
>
> These are the important consequences that derive from control of the narrative and the flow of information, which allows murderers to be transmuted into martyrs and villains into heroes. The ADL was founded just over a century ago with the central goal of preventing a Jewish rapist and killer from being held legally accountable for his crimes, and over the decades, it eventually metastasized into a secret political police force not entirely dissimilar to the widely despised East German Stasi, but with its central goal seeming to be the maintenance of overwhelming Jewish control in a society that is 98% non-Jewish.
>
> We should ask ourselves whether it is appropriate for an organization with such origins and such recent history to be granted enormous influence over the distribution of information across our Internet.[244]

---

243 http://www.unz.com/runz/american-pravda-our-deadly-world-of-post-war-politics/.

It will take quite a while for the work of Ron Unz to make it into any history textbooks, unfortunately, which one can doubtless say for our own work. However, our discoveries have managed to penetrate the pages of four books with which we are acquainted.

Alan Hart

Alan Hart, who died at age 75 on January 15, 2018, was a correspondent for the BBC's *Panorama* and for the major news service ITN, about as mainstream a news figure as one can be in Great Britain. He cut his journalistic teeth as a young man covering the 6-day war in 1967 in the Middle East and probably had as much first-hand knowledge of the conflict between the Israelis and the Palestinians as any person who ever lived. No Western journalist had more intimate access to leaders on both sides than he. He was very close to both Israeli Prime Minister Golda Meir and PLO leader Yasser Arafat. In 1984, reflecting much of his first-hand knowledge, he wrote a book about the latter, *Arafat, Terrorist or Peacemaker?*

To be a top Middle Eastern correspondent for such major organs also required a great deal of homework on his part, and one can see that he put in the time. More than that, in volume one of the three-volume set, *Zionism, the Real Enemy of the Jews,* entitled *The False Messiah,* he comes across as a thoroughly fair-minded man.[245]

It is a combination that is both remarkable for a mainstream journalist and lethal in a career field that is now so Zionist-dominated. It is perhaps telling that by the time he published his book on Zionism, the adjective "former" was already placed in front of those high positions of his in the Western opinion-molding industry. As we have seen with the 60 Minutes gerontocracy, at 71 years of age at the time, he was still a relative spring chicken in the field. It is hardly surprising that, as Hart

---

[244] http://www.unz.com/runz/american-pravda-the-adl-in-american-society/.

[245] Clarity Press, Inc., 2009.

tells us in the prologue to his U.S. edition, published in 2009 four years after the first publication in Britain, that he initially had to self-publish this book. That was so "despite the fact that my literary agent had on file letters of rare praise for my work from the CEOs of some of our major publishing houses."

It would appear that in his later years the British liberal Hart went the way of the late conservative American Joseph Sobran, discussed in Chapter Two, who in his declining years practiced his journalism in an unremunerated fashion through his web site. In virtual retirement Hart could say the sorts of things that he was not allowed to say by the BBC or ITN, and AlanHart.Net remains as a very good source for useful information, but his audience is perforce much smaller than before, probably along the lines of that for DCDave.Com.

The truth about Zionism, which Hart was finally free to tell, is, unfortunately, very ugly. How, really, can one put a rosy gloss upon the violent forcing out of a people from their ancestral homeland and the heavy-handed continued oppression of those who remain? Zionism, to anyone who has observed it objectively as Hart has, is a witch's brew of fanaticism, deceit, ruthlessness, and money.

Money and Gangsterism

Hart sees a big contrast among Jews between those who adhere to what he calls spiritual Zionism and the practitioners of political Zionism. Albert Einstein would have been a prime example of the former category, and they might well make up a majority of all Jews.[246] They are not the ones with the power, though. Most important of all for the success, up to now, of political Zionism has been the money that has been used to buy weaponry, public opinion, and political leaders, primarily where it has mattered most, in the United States. The Zionist control of the opinion-molding industries has made their thuggish control of the politicians less obvious. Money is half of the time-honored method of the underworld to

---

[246] See David Martin, "Dr. Einstein or Dr. Frankenstein?" http://dcdave.com/article5/171004.htm.

get its way with people in responsible positions. The Latin American drug traffickers call it *plata o plomo,* silver or lead. In English it boils down to bribery and coercion. The "bribery" might well be within the law in the form of campaign contributions, given or withheld or given to the politician's adversary. There is ample evidence, however, that the Zionists, in their completely amoral fanaticism, will freely commit murder if more moderate forms of coercion and intimidation are deemed insufficiently effective. We saw it with the assassination of the British governor general Lord Moyne and the lead UN negotiator on Palestine, Count Folke Bernadotte and with the bombing of the King David Hotel.

In his final chapter Hart reminds us that Begin's Irgun gang attempted to assassinate Foreign Minister Ernest Bevin of the UK in 1946, though he makes no mention of the letter bombs sent to the Truman White House by the Stern Gang in 1947. To his eternal credit, though, although it took us a while to discover it, he broke the book-publishing silence about our discoveries concerning the violent death of Secretary of Defense James Forrestal.

His concluding chapter is entitled "Forrestal's 'Suicide'," and it is important to note that he encloses the word "suicide" in quotation marks. In his account of Forrestal's determined efforts to remove the question of the creation and recognition of the state of Israel from U.S. domestic politics, Hart leaves no doubt that our characterization of Forrestal as the leading U.S. opponent of the creation of the state of Israel is an accurate one.

"I accessed his work by putting 'David Martin also known as DCDave' into Google's search box and readers can do the same if they wish," he tells us on page 317. It's a good thing that he does that because it allows the reader to read all the evidence for himself and make up his own mind. In spite of his extensive favorable reference to our work, including long quotes, Hart says at last, "In the jury of my own mind, the answer to the question of whether Forrestal committed suicide or was murdered is an open one."

The case is really open and shut. Forrestal was clearly assassinated, and the entire political and media establishment has conspired to cover it up. That latter point is extremely telling. Hart, as a mainstream establishment liberal, was still apparently hankering for "respectability" among the group that is complicit in this heinous cover-up. That forlorn desire would also explain why he takes gratuitous swipes at "holocaust deniers" in his book and apparently accepts the official 9/11 narrative (On his web site, though, he finally put some distance between himself and the 19-Arab-hijackers story, enough for his Wikipedia page to characterize this former British establishment wheel horse as a "conspiracy theorist.")[247]

The Zionist Grip on America

In the prologue to the 2009 American edition entitled "An Appeal to the American People," Hart writes, "As surely as day follows night, the Zionist lobby and other supporters of Israel right or wrong will make an awesome effort to limit distribution of this book in America, and to cause the informed and honest debate it was written to promote to be suppressed."

He certainly got that right, and the apparent success of that effort up to now demonstrates the futility of Hart's efforts to stay on good terms with the mainstream crowd. Their success in suppressing his book in the United States is illustrated by the fact that we had never heard of it until seeing it mentioned by Alison Weir in *Against Our Better Judgment,* even though he makes such long and favorable mention of my Forrestal work. The publisher, Clarity Press, Inc., of Atlanta, is hardly a household name. We have a wide circle of email contacts and our email address is freely available, yet no one had told us about the book.

I also live in an information center in suburban Washington, DC, but I find using WorldCat.org that the only library in the area that has the book is the public library in Alexandria, Virginia. No library in the Dis-

---

247 http://www.alanhart.net/911-open-letter-challenge-to-adl%E2%80%99s-abe-foxman/

trict of Columbia, Maryland, Delaware, or North Carolina has it. Currently, it is at one other library in Virginia, that of Eastern Mennonite University in Harrisonburg. By some small wonder, the Carlsbad City Library of Carlsbad, California, once made the book available to readers, but no more. They have already discarded it, no doubt as part of the "awesome effort" to limit the book's distribution. That discarded copy fell into my possession through an online used book purchase, where it has been put to good use.

By contrast, if I wanted to read a library copy of, say, *The Eichmann Trial,* by Zionist partisan Deborah Lipstadt, the nearest copy is within walking distance and there are six copies at libraries no farther than 20 miles from me. The Zionist grip on the United States, I'm afraid, is even firmer than Alan Hart realizes.

Alison Weir

We encountered Alison Weir in Chapter Six as the publicizer of the thwarted Jewish terrorist London bombing attempt. She is another former journalist, the editor of a small weekly newspaper in Sausalito, California, who has reported on our Forrestal findings. The child of a military family and a veteran of the Peace Corps and the Civil Rights movement, she became absorbed in the Israel-Palestinian dispute during the Second Intifada in 2000, when she noticed the great difference between the coverage of the event between the national news media and what she was able to learn through the Internet. She founded the organization, If Americans Knew, in 2001 after a visit to Gaza and the West Bank as the Intifada continued and continues to head up that organization while she has gone on to become the president of another activist organization, the Council for the National Interest. In 2014 she published *Against Our Bet-*

ter Judgment: The Hidden History of How the U.S. Was Used to Create Israel.[248]

Reading Weir, one notices a great similarity between Zionism and the attraction toward it of a certain privileged group of people and another misguided but powerful ideology, Communism. Those who fall for it fall heavily and have a tendency to subordinate all questions of right and wrong, truth and falsehood, and patriotism and disloyalty to the furtherance of this one "noble" cause. Not many people know it these days, but in the 1930s and early 1940s the Soviet Union itself got the sort of favorable coverage from America's leading newspaper that Israel gets today across the board, and numerous Americans were lured into betting their lives that Joseph Stalin's fiefdom really was a workers' paradise.[249]

The biggest victims of the Zionist zealotry have certainly been those non-Jewish residents of Palestine whose forbears had lived there for thousands of years, but the price that has been paid by others, particularly in the United States is of no small consequence. Weir makes a strong case that American entry into World War I was the *quid pro quo* of powerful Zionists close to President Woodrow Wilson for the British Balfour Declaration promising a home (though not a homeland) for the Jews in Palestine should Britain and its allies win the war. She supports her argument without relying once upon the Jewish apostate Benjamin Freedman so, taken together, Weir and Freedman support one another.[250]

The importance of the Balfour Declaration in bringing the United States into WWI against the Germans might not have been widely known in this country, but, according to Weir, it was well known in Germany and it engendered the sort of antagonism toward their resident Jews that

---

248 Alison Weir, *Against Our Better Judgment: The Hidden History of How the U.S. Was Used to Create Israel,* CreateSpace Independent Publishing Platform, 2014.

249 David Martin, "*The New York Times* and Joseph Stalin," http://www.dcdave.com/article5/080309.htm; David Martin, "American Victims of the Soviet Gulag," http://www.dcdave.com/article5/130226.htm; See also E. Michael Jones, *The Jewish Revolutionary Spirit and Its Impact on World History,* Fidelity Press, 2008.

250 "A Jewish Defector Warns America: Benjamin Freedman Speaks on Zionism," http://www.sweetliberty.org/issues/israel/freedman.htm.

one might expect. Opportunity for Jewish advancement had been greater in Germany than in any other European country.

From her book, it is hard to say which was the greatest big break for the Zionist cause, the persecution suffered by Jews under the Nazis, the Second World War's creation of hundreds of thousands of Jewish refugees ripe for the peopling of Palestine, or the death of President Franklin Roosevelt. FDR had been completely against the Zionist cause. Harry Truman was weak and unpopular and needed all the help from powerful Zionists that he could get to be reelected in 1948. Surprisingly, Weir makes no mention of the negative reinforcement that Truman received in 1947 in terms of the attempt on his life by the Stern Gang, which, as we have noted, sent a letter bomb to the White House. She also fails to mention Truman's long association with the Kansas City political machine of the gangster Tom Pendergast, a fact that we have noted would have made him easily subject to blackmail. In that regard, he was something of an archetype for U.S. presidents in the Zionist-dominated era in which we live.

There are heroes in Weir's book. They are the patriotic Americans within the foreign policy establishment of the U.S. government who energetically opposed the superimposing of what was essentially a European country upon Palestine, an act that these officials saw as in conflict with U.S. national interests and ideals. Theirs was the better judgment that Truman went against. A few names worthy of mention are State Department officers Edwin Wright and Loy Henderson and their superiors, Under Secretary of State Robert A. Lovett and Secretary of State George C. Marshall. Foremost among the patriots, though, would have to be Truman's Secretary of Defense, James V. Forrestal, and Weir gives the courageous Forrestal his due. He foresaw the Middle Eastern mess in which the United States has become entangled, and the cost in blood and treasure and moral capital that it would entail, and he paid dearly for his efforts to prevent it.

One might contrast Weir with a great earlier critic of the Zionist cause, the British journalist, Douglas Reed, the author of the extraordinary work, *The Controversy of Zion.*[251] Reed, deceived by the American press coverage and without the discoveries that this reviewer would later make, wrote that Forrestal, whom he otherwise gives his due, had committed suicide. Weir is aware of our findings, however, and refers her readers to our "Who Killed James Forrestal?" series on our web site. She also strongly recommends Chapter 12, "The Forrestal 'Suicide'," of Vol. 1 of *Zionism: The Real Enemy of the Jews* by Hart, which is how we discovered it.

Phillip F. Nelson

Since his retirement from the insurance profession, Phillip Nelson has been busy filling in a lot of the important gaps left by the courtiers who practice the history trade in academia. His subject has been President Lyndon Baines Johnson, and anyone reading Nelson on Johnson would have to conclude that there is no contest as to who the worst President in U.S. history was. His books, in order, have been *LBJ: The Mastermind of the JFK Assassination; LBJ, From Mastermind to "The Colossus"; Remember the Liberty! Almost Sunk by Treason on the High Seas; and Who Really Killed Martin Luther King, Jr.: The Case against Lyndon B. Johnson and J. Edgar Hoover.*

What we do in Chapter One, Nelson does in his Chapter Five, of *LBJ, From Mastermind to "The Colossus,* that is, he reports that Johnson paid a visit to Forrestal at his room in Bethesda Naval Hospital, to which the latter had been confined after he had experienced some sort of mysterious breakdown. He also makes explicit reference to our work on the subject. We can rule out that it was an innocent social visit by a well-wisher. We learned of the visit, recall, from *Driven Patriot: The Life and Times of James Forrestal* by Townsend Hoopes and Douglas Brinkley and they learned of it from an interview by the late Hoopes of Forrestal assis-

---

[251] Dolphin Press (Pty) Ltd., 1978, Durban, South Africa.

tant Marx Leva, who also told them that it was "against Forrestal's wishes."

Johnson and Forrestal were on far opposite sides of the fence over the question of recognition of the new state of Israel. Nelson speculates that the purpose of the visit might have been to subject Forrestal, in his weakened emotional state, to the notorious "Johnson Treatment," a combination of "supplication, accusation, cajolery, exuberance, scorn, tears, complaint, and hint of threat."[252]

He is suggesting, I suppose, that the intent was to drive Forrestal even further over the edge and perhaps to induce him to kill himself so others wouldn't have to do it. Since their political differences should have been well known and since Forrestal would have surely communicated to his doctors that Johnson's visit was unwanted, it amounts to virtual medical malpractice for the visit to have been permitted. Not surprisingly, the subject never came up when the Navy conducted its review. Furthermore, there is no mention at all in the Nurse's Notes to the Willcutts Report of that LBJ visit. That does not mean that Leva is wrong and that no such visit took place, because, as we have noted, we know of other people who visited Forrestal during his seven weeks at Bethesda who do not show up in the hospital record.

My own guess is that Johnson was brought in on that action in the manner in which a member of the Mafia becomes a "made man." Maybe he was asked to report on the means of access to Forrestal's room for the phony patients on the same floor who would eventually throttle him and throw him out the window. The role might have been wholly superfluous, but he had been made a party to a monumentally treacherous political act of the sort that would mark his entire political career, and it would have been done on behalf of the people whom he would serve throughout his life.

In the overall scheme of things, our differences with Nelson amount to little more than hair-splitting. Anyone who has read what Nelson has

---

[252] Nelson, p. 231.

written about the assassinations of the Kennedy brothers and of Martin Luther King, Jr. would readily believe that James Forrestal was assassinated. Others might need to read a few chapters of our book to come around.

Paul L. Williams

In a breakthrough for a book from a mainstream publisher, the award-winning journalist, Williams, citing my "Who Killed James Forrestal?" series, states flatly in his provocative *Operation Gladio* that Forrestal "was thrown out the window of the sixteenth floor of the Bethesda Naval Hospital, where he had been a patient." Consistent with the theme of his book, however, he hints implausibly, to my mind, that it was because of the influence that Forrestal had wielded as Navy Secretary three years before in getting Deep State-connected mobster, Charles "Lucky" Luciano, deported to Italy.[253]

---

[253] *Operation Gladio: The Unholy Alliance between the Vatican, the CIA, and the Mafia*, Prometheus Books, 2015, Chapter 2 at footnote 42 (Kindle edition).

CHAPTER 15

Deserted by the Church

Rendering unto Israel

There are those who pull strings in this nation
Who have a strong Israel fixation.
Many things become clear
That have taken place here
When one comes to this realization.

What is it about Catholic political leaders in the United States? The first Roman Catholic American president, John F. Kennedy, was assassinated. His younger brother, Robert F. Kennedy, who stood a good chance of succeeding Lyndon Johnson as president, was also assassinated.[254] The most prominent Catholic political leader in the United States before the Kennedys, Senator Joe McCarthy, was politically assassinated, and today, as a 20th century villain in popu-

[254] See David Martin, "Did Lyndon Step Down So Bobby Could Be Killed?" http://dcdave.com/article5/140923.htm; How RFK Could Have Saved His Life, and His Country," http://www.dcdave.com/article5/170206.htm.

lar imagination, his name ranks right up there with Adolf Hitler. Furthermore, there is a very good possibility that McCarthy's death at age 48 at Bethesda Naval Hospital was no more of natural causes than Forrestal's was an accident, in which case his assassination was not just political.[255]

The great Catholic monk and writer, Thomas Merton, was not a political leader, but his antiwar writing and his writing about the corruption of the American political and opinion-molding system had great political power. Hugh Turley and this writer have demonstrated beyond a reasonable doubt that Merton's death in Thailand on December 10, 1968, was not a result of accidental electrocution by a faulty (Hitachi) electric fan as those opinion molders would have us believe and that he, too, was assassinated.[256]

The Wikipedia page for James Forrestal says that he was Catholic, although he had not been a practicing Catholic since leaving Princeton University. He certainly had a strong Catholic upbringing. His father was a Catholic immigrant from Ireland and his mother fancied that he had the makings of a priest. As we have seen, furthermore, in his last few weeks alive he seemed to be making a serious effort to get back in touch with his Catholic faith. What is more, the Catholic press in the United States, which seems to be about as subservient to the ruling secular authority as the Polish church was under the Communists, has been about as active in covering up Forrestal's assassination as it has been of Merton's.

The most recent example, in the case of Forrestal, was posted on February 27, 2015, on the web site of *The American Catholic*. The subtitle under their masthead reads, "Politics & Culture from a Catholic Perspec-

---

[255] See Medford Evans, *The Assassination of Joe McCarthy,* Western Islands Press, 1970; David Martin, "James Forrestal and Joe McCarthy," http://www.dcdave.com/article5/110928.htm.

[256] Hugh Turley and David Martin, *The Martyrdom of Thomas Merton: An Investigation*, McCabe Publishing, 2018, http://www.themartyrdomofthomasmerton.com/.

tive." Attorney Donald R. McClarey wrote the article in question entitled, "James Forrestal and His Prophecy." [257]

Whether we might say that it is about a "fellow Catholic" or not, what "cradle Catholic" McClarey wrote in *The American Catholic* about Forrestal's death is an affront to the man's memory. It does violence to the truth. Everyone, Catholic or otherwise, should be appalled by it. Here are the offending lines:

> Appointed the first Secretary of Defense in 1947, Forrestal fought against budget cuts proposed by President Truman that he thought endangered the nation's security. He also opposed the proposal to unify the services which would gut the Navy and eliminate the Marine Corps. On March 31, 1949, Harry Truman, angered over Forrestal's opposition to his policies, fired him. Tragically, Forrestal, who had worked non-stop on Defense issues since he joined the Roosevelt administration in 1940, had a nervous breakdown. While undergoing psychiatric treatment he committed suicide by jumping from the 16th floor of the National Naval Medical Center. He left behind a note with a quotation from Sophocles' *Ajax:*

Then he repeats the lines found in Millis, Rogow, and Hoopes and Brinkley, ending in "nightingale."

There's really no excuse for anyone to be writing such things in 2015. We now have the Internet—*The American Catholic* is an Internet publication, after all. Since 2004 the official report on Forrestal's death has been available online, and the evidence that it contains shows beyond serious doubt that McClarey has repeated falsehoods.[258] Research these days begins with the Internet because it's so easy. Simply typing in the name "James Forrestal" into any search engine leads one quickly to our dcdave.com web site and the discoveries that we have made.

One might think that McClarey was just negligent. He was merely repeating what was in the 1992 Hoopes and Brinkley biography, after all, and Forrestal's death was only tangential to the subject of his article, which is primarily a sort of flag-waving defense of the U.S. Marine Corps. (Concerning that point, as we noted in Chapter One, had Forrestal's

---

257 http://www.the-american-catholic.com/2015/02/27/james-forrestal-and-his-prophecy/.

258 http://ariwatch.com/VS/JamesForrestal/WillcuttsReport.htm.

counsel been taken, the bloody battle of Iwo Jima, to which McClarey refers later on in his article, would likely never have been fought because Japan would have already surrendered.[259] The possibility that McClarey had made an honest error, more on the order of a sin of omission caused by insufficient research diligence underlay the email that we sent him a little over two months after his article first appeared.

Ten days passed and we received no response, so we concluded that the likelihood was great that McClarey's was a sin of commission from the beginning. The fact that his editor, Tito Edwards, at *The American Catholic* also failed to respond to our May 18 email to him virtually seals it, except for the Delphic "Update" that was appended later and that we have only recently discovered. We shall discuss that further on. Here is the latter email, which includes the original email to McClarey:

> Dear Mr. Edwards,
>
> On May 8, 2015, I sent the following email to a writer for your publication:
>
>> Dear Mr. McClarey,
>>
>> A friend has called my attention to your February article in The American Catholic. You seem not to be aware of what we have learned since the release of the official report on Forrestal's death in 2004. For starters, that poem transcription that you quote was in someone else's handwriting. Taken all in all, the evidence points heavily toward murder and cover-up and not to suicide. See my latest article on the subject here.[260] For a brief introduction to the subject see "New Forrestal Document Exposes Cover-up."[261] I believe that it is incumbent upon you to write a follow-up article correcting the record. I have come to expect government propaganda

---

[259] See also David Martin, "Forrestal Ignored: China Lost to Reds, Korean War Fought." http://www.dcdave.com/article5/110530.htm.

[260] At the word "here" I linked to the article, "Letter to a Court Historian about Forrestal's Death" as it appeared with illustrations and comments on the B'Man's Revolt web site, https://buelahman.wordpress.com/2015/04/08/letter-to-a-court-historian-about-forrestals-death/. That website, unfortunately, has fallen victim to censorship by Wordpress, so the article can now be read at my site, http://www.dcdave.com/article5/150407.htm

[261] Linked to http://dcdave.com/article4/040927.html.

from the mainstream press. The Catholic press should not abet them.

The first law of history is not to dare to utter falsehood; the second, not to fear to tell the truth. - Pope Leo XIII

Sincerely,
David Martin

I would have preferred to make my comment about the article online on your web site, but when I attempted to do so, I received a message that comments had been closed on the article. May I ask you why that is so? Looking at your site's "comments policy," I see nothing about any comments period or any reason for closing comments. What possible reason could there be for closing comments on any topic, but particularly for doing it so quickly after there had been so few comments on a topic of such great importance? I have taken note of your "three strikes and you're out," treatment of those you deem in violation of your rules, though I may not agree with them. Continuing the metaphor, how do you decide that a person will not even be allowed up to the plate?

Ten days have now passed, and Mr. McClarey has not responded to my email. I sent it through a lawyer referral service, so I have every reason to believe that he received it on the day I sent it. In case he didn't, would you please forward the message you see above to him?

Your responsibility hardly ends with fulfilling that errand request, however. Your web site has published information about the death of a great American public servant that is contradicted by the best evidence now available. The misinformation is so bad that the man who put it out is apparently unwilling to defend what he has written. If he will not do it, you have an obligation either to defend it or to retract it publicly.

Sincerely,
David Martin

All those practicing evil hate the light and will not come to the light lest their deeds should be exposed. - John 3:20

Mr. Edwards never responded, either, and no correction to the article or retraction was made.

Catholic Apologists for the State

Reflecting upon this non-response from a publication that displays an eagle and an American flag with the cross (not a crucifix) on its masthead, we are reminded that our local diocesan newspaper the *Arlington Catholic Herald* did not print our letter exposing arch-neocon George Weigel for the duplicity of an article of his that they had published.[262] We are also reminded that it is a rare American Catholic church these days that does not have an American flag in its sanctuary along with all the Christian iconography, and that the National Shrine of the Immaculate Conception in Washington, DC, has taken to hanging a massive flag from its bell tower on patriotic occasions like Memorial Day and Independence Day.[263]

The Catholic Church seems to have replaced the late Jerry Falwell's Moral Majority as the most consistent supporters of jingoism and militarism within our government, and McClarey's article is certainly consistent with that trend. With one issue, that of the undeniably worthy position against abortion, taking precedent over all others, the Church's support for rampant militarism becomes virtually inevitable. Parishioners are encouraged to support candidates who oppose abortion on demand, but those people are almost always Republicans who are also the biggest supporters of an aggressive foreign policy, although, in recent years, Democrats and Republicans seem hardly indistinguishable in that regard.

Even if it is genuine, the Church's effort to obtain a Supreme Court majority to overturn Roe v. Wade is doomed to failure as long as it gives a pass to the powerful opinion molders in favor of abortion. The annual March for Life would be much more effective if it ended up in front of the *Washington Post* building instead of the Supreme Court Building

Most disturbing of all from a Christian standpoint is that the Church's embrace of the government and its flag has entailed a growing divorce

---

262 "The Brazen Duplicity of George Weigel," http://www.dcdave.com/article3/000330.html.

263 http://www.dcdave.com/article5/ShrineFlag.jpg.

from the truth. That is because the government's foreign policy, in particular, is built upon an ever-growing edifice of lies. Furthermore, it is a foreign policy that, at least since the assassination of John F. Kennedy, is much more in the interests of Israel than it is of the United States. It would be more honest if the flag being waved in support of the mindless patriotism that the Catholic Church has fostered were the one depicting the Star of David instead of the Stars and Stripes.

It is at this point that the misbegotten foreign policy and the disregard for truth come together in *The American Catholic.* James Forrestal, as we have noted repeatedly, was the leading opponent within the United States government of the creation of the Jewish-supremacist state of Israel in Palestine. Parroting the propaganda line as it has developed, starting with that fiftieth anniversary article in *The Washington Post* in 1999, *The American Catholic* not only makes no connection between Forrestal's death and his principled position on Israel, but it also completely avoids mentioning that fact as a major reason for the vicious press that he received in the last year of his life, culminating in his firing by President Truman.

Now let us discuss the belated and very curious reaction that *The American Catholic* made to our letters. As of this writing, it is at the bottom of the article, and it reads as follows: "Forrestal's suicide has ever been a feeding ground for conspiracy theorists. Go here for a prime example."

The lawyer McClarey appears to believe that the mere invocation of the "conspiracy theorist" epithet effectively trumps hard, irrefutable evidence. Under the word, "here," you see, *The American Catholic* has embedded a link to our article as it appears with illustrations on the B'Man's Revolt web site.[264] The article, which is primarily what we have in this

---

264 David Martin, "*The American* (Establishment) *Catholic* on Forrestal's Death," https://buelahman.wordpress.com/2015/05/28/the-american-establishment-catholic-on-forrestals-death/. Unfortunately, though as previously noted, the entire Buelahman web site has now been taken down, and the article can now only be found at my dcdave.com web site.

chapter, effectively destroys the suicide conclusion to which McClarey has leaped in his article (along with the factually incorrect statements that Forrestal "jumped" from a window and that he had suffered a "nervous breakdown."). Did he and the editor Edwards not even bother to read the article or the letters that we wrote to them? Are they severely challenged in reading comprehension skills, or are they both so contemptuous of the Catholic "flock" making up their readership that they believe that their authoritative sounding repetition of the "suicide" mantra and their "conspiracy theorist" slur will blind their followers to the actual facts? Could Edwards and McClarey not realize how bad this makes them look in the eyes of anyone with the ability to think clearly and with the courage to resist the mentality of the herd?[265]

Such a shoddy performance, participating in the cover-up of the assassination of the great public servant, James Forrestal, whether he was a Catholic or not, by people who wear their Catholic religion on their sleeves, hardly reflects well upon these prominent representatives of the American Catholic Church. It is a good deal worse than a Catholic organization giving a platform to a Jewish writer to slander Forrestal by writing falsely that he had "anti-Jewish sentiments" and that possessing such sentiments amounted to a "character stain," described in Chapter Two. At least that article has since been taken down.

---

[265] See David Martin, "Children's Fantasy Writers," http://www.dcdave.com/article1/081498.htm.

CHAPTER 16

Conclusion

Occupied Country

Like the Germans we now know how it feels
To be by foreigners bossed.
It's like we'd fought a big war with Israel,
And we had, unfortunately, lost.

Who is strong enough to remove the gun ever-pointed at the White House by the combined hands of supine politicians, the controlled media and the Zionist lobby?
- Alfred Lilienthal[266]

From its inception, political Zionism has made great use of terrorism. The following observation is from the biography of General Patrick J. Hurley, who was President Roosevelt's special envoy to the Middle East in 1943:

266 *The Zionist Connection II,* p.808

> While throughout the world Zionism was represented as a religious movement "based on humanitarian concern for a persecuted people," within Palestine it was a terrorist organization using tribute, coercion and assassination as its weapons. Foreign businesses, including American, operating in Palestine were forced to contribute monthly payments to the Zionist organization's treasury for permission to remain in business unmolested and un-boycotted. And when Hurley refused to publicly endorse the Zionist movement during his stay in Jerusalem, *the personal representative of the United States was threatened with kidnapping and assassination.* [David] Ben-Gurion, nominal head of the Zionist movement in Palestine, admitted that he was not sure of his ability to control the terrorist Zionist groups.[267] (Emphasis added)

The reader should be reminded that these observations were made and events took place before the assassinations of Lord Moyne and Count Folke Bernadotte, the attempted assassinations of Bevin and Truman, the bombing of the King David Hotel, and the slaughter of the residents of the village of Deir Yassin and numerous other smaller atrocities around that time, and Qibya in 1953. Contrary to the apparent belief of Albert Einstein and the other signers of that 1948 letter to *The New York Times*, Menahem Begin's terrorist Irgun was hardly a minority extremist element within political Zionism.[268]

Canadian author Greg Felton writes persuasively of how the Israeli government under former terrorist and assassin Yitzhak Shamir plotted to assassinate President George H.W. Bush at the Madrid Conference in 1991 because of the pressure that Bush was putting on them to make concessions to the Palestinians, only to have the plot thwarted by the dissident Mossad agent, Victor Ostrovsky.[269] Books by Michael Collins Piper and Salvador Astucia complement one another on the involvement of Israel in the assassination of President John f. Kennedy.[270]

---

[267] Don Lohbeck, *Patrick J. Hurley*, Henry Regnery Company, 1956, p. 193.

[268] Green, *Taking Sides*, p. 47.

[269] Greg Felton, *The Host & the Parasite: How Israel's Fifth Column Consumed America*, Money Tree Publishing, 2017, pp. 124-128.

[270] Michael Collins Piper, *Final Judgment: The Missing Link in the JFK Assassination Conspiracy*, The Center for Historical Review, 2000; Salvador Astucia (a pseudonym) with Stephen A. Zarlenga, editor, *Opium Lords: Israel, the Golden Triangle, and the Kennedy Assassination*, Amazon Digital Services, 2015.

Bringing the subject of Israeli assassinations up to date, National Public Radio began a program on January 31, 2018, this way:

> This is FRESH AIR. I'm Terry Gross. Our guest, Israeli investigative reporter Ronen Bergman, says that Israel has developed the most robust streamlined assassination machine in history. His new book, based on a thousand interviews, chronicles decades of shootings, poisonings, bombings and drone strikes. The targets were perceived enemies of the Jewish state, ranging from British colonial officials in the 1940s to leaders of Hamas, Hezbollah and the PLO to Iranian nuclear scientists. Bergman describes the planning and approval process for targeted killings, which typically involved young military and intelligence operatives making the case for a strike to the country's prime minister.[271]

Ronen Bergman is a prominent Israeli journalist and author of *Rise and Kill First: The Secret History of Israel's Targeted Assassinations.*[272] Many of the assassinations that he describes were secret ones, with the deaths made to appear as the result of something other than murder. The Israelis would like to boast that they originated these techniques, but most are right out of the CIA assassination manual.

The names of the victims on the Wikipedia "List of Israeli assassinations" page actually stretches for pages and pages.[273] As of this writing, the site has 268 endnotes. The murderous reach is global. Here are a couple of examples:

Heinz Krug, West German rocket scientist assisting Egypt with its missile program. On September 11, 1962, he was abducted from his company offices on Munich's Schillerstrasse. His body was never found. Swiss police later arrested two Mossad agents for threatening the daughter of another scientist and found that they were responsible for the killing.

Syrian General Muhammad Suleiman, National Security Advisor and Presidential Advisor for Arms Procurement and Strategic Weapons. He was,

---

[271] https://www.npr.org/2018/01/31/582099085/journalist-details-israels-secret-history-of-targeted-assassinations.

[272] Random House, 2018.

[273] https://en.wikipedia.org/wiki/List_of_Israeli_assassinations.

"killed by sniper fire to the head and neck. Israel denied responsibility for the killing but was widely suspected of involvement. According to an NSA intercept published by Wikileaks, the NSA defined it as the 'first known instance of Israel targeting a legitimate government official.'"

Most of the assassination victims have been Palestinians, of course, many of them important leaders, and the list stretches on at truly sickening length.

FRESH AIR's Dave Davies manages to shine a light on the mentality behind the Israeli policy of assassinations with the following exchange:

> DAVIES: And to what extent do you think the Israeli willingness to embrace targeted assassinations is rooted in the horrors of the Holocaust and a determination to avoid that ever happening again?
>
> BERGMAN: Profoundly. David Ben-Gurion, the most important Jew in the last 1,000 years at least, objected the use of targeted killing [sic]. He said this is not the weapon that the Jewish people should embrace, but that changed after the Holocaust, even before Israel was established as a state. I think that the new Israelis - those who build [sic] the nation, those who built Israel, those who established Israeli Defense Forces and intelligence community - and for that sake, all Israelis - I myself, I'm the son of both Holocaust survivors, both my parents are Holocaust survivors - the new Israelis came from the Holocaust with three main lessons.
>
> The first is that there will always be a gentile, a goy, who is after us to kill us. The second is that the - all the other gentiles, the goyim, are not going to help us. They're going to stand aside, if not helping the first one. And the third is that we should do everything to have a safe haven, to have a homeland, to have Israel and defend it with whatever price.

That is to say, the Zionist experiment must be defended at the price of the sacrifice of the most basic standards of decency and morality because, as the arch-Zionist Forrestal biographer Arnold Rogow put it, "Jew-baiters and anti-Semites of one variety or the other—Greek, Roman, and Christian—have largely dominated the Gentile world, and as a result that world has been one in which the Jew has always had to move cautiously and, more often than not, live dangerously." Putting it another way, it's us against the world, so anything goes. It's truly chilling that there are people who harbor such atavistic, tribal attitudes, especially when one considers the power that they now wield in the most powerful country in the world.

Perhaps the most important power, mentioned in Chapter 12, is thoroughgoing control of the NOMA, the national opinion molding apparatus. Controlling the GAME, the government, academia, the media, and the entertainment, enables control of the NOMA. The media, it should be pointed out, also includes book publishers. Thus, the national eyes remained shut and the national mouth closed when the government kept its feeble official inquiry into James Forrestal's death secret for 55 years. One need only ask in whose interests was that secrecy. It was certainly not that of the American people. One might as well ask in what one country in the world did the majority of the population favor America's invasion of Iraq. It was certainly not the United States or Iraq or any of those countries that were fashioned "the coalition of the willing."

Interestingly, the part of the GAME that gave way with the Forrestal death secrecy was the government when the Navy JAG office released the Willcutts Report to this writer in 2004. Then the ranks closed and with the very tiniest of exceptions, they have all dummied up about it. In this instance, the media include virtually all of what has come to be called the "alternative media" as well, a fact that should really give one pause.

How really important *was* this assassination and how completely *is* our information controlled?

James V. Forrestal was a very prominent and popular man in his day. As we noted in the Introduction, as Under Secretary of the Navy he had overseen the massive procurement effort that furnished the war's vital weaponry, particularly in the Pacific Theater. But his image went quickly south as shaped by the NOMA when he took his stand against the Zionists.

Also, as we observed in the Introduction, Forrestal is hardly the only person upon whom the Zionist-controlled NOMA has exercised its power in a very negative fashion. Consider this opening sentence from Wikipedia concerning one of the people on the list of those who have been smeared:

> Dorothy Celene Thompson (July 9, 1893 – January 30, 1961) was an American journalist and radio broadcaster, who in 1939 was recognized by *Time* magazine as the second most influential woman in America next to Eleanor Roosevelt. She is notable as the first American journalist to be expelled from Nazi Germany in 1934 and as one of the few women news commentators on radio during the 1930s. She is regarded by some as the "First Lady of American Journalism."[274]

Dorothy Who? Scroll down to the "Fame and controversy" section on Wikipedia and you'll see what happened:

> In 1941, Thompson wrote "Who Goes Nazi?" for *Harper's Magazine*. She was a keynote speaker at the Biltmore Conference, and by war's end was regarded as one of the most effective spokespersons for Zionism. Thompson switched her views round radically after a trip to Palestine in 1945, and ran into difficulties, including accusations of anti-Semitism, which she strongly rebuffed, after being warned that hostility toward Israel was, in the American press world, "almost a definition of professional suicide." She eventually concluded that Zionism was a recipe for perpetual war.

And as we have seen, she was right, and so were the people who warned her what she, like Forrestal, was in for if she were to stand up for the truth:

> Before long, her column and radio programs, her speaking engagements, and her fame were all gone. Today, she has largely been erased from history.
>
> In the coming decades, other Americans were similarly written out of history, forced out of office, their lives and careers destroyed, history was distorted, re-written, erased, bigotry promoted, supremacy disguised, facts replaced by fraud.
>
> Very few people know this history. The excellent books that document it are largely out of print, their facts and very existence virtually unknown to the vast majority of Americans, even those who focus on the Middle East. Instead, false theories have been promulgated, menda-

---

[274] https://en.wikipedia.org/wiki/Dorothy_Thompson.

cious analyses promoted, chosen authors celebrated, others assigned to oblivion.[275]

To their great credit, with their widely acclaimed 1992 Forrestal biography, Townsend Hoopes and Douglas Brinkley went a long way toward restoring Forrestal's reputation, which had been so badly damaged by the journalists Drew Pearson and Walter Winchell and the rest of the pack, and later by the first biographer, Arnold Rogow, and the others that we have mentioned. Their chosen title truly sums up their accurate characterization of one of the greatest public servants this country has ever had, *Driven Patriot.*

Hoopes and Brinkley also give credit to Forrestal for his farsightedness in urging a more lenient policy toward Japan toward the end of the Pacific War as a means of ending the bloodshed and blocking Soviet penetration into the Far East.[276] They credit him, as well, for coming up with the war-ending clever response to the Japanese offer to surrender that

---

[275] Weir, p. 93. It wasn't anti-Zionism that did them in, but the Thompson story reminds us of a couple of other journalistic lions of the period destroyed by our powerful NOMA, John T. Flynn and Percy Crosby. In their case it was opposition to U.S. involvement in World War II and to the man responsible for it, President Franklin D. Roosevelt. See Hugh Turley, "Antiwar, Anti-FDR, John T. Flynn," http://www.dcdave.com/article5/121212.htm and search his name on dcdave.com. Crosby was the most famous cartoonist of his day, the creator of the extremely popular Skippy comic strip. Like Flynn, he was a liberal Democrat who initially supported Roosevelt. After he publicly turned against FDR, a bankrupt California peanut butter company stole his Skippy trademark and Crosby was committed to a mental institution where he spent the last sixteen years of his life. His daughter, Joan Tibbetts, is still fighting for justice in the case. See David Martin, "Roosevelt's Revenge?" http://www.dcdave.com/article5/061210.htm; "Percy Crosby on Franklin Roosevelt," http://www.dcdave.com/article5/101003.htm; "Forrestal, Skippy Creator Shared Similar Fate," http://www.dcdave.com/article4/030929.html; Hugh Turley, "A Tale of Two Cartoonists," http://www.dcdave.com/article5/090410a.htm; and the Skippy web site, http://www.skippy.com/.

[276] Hoopes and Brinkley, pp. 208-209.

allowed them to keep the Emperor while placating the American public by fashioning the surrender terms as "unconditional."[277]

But to the people who took his life and to those who covered up his assassination, the great statesman and the great patriot James Forrestal was just another person who stood in the way of their ambitions.

[277] Ibid., p. 214.

Index

ABOUT THE AUTHOR

David Martin is the author with Hugh Turley of *The Martyrdom of Thomas Merton: An Investigation.* His web site of longstanding is dcdave.com.

Forrestal's Resting Place in History

He was brought before his time
To Arlington to reside.
Now, at last, the truth is known:
It wasn't from suicide.